Oh! I Remember Him

Mike McClean

Michael Greco, Actor, EastEnders.

"Top banter from one of the good guys in show business. They broke the mould with squeaky. Rare entertainment at its best."

Larry Lamb, Actor, Gavin and Stacey.

"If you're not going to work with him, reading this will be the next best thing."

Linda Robson, Actress.

One of the funniest men I have worked with. (Even when he's looking up my skirt!)

Marcus Collins, X-Factor finalist.

"Mike squeaky McCLean has a reputation that is anything but, I don't care what anyone says about him... I think he's a decent guy."

Anthony Costa, boy band 'Blue'.

Mike was our first ever tour manager when we did the Big Breakfast, he was a cross between Arthur Daley and Dell Boy. A very funny guy that will have you laughing for hours., I know I have spent many of those hours with him.

Gary Bushell, television critic.

Funnier than Richard, sexier than Judy, not quite as squeaky as Pasquale.

Alan Cohen, director.

Mike has a great, and rare, quality of natural warmth onstage that all his audiences respond to. I love directing him – he's inventive, supportive, and a great company member.

(Shame about his choice of football team though!)

Ken Oldfield, West End director.

Well what can I say about Mike? nothing so I'll shut up!

One of funniest guys I've had the pleasure of working and writing with. His personality knocks me for six every time I'm around him.

A truly gifted comic genius and an amazing guy.

If you need a good laugh … see him Live !!! or better yet read his Autobiography. Ohh you are.

Ian Cheeseman, BBC Radio Manchester.

Mike is funny even when he doesn't mean to be.

ACKNOWLEDGEMENTS

There are so many people I need to thank. First and foremost, big hugs and kisses to my two boys – Carter and Cooper - who I love so much, and who bring immeasurable joy to my life. I want to thank my soulmate, Kate, for being a truly wonderful person and my best mate. To my mum and dad for bringing me up and supplying me with years of laughter. My lovely sister Aurora has been my rock over the last few years, and her daughter, my niece, Nicole. Finally, not forgetting my fabulous extended family, both in Spain and Ireland, all of whom I love dearly.

I'd like to thank Joe Rozich for giving me my first summer ever season to also thank Harry Robson, one of the nicest men in magic and a lovely friend.

A big shout-out to my friends, too, who have always been there for me, namely Degs, Les, Stevie and Dave (even if the latter is a Manchester United fan).

I'd also like to thank the fantastic Charlotte Hamilton for being a brilliant agent, as well as Gaz Cornick and Paul Connolly for being the best people I've ever had the pleasure of working with in television. I'm very grateful to Amanda and Simon Ross for the six-and-half years I spent working on Richard & Judy, and I'd like to express my sincere thanks to the King and Queen of TV themselves, of course, who are among the loveliest people in the business. Additionally, my thanks go to John Spillers for teaching me the art of panto, to Ben Rigden for being the best executive producer anyone could wish for, to Graham Haye for helping me get back on the stand-up circuit, and to David 'hot nuts' Hahn for dishing out the finest advice and guidance. I'm also indebted to Emma and Ron at The Hub who gave me the opportunity to perform at one of the best comedy clubs in London; to Ian, Martin and Craig at The Comedy Club for getting me some great gigs, and to Gerry Kaye and Ryan McDonnell for being funny fuckers and brilliant mates. A big thank you to Roy Yates – not a bad bloke for a Liverpool supporter – for introducing me to the wonderful world of cruise ships. Not forgetting all the co-medians I have had the pleasure of working with on the cir-cuit.

I'd like to thank Jo Lake for helping me to edit and to Taryn Johnston for publishing this book!

Finally, I want to thank YOU!! for reading this book. If I have made you laugh throughout it, or you have smiled then that's fine by me.

There is always so many people to thank so if I have for-gotten anyone.

I AM SORRY.

DEDICATION

I need to express a heartfelt thank you to the most inspira-
tional mentor one could ever ask for - the late, great Peter
Woolley – who's in my thoughts every single day. (I Still miss
you, Peter.)

FOREWORD

by

Richard Madeley

Judy and I first met Mike when he was presenting The Big Breakfast on Channel 4 – they sent him to hand us a leaving cake outside as we left our ITV This Morning studios for the last time. Twelve months later, Mike would become our roving reporter on our new Channel 4 show, Richard and Judy, a role he would perform for almost seven years.

By then we'd learned that, as show hosts, you need to find the right people to work with. Mike defined that requirement. He brought with him something that is incredibly difficult to find in a presenter; a unique blend of humour, comic timing and huge likability. Our viewers embraced him no matter where we sent him or what we made him do. They loved him.

Mike has a lovely way with ordinary people on the street; he extracted comedy gold from them. Not many people could get a 90-year-old woman to wing walk on a Utterly Butterly plane or convince a man who survives by eating roadkill to tell us about it on live TV! We always loved seeing what Mike brought to the show.

Mike is, of course, at heart a down to earth working-class lad from Manchester. Hard work and persistence has been key to him achieving his goals. This book has some incredibly funny stories and, combined with Mike's characteristic self-deprecation, they make it a joy to read. The journey he sets out in "Oh I remember him" will have you laughing from beginning to end. I am so pleased that Judy and I feature in it - without having to consult our lawyers.

It has been a pleasure working with Mike. We consider him not just a colleague, but a friend.

Richard Madeley.

CHAPTER 1

The Early Years

It was in August 1969, in a tiny hospital in San Sebastian, that I made my very first public appearance, popping out of my exhausted mum, Amparo Breijo Parierra, who'd been in labour for fourteen hours until the midwife realised she still had her tights on (ok not really but I'm just warming up here). My dad Peter soon arrived at the maternity ward - he'd been on a bus heading to the hospital during the birth – and had promptly run out to the phone box to inform his Spanish in-laws that his first-born was a boy, and that he'd be called Michael.

My mum hailed from a beautiful town called La Coruna, situated on the northern coast of Spain (pinpoint Portugal on a map, keep heading north and you'll find it). It's the most amazing part of the world, with some of the finest beaches in Europe and some of the best seafood in the world. Mum had a hard upbringing, living in a small flat that had more family members than rooms. Sadly, her father passed away at a very early age, and my nan had to cope alone, bringing up six kids (five of her own and one adopted). Mum left Spain when she was seventeen, to join her sister Bene who'd headed to England to escape a violent marriage. Mum wasn't allowed into the country when she first arrived – she was still deemed a child - so my Auntie had to collect her from the port authorities in Dover, something that we still remind her of today.

My dad had a comparatively awful start in life. From the age of four he was brought up by nuns in Belfast, his parents

1

– for some unknown reason - having put him, his brother and his two sisters into an orphanage called Nazareth House in Belfast. These nuns probably reckoned they were full of the Lord's blessing but, in reality, they were mentally and physically abusive to these poor little kids. My father was never harmed, thankfully, but he was clearly one of the lucky ones. It took decades for the truth to filter out about the shocking neglect that took place within Nazareth House.

One day my dad decided he'd had enough so off he went. He walked all the way to the Belfast docks, sneaked onto a coal boat and headed over as a stowaway to Scotland, arriving in the port of Stranraer. He then headed down to London, where he would eventually meet my mum. They were both working in a hotel in London called the Royal Over-Seas League, which still exists to this day. My dad was already engaged to another woman called Eva (I only know that as the idiot still has her name tattooed on his arm) but once he'd clapped eyes on Mum he was smitten.

'Absolutely stunning, with a great arse,' were the first thoughts that came into his head, apparently.

Peter and Amparo fell in love, got married, and within four years were the proud parents of me. Mum was keen to spend her first pregnancy in Spain – she'd understandably wanted to be near her mother and close family - so Dad quit his job at the hotel, packed his suitcase and went abroad with his wife. For the next two years our little family unit lived happily in La Coruna, my Uncle Eladio managing to get Dad a job in the local fish market, despite the fact that he couldn't speak a word of Spanish (my dad, that is, not my uncle). Keen to integrate as best he could, Dad bought himself a Spanish-English dictionary and, whenever he didn't understand a word, would look it up and write it down for future reference. It certainly had the desired effect, because, over time, my dad learned to speak and write the language, a pretty massive achievement for someone who'd left school without any qualifications to his name, and without a trade to speak of.

In early 1971, however, my Dad made the decision to take the family back to England. He'd relocated to San Sebastian on the premise of there being plenty of work, but it turned out not to be the case (my uncle had told a few porkies, it transpired) and after spending a couple of years struggling to keep us fed and clothed, he'd had enough.

'Bollocks to this!' he'd said as he'd flung open our suitcases, thrown in our belongings and headed to the ferry terminal. A strong, proud Irishman, he was not prepared to bring up his son in a household with no money or security, and my mum, perhaps reluctantly, agreed with him.

He promptly contacted his best friend, Peter, asking him if it was okay for the McClean clan to stay at his place in the Manchester suburb of Levenshulme until we found somewhere else to live. His mate obliged, and our trio moved in. It was a tough time for my mum, by all accounts. She hardly spoke any English, had a demanding toddler to look after and was camping out in a complete stranger's house. Not only that, she'd found herself in a big, unfamiliar city that had rain-soaked days and dark, dirty rivers, instead of the wall-to-wall sunshine and the long, golden beaches of her birthplace.

In time, Mum would become ridiculously fond of her adopted 'home' city, but it took a few years to acclimatise. I found it much easier to settle down, apparently. Helping matters was the fact that the house, on Kettering Road, wasn't far from a massive playing field, in Greenbank Park. To me, it was better than any beach, and I'd spend a huge chunk of my childhood running around the park, often with a football at my feet.

Dad was true to his word. Within weeks he'd secured himself a job on the railways and, with money in his pocket, had moved us out of Pete's house and into a tiny little flat. I remember dashing around our new abode thinking *"Wow, this place is massive",* but I suppose everything looked huge to a little 'un like me. On 2nd July 1971, however, I'd find myself fighting for space with a new arrival. My sister, Aurora, was born in St Mary's Hospital, weighing next-to-nothing (she remains skinny to this day; in fact, she's so tiny she travels by fax). One thing about her, as she grew up she had these lovely freckles on her face, which everyone used to comment on, she was and is truly lovely, just don't tell her I said that!

Eventually, having sensibly saved up his wages, Dad was able to put down a £2,000 deposit on a three-bedroomed terrace on Kettering Road. Back then it was a lovely district: clean, safe, and swarming with salt-of-the-earth characters, many of whom were part of the large Irish community that had settled in that area. Located two miles from the city centre, Levenshulme straddled the busy Stockport Road which boasted an array of shops, pubs and cafes, alongside other attractions like the bingo hall and The Palace nightclub.

My sister and I both attended St Richard's RC Primary School, on Wilpshire Avenue. Growing up there was only the two of us, I'd sometimes wish I had a brother to play football with and like most brothers and sisters we fought. But she was my sister above and beyond anything, I remember one occasion she came back crying because one of the boys in the street had hit her. I dashed straight outside, went up to the lad, called David Turner and punched him in the face, I told him that every time he hit my sister I would hit him.

Neither a boffin nor a dunce, academically I was somewhere in the middle. I did, however, have an uncanny knack of picking up random nuggets of trivia that would either amuse or interest me: Sir Walter Raleigh, I learned, was born in rural Devon. Astronaut Neil Armstrong had been an officer in the US Navy before he'd changed vocations. And, as I'd tell anyone who cared to listen, there were 206 bones in the human body.

St Richard's was run by a strict, sergeant major-like headmaster called Mr Welsby. In the mid-to-late 1970s, many schools still advocated corporal punishment which, in our case, either comprised a whack from a slipper or a smack on the backside. One particularly fearsome teacher, Mr Bond, loved a bit of slipper action. The crazy fucker even used to take a run up, and if by the time he got there he found you weren't touching your toes, you received a double dose. I vividly remember getting the slipper in the third year, when I was about nine or ten.

'Why are you late getting into the classroom?' he'd once demanded after I'd nipped out to the toilet. 'You should have asked for permission.'

'You wouldn't have been happy if I'd weed all over your floor,' I replied, which got the whole class laughing.

'Think you're funny, McLain?' he said, pronouncing my name wrongly, which never failed to piss me off.

'It's Mc-CLEAN, Sir, not Mc-LAIN,' I countered, which again got my classmates sniggering.

Mr Bond then told me that he was going to 'wipe the smile of my face', before rummaging in his desk drawer. I honestly thought he was going to bring out a hankie to quite literally wipe off the grin that was annoying him so much, but out came the dreaded slipper instead.

'Bend over and touch your toes, McLain,' he demanded sternly, as the whole class stopped giggling and took a sharp intake of breath. I did as requested and, as I peered through my legs, could see him taking his run up in his tracksuit, slipper in hand, like Daley Thompson going for pole vault glory. He'd have probably dusted his hands in white powder if he'd have had the chance. I closed my eyes, I gritted my teeth and, before I knew it, he'd hit my arse with such a force the whole class went *oooooohhhhhh*. Then he said possibly the daftest thing a teacher has ever said to me.

'Do you want another one, McLain?'

What did he expect me to say, the stupid bastard? *Oooh, yes please, Mr Bond, but this time could you possibly take a bigger run-up and perhaps use a size 10 slipper instead of a size 8, for maximum impact?*

One was enough, thank you very much. In fact, my arse was so red, pupils were coming up taking pictures of it so they could colour match it at the Dulux paint counter.

Mr Bond also happened to organise a lot of the sports at St Richard's. I loved football and athletics, and found myself representing the school in both. My slipper-wielding arch-enemy managed the football team, and for some reason – maybe he just didn't like me - always chucked the number 2 shirt in my direction, ordering me to play at right back. I fucking hated being in defence. I was a tough-tackling midfielder who liked getting stuck into challenges and scoring the odd goal, like my Manchester City hero Dennis Tueart. The more I pleaded to be deployed further up into midfield, however, the more Mr Bond resisted.

'I'm the manager,' he'd snarl, 'and I decide who plays in which position. Do you understand, McLain?'

'I understand, Sir, yes,' I'd reply. I also understood that he was the biggest prick in Levenshulme, but I'd never dream of saying that to his face.

We'd play our school football matches in my beloved Greenbank Park. Despite it being a stone's throw away from our house, my mother and father rarely joined the other parents on the touchline. Mum was far too busy preparing our dinner in the kitchen, and Dad was often waylaid at work. On the rare occasion that he turned up, he'd watch the match but barely comment afterwards, other than a 'did you enjoy that, Michael?'

I'd see the other blokes putting their arms around their boys' shoulders and saying 'I'm proud of you, son,' and 'You played well, lad,' but that just wasn't Dad's style. Don't get me wrong, he'd often take me out on the fields for a kick-about – he wasn't the best footballer yet could strike a shot or two – but he wasn't the type to push me or urge me on.

He never claimed to be a big football fan, to be fair, and was much more interested in horse racing. If his son had been a budding jockey rather than an aspiring footballer - I was definitely small enough - no doubt he'd have been at every race meeting, telling me to dig in deep like Lester Piggott and encouraging me to pass that finishing post.

He absolutely adored the nags, and would be glued to *World of Sport* on a Saturday afternoon for live coverage from Aintree or Newmarket. In the morning he'd leave the house at 9 a.m. to get Mum's shopping (usually returning with all the wrong items) before heading to the bookies' on Stockport Road. There, he'd read *The Sun's* racing page and place his bets.

****

Once my seven years at St Richard's had come to an end, it was time for me to head to senior school. St Alban's RC High School in Gorton was a fifteen-minute walk from my house and was a decent enough place, run by an even stricter headmaster called Mr McFadden. I liked the guy, along with a few other teachers like Mr Brown (a very funny Irishman who'd let us take the piss out of him) and Mr Whatmough, our PE teacher with *Incredible Hulk* thighs and a don't-fuck-with-me attitude. And not forgetting Mr Johnson, our metal-work teacher, who'd let you have a sip of his tea, despite the fact that he'd laced it with whiskey; on a pre-lunch stomach filled with nothing but partially-digested Frosties, you could actually get quite pissed.

I was eager to be a model student at St Alban's, though, and remember trying to look as smart as I could in my brand new uniform, which comprised a navy blue jumper, a light blue shirt, grey trousers and a dark blue tie. Any student who forgot their tie would be frog-marched to McFadden's office to experience a higher grade of corporal punishment, namely The Strap. This teachers' weapon was made of tough brown leather, and would be whacked upon your hand, palm facing upwards, as you tried to stifle your yelp.

Despite not being the most academic of kids, I tried my best in class. My school reports, however, would always trot out the same line.

'*Mike's a very polite young student*,' a teacher would write, '*but he just needs to concentrate on his work rather than trying to make the class laugh…*'

In the early 1980s my love of comedy really started to gather pace. I'd love watching all the best 'funnymen' on TV - particularly Laurel and Hardy, Tommy Cooper and Les Dawson – and would enjoy nothing more than parking myself on the settee and watching a star-studded light entertainment show. *Sunday Night at the London Palladium*, *The Royal Variety Performance* and *Seaside Special* were all favourites of mine, as were any other programmes that featured comedians who made me roar with laughter. What also used to make me laugh was Aurora getting up between commercial brakes and performing a dance routine for us, she really was a Tiny Dancer but maybe somewhere there's performance in our blood.

I'd listen to the radio, too; I was a big fan of Radio 1's comedy segment and would write down all the funniest lines into a notebook to use at school the following Monday. Describing myself as a 'class clown' may be a bit of an old cliché, but that's what I was. To me, the classroom was a stage, and the pupils were like my own personal audience. I loved the feeling of making twenty-five kids laugh (and, occasionally, the teacher too).

I soon forged a close friendship with a fellow pupil, Anthony Beaman, who was a couple of years above me. For some reason we just clicked; he lived on Broom Lane, just over the field from me and his mates and I would spend our weekends and school holidays playing over-upon-over of cricket in the park, or staging football matches on the council-built five-a-side pitch. The fact it had floodlights meant that Anthony and I could stay out until 10 p.m.

I nicknamed him 'B' – for Beaman - and he used to call me 'Mouse' because I was so small.

'Is Mouse in?' Anthony had once asked my mum when he knocked on our front door one afternoon. This confused the hell out of my poor mum, whose command of spoken English was still pretty basic, and who couldn't read or write in the language.

'Sorry, dew wanta de mouse? I don't hab de mouse,' she said, before I ran down the stairs, with my football under my arm, to explain.

B was a great character, a proper one-off. He didn't give a shit and would change his appearance on a whim; I remember him frightening Mum to death when he turned up to my gaff with a shaved head, jeans covered in zips, Doc Marten boots and a leather jacket, like Kenny Everett's Sid Snot.

It was during a particularly boisterous five-a-side match that I made another good mate, a lad called Jock (his real name was actually Steven, but he'd just moved from Scotland to Manchester, hence the highly original nickname). I'd gone in for a challenge, and Jock had inadvertently booted me in the mouth.

'Ye all right, wee man?' he'd asked, looking down on me as I writhed on the deck.

'Fine mate,' I'd replied, as the blood gushed from my mouth.

It wasn't an ideal start to a friendship, but from that day on Jock and I became as thick as thieves (we still are really and I see him most Man City games). I introduced him to B and his mates, and he became one of the crew who'd meet up to play footy most days, and drink cans of lager every Friday night.

One particular weekend in May, a local fair came to Greenbank Park, the travellers parking their gaudily-painted trucks on a Levenshulme side road before rigging up all the various rides and stalls. As Jock and I watched them set to task, he came up with the bright idea of, later that night, nicking the light bulbs from the Helter-Skelter so we could sell them and make some money.

Being the smallest and most agile, I was designated to do the dirty deed. However, as I shinned down the Helter-Skelter, with a handful of unscrewed bulbs stuffed in my pockets, I spotted a police van heading in our direction.

'Shit... leg it,' I yelled to Jock, but as we ran through the park we found another van waiting for us. Busted.

I think the officers found it all fairly amusing – at one point we thought they were going to let us off, and send us on our merry way – but they insisted on driving us back home in the big van, knowing full well that our parents – or our curtain-twitching neighbours - would get wind of our misdemeanours.

The next day I had no choice but to tell my mum. You'd have thought that I'd committed some barbaric murder and buried my victim under the patio, such was her tearful reaction.

'A poleez ban at my house?' Mum wailed (she'd always had issues pronouncing her 'v's). She then started a long, angry Spanish rant - interspersed with a few English 'Ohmagods' – before chasing me around the front room table with a frying pan.

My dad, in contrast, was surprisingly calm when it came to punishment. He'd never lay a finger on me, but had the ability to utter one simple sentence that would make my blood run cold.

'Because of that, you're to be in every night at seven o'clock, Mike,' he'd say, as I shook my head. There was nothing more embarrassing than telling your friends that you had to be home early, and Dad knew it.

CHAPTER 2

Love Man City

At a very early age I'd decided that football was my sport of choice, and I made it my ambition in life to play for the mighty Manchester City. I chose them as my team, as opposed to Manchester United, because I loved their sky blue and white Umbro kits, especially the diamonds that went down the arms. I became the captain of the St Alban's school team - either playing in midfield or in goal – and simply lived, breathed and ate the Beautiful Game.

At one stage, probably when I was about thirteen, I was hand-picked by a Manchester City talent scout to attend the club's ten-week junior training camp, held at their Platt Lane ground. Wow! Can you imagine the thirteen year old me? In my mind I was already destined to be on Match of the Day!

'If you impress the coaches, you'll be able to train on a more permanent basis,' I was informed.

After the final school bell, I'd cycle like hell to get to Rush-olme for 4.30pm, when former City player Brian Kidd would begin the session. While I always trained hard with the other lads, I got the feeling that my small stature put me at a disad-vantage; in those days – unlike now - height and bulk seemed to be the most important player attributes.

I was utterly devastated therefore when, at the end of the ten weeks, my name wasn't among the successful candidates. I cycled home to Levenshulme in tears, truly feeling like my life had just been blown apart. I dusted myself off, though, and carried on turning out for my school team and the Junior Blues side, and even made a few appearances for Manchester Boys.

I loved watching football as much as playing it and, each year, Mum and Dad would present me with a Maine Road season ticket for my birthday.

'Thanks so much,' I'd say, grinning as I opened the envelope to unveil my 'surprise'. My parents were by no means well off; in the early 1980s Mum was working as a school cook and Dad, due to the unstable economic climate, was in and out of various manual jobs. Somehow, though, they managed to scrape enough money together. On occasion, I think Dad had to resort to borrowing extra cash, as I seem to recall a 'money man' visiting us on a Saturday for his weekly payment. When I look back and think about it now, it's those small details that make realise just how much they really did do their best.

There were limits as to how much football gear I could have, however, and I remember one year being told that my parents simply couldn't afford to buy me a brand new City kit. As a compromise, however, Mum bought me a sky blue shirt from the market (upon which she sewed the official club badge and drew the Umbro logo) as well as some sky blue shorts and socks. Amparo McClean was making knock-off replica strips well before anyone in the Far East jumped on the bandwagon, but little did she know that her creation was mocked by every kid that saw it, especially my United-supporting mates. I didn't give a monkey's, though; in my eyes it was a Manchester City kit, and I felt proud as punch wearing it.

My first visit to Maine Road was just amazing. I went with my mate Alan, a fellow Blue, and can still recall that walk through Moss Side to the stadium, soaking up all that pre-match atmosphere. Once we got to the stands, we'd grab ourselves a hot drink and a steaming pie before watching our heroes emerging from the tunnel.

****

Life in Kettering Road continued to be good. Thanks to Mum, our house was always immaculate and we ate the best food ever, most of it of the Spanish variety. We ate lovely pan-fried fish with roasted vegetables, mussels in hot, spicy sauce, and Spanish omelette with chorizo sausage before it became a foodies' favourite. We always had wine on the table, too.

Whenever my mates came around Mum would invariably want to feed them, and growing lads like B and Jock would always be well up for some tasty Spanish fare. That was until the day she presented them with a plateful of squid.

'What's this?' I remember them saying, regarding their meal like it had landed from outer space. 'You don't really eat this stuff do you, Mike?'

All our meals were freshly made; Mum would never buy packet food and my sister Aurora and I were forbidden from eating at our local McDonalds.

'You want a hamburger, I will make you one,' Mum would say, thinking she was doing us a huge favour.

'Yeah, but yours are about seven inches thick and three feet wide, Mum,' I'd whine.

The only time we were able to eat 'convenience food' was on a Friday night – otherwise known as 'Chippy Night' – when Dad would visit the chip shop on Barlow Road and Mum would have a well-earned break from her kitchen duties or when I grabbed a pie at the footie.

I'd get the chance to experience even more of Mum's Spanish heritage during the summer holidays, when Mum, Dad, Aurora and I would visit the family in La Coruna. They were the only relatives I had, really, since my father had lost touch with most of his.

I remember, when I was about ten, travelling to London to stay with my Auntie Bene, before catching a coach to Luton Airport and flying out to Spain. My Uncle Mario and his wife Lola met us at the airport; it was the first time my mum had seen her brother for years and they were both crying like babies. All six of us headed to my uncle's flat in a little Corsa, every single adult puffing on a cigarette as we did so (weren't the 'Eighties brilliant?). Waiting for us was my lovely nan, or 'Abuela' in Spanish. I'd never met her before – I'd only seen her in black and white photographs - yet on this occasion she was a vision in glorious 3D Technicolor.

Aurora and I had a brilliant summer, spending hour after hour playing on the beautiful golden beaches and swimming in the crystal blue waters. I got to know my cousins well, including the boys (I shared a top bunk with José Ramon while Pedro slept in the bottom bunk) and the two girls, Sonia and Lolli. José took me under his wing - he was like a big brother to me – and would drive me around the town on his scooter, neither of us bothering with anything as sensible as a crash helmet.

A couple of years later, in 1982, Spain were due to host the World Cup finals.

'D'you fancy going over to Spain for the summer, Mike?' Dad had asked one day, completely out of the blue. 'You can stay with the family and watch the footy.'

I couldn't believe what I was hearing. Not only would I be living in Spain for three months, I was going to be excused from St Alban's High School, too, the plan being that I'd attend a school in La Coruna in order to learn Spanish. Then, in August, mum and Aurora would come and join me while Dad held the fort at home, where no-one would be able to nag him about spending every Saturday in the bookies'.

'How cool is that?' said my mate B when I told him about my travels. I know for a fact that some of my teachers were pretty envious, too.

I felt all grown up on the flight over to La Coruna, and I remember the lady sitting next to me laughing her head off when I asked the air stewardess for a red wine (I was deadly serious; we drank it at home all the time). I was met at La Coruna airport by my Uncle Mario and cousin Lolli, neither of whom spoke a word of English apart from 'You like?', 'Yes please' and 'Fuck off'.

How the hell am I going to manage? I remember thinking.

I stayed with my cousin José Ramon, who lived in a flat with his girlfriend Conchi and their baby girl, Vanessa. The routine, supposedly, was that I'd have breakfast at my Nan's every morning before going to the local high school with Lolli. This plan lasted for about a week. I couldn't understand a bloody word they were on about, so I decided to sack the education bit and just have one big jolly. I swapped the classroom for the beach, and every day would don my kit, grab a football and spend hours practising my skills on the sand, come rain or shine. Of course, my family knew but they never said anything.

Just because I'd binned school didn't mean that I wasn't learning Spanish, though. By living with the family in La Coruna, and by playing with the kids in the neighbourhood, I couldn't help but pick up elements of the language. I'd teach them English words, they'd teach me simple Spanish phrases like *hijo de puta* – son of a bitch - and after a month I was able to communicate quite well.

As the World Cup loomed – it began on June 13th – my excitement mounted. La Coruna happened to be one of the host towns, so I got to see Cameroon, Italy, Poland and Bulgaria in action. Argentina's Diego Maradona was the main man that tournament, though, and I just loved watching him play on the telly; the guy was a genius of a footballer.

After the final - Italy beat West Germany - my uncle took us away to a camp site that overlooked the most beautiful bay I'd ever seen. With my Spanish improving by the day, I found that I could chat to other kids in the resort as long as they spoke slowly (most Spaniards speak like they're on fast-forward). Most of my playmates were all right, but having an English accent wasn't exactly a badge of honour in 1982.

'You start Falklands War,' I remember one kid saying, before spitting at me.

I wasn't having any of that.

'Listen, *hijo de puta*,' I replied. 'Firstly, I'm not English, I was born over here and I've got an Irish dad. And secondly, not that I'm a grass or anything, but I think you'll find Thatcher started it, not me.' I think he muttered something in garbled Spanish that was unlikely to be complementary, then left with his ball.

José Ramon's flat wasn't far away from the town's red light area, where all the prostitutes plied their trade. Following a game of football on the nearby pitches, my friends and I would watch the soldiers from the army barracks head into a cheap hotel to get their fill (I remember us wolf -whistling the good looking ones; the girls, not the soldiers). I also clearly recall my nan taking me shopping for some shoes one day, and making a detour the 'back way', through the red light area. As we did so, every single prostitute let onto her.

'Hola, this is my grandson... he's from England,' said Nan, as the girls kissed me on each cheek.

Holy shit, I thought. *Are we really going shoe shopping? Is it code for something else? Is my nan a pimp? Is she about to get me a prostitute?*

Much to my relief, it was nothing of the sort. It turned out that everyone in the town knew my Nan; in her younger days she'd cleaned the steps of that hotel (and others around La Coruna) and had become something of a local celebrity. I did get my shoes, by the way, and I bloody hated them (sorry Nan).

The summer just flew by, and it wasn't long before I had to return home to England. I had mixed feelings, really. On the one hand I was so excited to see my dad – I'd spent nearly fifteen weeks away, and had missed him terribly – but on the other hand I was sad to leave my Spanish family. On my last

19

night my auntie cooked us all my favourite meal - octopus with boiled potatoes – and I took the chance to say all my thank yous and goodbyes to everyone around the table. My cousin José was sad to see me go and his wife Conchi started to cry. They'd loved having me live with them, apparently, and my broken Spanish had made them laugh.

'I've loved every minute,' I said, 'and I'll never, ever forget this summer.'

And I never did. If I had a time machine, I'm pretty sure that La Coruna, in that long, hot summer of 1982, would be the place that I'd want to go.

****

Somewhat reluctantly, I returned to St Alban's RC High School in September. Around the same time, I discovered a little book that would go on to change my life. At school we'd often be handed a mini-magazine, its pages full of cut-price hardbacks and paperbacks that I'd occasionally buy with my £1 pocket money. One morning I distinctly remember one title catching my eye: *More Magic* by Paul Daniels. *I'm having that*, I thought.

At that time, Paul Daniels was in his heyday. Eighteen million viewers would regularly tune in to his peak-time Saturday night TV show on BBC One, and I was always among them.

'Woah, how did he do that?' I'd say to my sister as the little magician performed brilliant vanishing card tricks, and pulled mad stunts involving hats and live white rabbits.

As a kid, I'd never read a book from cover to cover, but I couldn't put *More Magic* down. I mastered every single trick and I'd start off by showing them to Aurora at home. Once I got brave enough, I'd perform some of them to my school friends, completely baffling them (my classmates weren't the brightest, to be fair; I could have either waved a wand and conjured up a bloody elephant or marble and their expressions would have been the same). Performing tricks made me feel so euphoric, though, and in a funny way, my new-found talent softened the blow of being rejected from Manchester City. I promptly abandoned my plans to become the next Dennis Tueart; I now wanted to become the next Paul Daniels.

In order to expand my repertoire of tricks I tried to get my hands on as many magic books as I could, even becoming the first member of my family to join a library. My favourites became the Chop Cup - basically comprising a silver beaker and a ball that you had to try and follow - and the Burnt-and-Restored-Five-Pound-Note, whereby the money would reappear inside a piece of fruit. Such was my devotion, I stopped playing football in the evenings, preferring to spend all my spare time practising the tricks in my bedroom (well that's what I told my parents, anyway).

I also enrolled myself into a proper magic club, based in Moston, which led to me being entered into an official Magic Circle stage competition at the tender age of thirteen. I remember that night so clearly. My parents bought me a dinner suit specially for the occasion, and my dad agreed to come with me to offer some moral support. As he took his seat in the audience at the Moston Methodist Church, I remember feeling petrified. I'd never stood on a stage before, and my forklift truck driver father and dinner lady mother didn't exactly equate to your average showbiz family. I managed to get through my ten-minute routine, although I didn't win a prize.

'Better luck next time,' said a fellow magician.

My first ever paid 'gig' took place a few months later, on New Year's Eve at the Levenshulme Conservative Club. An act had pulled out at the last minute, and I was asked if I wanted to do a spot.

'Yes please,' I said, jumping at the chance.

I walked on the stage with my table, my props, and without a clue what to do. Within the first five minutes I found myself getting heckled by an audience member who probably thought this tiny teenager would buckle under the pressure. Little did he know that I was forearmed with an array of put-downs.

'Thank you for your undervalued opinion', I said. He then gave me some more stick, to which I replied 'Please stop shouting, mate, otherwise I'll stop getting punters for your sister.'

The audience laughed and clapped, seemingly amazed that this cheeky little scamp was standing his ground. I continued with my spot and left the stage to a huge round of applause. It felt amazing. Wow! I had just stood on a stage and made people laugh, I felt 6 foot tall and I'd got paid. I knew right there that getting paid for something you love doing was always going to be the icing on the cake.

'Thanks, Mike,' said the club secretary as he handed me a fiver. 'You were great, son.'

I put the note in my coat pocket before legging it back home. When I reached into my pocket to proudly show Mum and Dad my fee, however, there was no sign of it. *Damn*, I thought. *I must have lost it on the way.* I ran back to the club to ask if anyone had handed in a fiver, only for the security guard to shake his head.

'Don't lose this one, though,' he grinned, delving into his coat and handing over another. A few days' later I found the original, so technically I'd earned the grand sum of £10 for my first professional appearance.

CHAPTER 3

Now That's Magic

I continued to enjoy life at St Alban's, particularly the drama lessons. Our teacher, Mr Feeney, assembled a drama group which would devise little plays and routines, usually based on improvisation rather than scripts. Once, we were asked to produce a doctors' waiting room sketch for the upcoming Parents' Evening. I loved the whole process, from coming up with funny lines to sorting out the stage directions, and it turned into quite an amusing little skit which got loads of laughs.

Mr Feeney seemed impressed with my enthusiasm, and invited me to do a ten-minute magic spot that night, too. In a school hall packed to the rafters with pupils, parents and teachers, I performed one of my favourite tricks. Firstly, I asked the headmaster, Mr McFadden, to join me on the makeshift stage.

'Have you got a lot of money?' I asked him.

'Erm, no...' he replied

'You must have, surely,' I said with a wink, 'because you clearly don't spend it on your clothes, sir...'

At this, everyone laughed, even him. I then asked him to get hold of a pound note (remember them?), told him to write down its serial number, before placing it in an envelope. I proceeded to hold up a sign bearing the letters 'M.M.M.M' which stood for 'MIKE'S MUNCHING MONEY MACHINE', which was basically a pair of scissors. I asked him to choose one of three envelopes, one of which apparently contained the pound note, and I destroyed the other two.

'Okay,' I said, 'open the envelope, take out the pound note and show everyone. Mr McFadden did as he was told and brought out a blank piece of paper.

'Once you've got out your pound note,' I continued, 'show the audience that it matches the serial number you gave me at the beginning.'

The kids and parents started to laugh nervously as they saw that the 'note' was in fact a slip of paper. They thought I'd messed up the trick, and that it had all gone pear-shaped.

'Guess who'll be in detention tomorrow,' said Mr McFadden who, it appeared, had lost his money. I remained deadpan.

'I'm so sorry, sir,' I said, feigning disappointment, before asking him to come to the side of the stage, where there was a balloon attached to a piece of string.

'Has anyone got a lighter?' I asked, before setting the string alight. The flame burned up to the balloon and popped it, and out came a little plastic Action Man-type figurine affixed to a little parachute. Tied to his parachute was the head-master's pound note, bearing exactly the same serial number that he'd jotted down.

The applause was deafening. Mr McFadden stood there, his mouth agape.

'Okay, McClean, he said after everyone had filed out of the hall. 'How the hell did you do that?'

'Can you keep a secret?' I whispered.

'Yes, of course,' he answered.

'Well so can I, sir...' I grinned, before packing up my props, turning on my heels, and walking off. Back to school the next day all the teachers kept asking me how was it done, but I was a true professional and never told.

With my confidence growing, I began to enter more local talent shows and tried to perform in public as much as I could. I was asked to do a show for my mum's friend, for example, who worked at an old people's home. Let's just say it wasn't my best career move. It was bonkers. I had one man randomly standing up and yelling 'I can see dead people' at the top of his voice, a woman screaming 'Don't touch me!' at every opportunity, as well as another fella who, right in the middle of my act, hobbled over and asked me to take him to the toilet. And not forgetting the frisky old sod in the corner who decided to get his cock out, much to the amusement of the old dears sat beside him. I think the majority of them were more bothered about getting their medication rather than watching a magician, although they did all clap at the end, no doubt pleased that I'd finally finished and they could get back to *Pebble Mill At One*.

At the time it all felt pretty traumatic for a fourteen-year-old but, looking back, it was a huge learning curve for me; if I could get through a gig in a care home, where they could barely remember which fucking card they'd chosen, I could do a gig anywhere.

On another occasion, I saw an advert in he *Manchester Evening News* that was recruiting acts to take part in a talent show in a pub just off Pink Bank Lane, in nearby Longsight.

'Have you heard of a pub called The Garratt?' I asked my dad, telling him that I was thinking of throwing my hat into the ring. I thought he was going to faint on the spot.

'You bloody what?' he yelled. 'No son of mine is doing a gig in that place. Some fella got stabbed there a few weeks' back...'

After some pleading – I was desperate to take part - I managed to persuade Dad to chaperone me to The Garratt. The following Tuesday, at seven o'clock, we arrived at an empty pub, however, causing me to wonder whether I'd got the right night.

'Is the talent show on here tonight?' asked Dad.

'Oh aye, yeah,' said the guy behind the bar.

'Then I'll have a nice pint of Guinness, and he'll have an orange juice,' he said, beckoning for me to sit on a nearby chair while he had a chat with the bartender. Dad explained to him that I was one of the acts, and that I did magic. At this, the guy behind the bar let out a huge belly laugh.

'A magician,' he guffawed, looking over at me. 'I wish your lad all the best. They're animals in here, mate, *animals...*'

Dad returned with the drinks, white as a sheet.

'You better be bloody good,' was all he said.

Within an hour, the pub was packed. On the same bill, I discovered, were two singers, a reggae band, a dance troupe and a comedian. We drew lots and I was due on third.

That's not so bad, I thought.

The first two acts – the comedian and one of the singers - both died a slow death. I could hardly drink my orange juice my hands were shaking so much, and had to ask Dad to get me a straw.

'Up next,' said the compere, 'is a teenage magician from down the road in Levenshulme...'

Well, they started laughing before I had even got on the stage. *Please don't say he's come with his dad...* I remember thinking.

'...so let's all give a great welcome on stage to young Mike McClean...'

I can safely say that I was shitting myself. Not even a war correspondent would have done a live report from this pub, yet here I was on a stage with a hundred-or-so rough-arse locals demanding to be entertained. Meanwhile, in the corner, my dad was making the sign of the cross and flicking through a brochure for headstones.

I started off with a card trick and asked someone to pick a card and show it to the audience. The drummer of the reggae band, a big black guy, walked up to the stage, chose a card as requested, and – out of the fifty-two cards - held up the ace of spades.

The pub promptly erupted. Everyone was pissing themselves laughing - including the reggae band, the compere and the drug dealers in the corner - and I didn't have the first clue why. I remember standing there, confused as hell, surrounded by all this mirth, thinking *What did I do? What did I say?* I just carried on with the rest of the trick, ripping the card up, giving him one piece and making the pieces vanish.

I became even more perplexed as the trick progressed to its next stage. I had with me a bag of fruit, which contained an apple, an orange and a banana. I asked him to put his hand in and grab one, and out came the banana. People were now shrieking with laughter – 'It's feeding time, Lennie,' shouted one of his band-mates – and I tried to soldier on as best I could, peeling apart the banana to reveal his ace of spades card, as he still grasped its missing piece.

Lennie left the stage to a massive round of applause, yet I still felt totally and utterly bewildered.

Looking back, I think my naivety, innocence and genuine confusion probably added to the hilarity, and probably defused a potentially awkward and offensive situation. Put it this way, I'm pretty sure there'd have been a wholly different response from Lennie and the band had I been an older, more knowing magician.

My final trick was the age-old 'head chopper' routine, when a magician gets a woman to put her head in a guillotine, and appears to slice a blade through her neck while simultaneously scything some carrots in half. I selected a woman to come up onto the stage, wheeled on the guillotine and demonstrated how it could chop things up, placing a big carrot in the middle of the blade and standing behind it.

Yet again, everyone began to laugh. *Not again*, I thought. *What the hell are they laughing at now?* Even Dad was chuckling, which wasn't like him. I reached around and grabbed hold of the carrot, prompting my audience to start crying with mirth. It's only then when I twigged – it clearly looked like I was holding my penis – and I just tutted and shook my head before slamming the blade through the carrot, cutting it in half.

I glanced over at the woman, who had turned white as a sheet.

'I am not putting my fucking head in there,' she said.

'Yes you fucking are,' shouted her partner.

'Fuck off,' she replied.

'No *you* fuck off,' he countered.

This Longsight domestic carried on for a few minutes before she eventually relented. She knelt down and placed her head in the guillotine, after which I put a bucket near her backside.

'If you shit yourself this'll catch it all,' I said, my confidence growing by the minute. Yet more gales of laughter. I was *on fire*.

Because I was getting a bit cocky and had probably taken my eye off the ball, I'd overlooked the fact that this woman had long hair, something that you'd generally try to avoid with this kind of trick. As I'd casually put her head inside the guillotine, and as I'd knocked the safety hatch down, I'd not paid enough attention to her flowing blonde tresses.

After building up the tension by getting the audience to perform a countdown ('three...two...one...') bang, I slammed the blades down. BANG.

'*MY FUCKING HAIR...!*' the woman yelled, as I hacked through the carrot and most of her hairdo. I tried and failed to release the blade, since the remnants of her hair had jammed the machine. By now everyone was screaming with laughter - apart from me, of course - and this only became louder when she finally wrestled free of the guillotine and glared at me, sporting her new, lopsided Human League-style hairdo.

'Ladies and gentlemen, you've been a great audience,' I said, quickly ushering her back to her seat. 'I'm Mike McClean, good night!'

I walked back to my seat near the bar – past the compere, who was wiping away tears from his eyes – and re-joined my dad.

'That was bloody funny, son,' he said.

'Funny? It wasn't meant to be funny,' I snapped. 'I'm a serious magician.'

Then the comedian came over, asking me if I wrote my own stuff, and telling me that I'd go a long way in this business. *Write my own stuff? What the hell was he on about?*

I then went to the toilet, and found myself standing next to the black guy who'd done the card trick.

'Man, that was funny,' he grinned. 'The ace of fucking spades, you cheeky fucker...'

I came second that night – behind one of the singers, and in front of the reggae band – and walked away thirty quid better off.

That night a few things dawned on me. Nobody wanted to see a serious magician; they wanted to see a funny one. I also realised that I could probably make money from this showbiz lark, and that comedy was definitely for me.

CHAPTER 4

Get A Bloody Job…

The next day I went to school with a spring in my step, and a head brimming with ideas. I knew that my whole routine had to change and that, in order to stand out from the rest, it had to be funny. I began to hone my act, continuing to attend my monthly magic club and entering its junior stage competition. I put together a ten-minute routine, and did my best to add some comedy to the tricks.

I was a bit disappointed to come third in the contest, but was pleased to learn that my act had been reviewed in an entertainment magazine by a fellow magician, Les Greenhall. 'This man will go far if only he keeps at it,' he'd written. I still have the article hung up in my toilet.

Les had also introduced himself to me after the show. He was a short, grey, oldish guy who was always immaculately dressed.

'I've been doing magic for donkey's years, Mike,' he'd said, 'and I'd love to teach you some more. Come over to my house whenever you like.'

I appreciate that, to some, such an offer might have sounded a bit dodgy, but Les was completely legit and totally genuine. He was a committed family man, married to a really lovely lady, and simply wanted to help a young lad produce some decent magic. I took Les up on his offer, and, armed with my bag of tricks, would visit his house in Crumpsall.

There, he'd give me some hints and tips and would help me create some routines. He was a master of the 'pea under the shell' trick, often practiced on street corners, whereby people would be challenged to bet which shell the pea was beneath, and would invariably lose all their money. Les' amazing sleight of hand meant that I'd choose the wrong option every time, without fail.

'I think you should enter the *Junior Close Up* competition, Mike,' Les suggested one evening. This was a very prestigious magic contest to which only the best youngsters were invited, and it was also the first time they'd staged a junior version. For the next few weeks, Les painstakingly went through everything with me, telling me what to do, what to say and how to do it.

On the night of the contest I asked my parents if they wanted to come along, but they both declined. My mum was addicted to her soap operas, bless her, and that evening I think there was a massive storyline in *Coronation Street* that she didn't want to miss. As for my Dad, he 'just fancy a night in, Son.'

Deep down, I was gutted that they'd both preferred to sit in front of the box rather than support their son. In fact, my mum never once came to see me in any competitions - maybe it was just a Spanish thing – but I remember feeling quite upset about it at the time.

'Good luck, Son,' mumbled Dad as I left the house to catch the first of two buses that would take me to the north Manchester suburb of Moston.

'Aren't your parents coming?' was the first thing that Les asked when I arrived at Moston Methodist Church, shaking his head sadly when I explained the situation. Looking back on it now I know that without a doubt they were both very proud of me and still are, they just didn't realise the importance and to be fair patents in our generation weren't under the same pressure to attend everything their child does for fear of parental failure.

I got changed, and soon found myself up on the stage. Was I scared? Yeah, just a little. Put it this way, had Pampers Pull-Ups existed back then, I'd have worn three pairs. I performed my ten-minute routine – honed by Les – and, once all the acts had done their turn, there was a little break before the results were announced. I soon discovered that I wasn't in third place, and that I wasn't in second place, either.

'The winner of the inaugural Junior Close-Up competition,' announced the compere, before a dramatic pause, 'is... Mike McClean!'

My jaw dropped to the floor. *I'd come fucking first.* I'd never won anything in my life, apart from the 1500 metres on school sports day and the occasional game of 'I-Spy' with my sister.

'Congratulations, young man,' said Les after I'd gone up to collect my award. 'But remember this, please. Just because you won doesn't make you the best. It just means you were the best out of a bad bunch.'

His reaction totally floored me, and wiped the beaming grin off my face. There I was, basking in my moment of glory, and Les had chosen to piss on my chips. But if he'd purposely said it to stop me from getting big headed, it worked, because from that day, on I neither took my competitions, nor my rivals for granted.

Incidentally, Les sadly died a couple of years, later, and I was really touched when a friend of his told me that he'd often talked about me in glowing terms, and that I'd made him feel extremely proud.

That night I boarded the bus from Moston and headed home, sporting a smile that stretched from Land's End to John O'Groats. Once I reached Levenshulme I ran all the way home, desperate to relay my good news to Mum and Dad. While they were both pleased enough to see me clutching my trophy, there were no kisses, handshakes or back slaps. It didn't take them long to turn their attention back to *Corrie* on the telly. They simply weren't the demonstrative parents that maybe others had, but I knew they were happy as long as I was happy.

My teachers seemed far more impressed, however, and Mr McFadden even gave me an honourable mention in assembly. Word must have travelled, though, because that same day I also got a call from the *Manchester Metro* newspaper, requesting an interview and photo session. They duly sent a reporter and snapper to my house and, lo and behold, a few days' later my achievement was splashed over the front page.

'YOUNG MAGICIAN WINS PRESTIGIOUS MAGIC COMPETITION' trumpeted the headline.

In the aftermath, I was treated like a celebrity at school, especially by the girls (most of them wanted to see my trick rather than my dick, more's the pity). Not everyone at St Alban's was impressed, though, and I was subject to a lot of snidey comments, too, among pupils and staff alike.

'Not done your homework, McClean?' asked my Social Studies teacher, Mr Body, one morning. 'Well, maybe you could magic it to my desk in the next ten minutes.'

On this occasion, as was often the case, my cheek got the better of me.

'No sir,' I replied, looking him up and down, and surveying his dodgy clothes. 'If I could do any magic in the next ten minutes I'd magic you into some ironed trousers and a pair of nice shoes.'

The whole class pissed themselves laughing, but Mr Body wasn't happy.

'I tell you what, why don't I magic you to the headmaster,' he countered, and I soon found myself standing outside McFadden's office.

Much to my surprise, the first thing he did was congratulate me on winning my competition, before asking me if I'd be able to perform the same act at the next Parents' Association meeting. Then he bollocked me for what I said to Mr Body, and reached into his drawer for the dreaded strap. Immediately I seized my opportunity.

'Sir, when exactly is the parents' meeting?' I asked.

'Tomorrow night,' came my his reply.

'The thing is, sir, if I get the strap I won't be able to perform, as I need the use of my hands.'

He smiled, before slowly returning the strap to the drawer.

'Very, very good, McClean,' he said. 'Just get out of my office before I change my mind.'

The next day, having done a great show in the school hall, Mr McFadden invited me back into his office.

'Well done,' McClean,' he said, telling me that my act had gone down brilliantly with the mums and dads. I thanked him and was just about to leave when he stopped me in my tracks.

'Ah, McClean, when's your next show?'

'Not for a while sir,' I replied.

At that, he reached into his drawer and pulled out his strap.

'I couldn't give you this yesterday, but I can today,' he said.

The man was two steps ahead of me, not one, and despite the stinging pain of leather on skin, my respect for him grew that day. I'd like to think that the feeling was mutual.

I continued to do more and more magic shows – doing my best to swerve any bookings for old folks' homes – and was even asked to perform in front of the Lord Mayor of Manchester at the Town Hall. It was only a twenty-minute slot, and there wasn't any fee involved, but the thought of doing my act in front of a VIP audience was reason enough for me to say yes. For once, however, I was glad that Dad had chosen to stay at home, because that night he may well have committed murder.

My act that evening went down a storm, and the Town Hall staff were so impressed that they organised for me to be taken home by the mayor's driver, in the big black official car.

I was made up, firstly because it was always a real pain to haul my props and my table onto the bus, and secondly because I couldn't wait to draw up outside my house in a posh Daimler. The driver helped me pack up my stuff, chattering away as he did so – *what I lovely fella*, I remember thinking – before ushering me into the nearby lift. As soon as the heavy doors closed, however, his mood seemed to shift.

'Loved your show, very funny,' he smiled, looking me up and down and slowly edging towards me.

'Thank you,' I replied uneasily, as he began to invade my space.

'I bet you've got a big one,' he leered, eyeing my crotch as the lift started to descend.

I just froze. *Oh my God*, I thought. I pretended I didn't hear him and just looked away.

'I said I bet you've got a big one,' he repeated, this time with a wink. 'Go on, Mike... why don't you show it to me?'

The lift seemed to take an eternity to go down – the countdown of red floor numbers took ages – and I remember shaking with fear, petrified that he was going to try and touch me. I decided to scream and kick him in the bollocks if he did.

'I'd *really* love to see it,' he said. At that moment, the lift shuddered to a halt as it reached the ground floor, and the doors opened. 'Wait here,' he said, 'and I'll go and fetch the car.'

As if I'm going to hang around for you, you fucking pervert, I thought, and as soon as he turned his back I legged it to the nearest taxi rank, clambered into a cab and told the driver to put his foot down, all the way to Levenshulme. Little did I know that it was happening all over the place. It's taken nearly 40 years for it to all come out. The celebs that you thought you could trust were all perverts. I don't need to name them, we all know who they are.

'How did it go?' asked Dad when I arrived back home.

'Great,' I said, before making myself a cup of tea and heading straight to my bedroom. I never breathed a word to my parents; had I done so, I know for a fact that Dad would have stormed over to the Lord Mayor's office, dragged out that dirty old driver and lamped him on the spot.

****

In 1985 I turned fifteen, and my final day at St Alban's was fast approaching. Unfortunately, I had to miss out on the school's annual skiing trip to France because my parents couldn't afford it. That year my dad had been made redundant from Johnson and Nephew's iron works although, bless him, when he'd received his final pay packet he'd put £5 in an envelope and sent it anonymously to a children's home (that was him all over). Sadly, Dad remained reluctantly unemployed for a further two years. An out-of-work Irishman was virtually unheard of in his world, and he hated every minute of it.

In order to avoid asking my parents for cash, I took on some extra jobs. I started a daily paper round and also worked at Maine Road, selling City's match day programmes (sometimes I'd bring home a few spares for Dad to flog in the pub). And, while I was proud of the fact that I was generating my own income, even I couldn't stump up enough for an Alpine holiday.

The time had also come for me to think about my post-school career path. Unlike many of my classmates, I knew exactly where my ambitions lay: I wanted to be an actor, a performer. I'd already had a small taste of 'showbiz' with my magic act, but my appetite had also been whetted by the various theatre trips that I'd attended with school, to venues like the Davenport Theatre in Stockport and the Library Theatre in central Manchester. I'd be enraptured as I watched the actors prowl around the stage and, during the post-show Q&A session, would barrage them with questions about their methods and their craft. During Dad's employment at Johnson and Nephew's, the firm would treat their staff and their families to a Christmas pantomime trip, which I loved. All that, together with my long-standing TV addiction, fuelled my desire to perform, and persuaded me that my future lay in light entertainment. Not everyone shared my faith and enthusiasm, though.

'I'm going to be an actor or performer, sir,' I once said to Mr Brown, our careers teacher, which prompted everyone in the classroom to fall about laughing.

'No one becomes an actor,' was his response.

'Really, sir? Where do they all come from in the films, then?

'America,' he said, glaring at me. 'They all come from America.'

Mr Brown then explained that, as part of the careers' curriculum, we had to organise our own work experience placement, for a whole fortnight. One classmate said he wanted to drive a white delivery van – *aim high, lad*, I remember thinking – and another boy – who was as thick as shit – said he hoped to work as a vet. He had more chance of winning Miss World, the poor bastard.

'If you're having problems sorting out a placement, speak to me,' said Mr Brown. 'I've got local firms that can offer you work.'

I set to task. In the spring of 1985 I'd managed to secure myself a stand-up gig at the Contact Theatre in Manchester, doing a half-hour routine before the main show for £5. One evening I decided to bite the bullet, asking the artistic director, Tony, if I could do my work experience there.

'Of course, Mike,' he smiled. 'No problem at all.'

The next day I went in search of Mr Brown to tell him my glad tidings.

"Sir, I've sorted out my work experience," I grinned, collaring him as he was having his lunch in the dining hall.

'McClean, can't you see I'm eating,' he growled. 'And anyway, I've already got yours planned. You start at Kwik-Fit next week. Now go away.'

I walked away, fuming. *Kwik-fucking-Fit?* He had to be joking. He knew damned well I wanted to work in the theatre, not change some twat's front tyre.

The next day, it was Mr Brown that found me in the canteen.

'Ah, there you are, McClean,' he said.

'D'you mind, sir, I'm having my lunch,' I replied, before turning my attention to the food on my plate.

'My office... NOW,' he yelled.

'But I'm still eating, sir,' I said.

'You'd better be in my office when you've finished,' he replied, before storming off.

I was given a full dressing down by Mr Brown, who accused me of ingratitude after he'd spent all that time organising my work placement. I wasn't having any of it though, and stood my ground. To be honest, towards the end of my school life I'd become sick to death of the way some teachers seemed to enjoy belittling their students.

'On Monday I'm starting my work experience at the Contact Theatre, not Kwik-Fit, and no one's going to stop me,' I said, giving the knobhead a withering look before walking out of his office.

During my first week at the Contact I was generally office-bound, doing all the menial jobs like filing and tea-making. The following week, following a grand tour of the theatre, I was allowed to spend time in the workshop, where all the sets for the various productions were constructed. Each day I'd help the head carpenter, a fantastic guy called Alan, as he built the props and scenery, and I relished every minute (many years earlier, my dad had worked briefly as a props master at the Opera House in Manchester, and he'd loved it too).

I started at nine o'clock in the morning – I'd have Alan's brew ready and his tools arranged before he arrived - and I would finish whenever he did, which could often be past 8 p.m. In fact, I enjoyed my work experience so much, I asked if I could extend it, and worked throughout the Easter holidays.

My affection for the theatre was growing by the day. I simply couldn't get enough of it. I felt at home.

CHAPTER 5

I'm Going To Be An Actor Darling

In May 1985, at the age of fifteen, I left St Albans's RC High School with no job to go to. Thanks to Maggie Thatcher, the country was a mess. People were getting laid off left, right and centre and, for the best part of a year, the Conservative government had chosen to pick a fight with the National Union of Mineworkers, spearheaded by Arthur Scargill. The NUM was decisively defeated and, as a result, coal mining virtually disappeared as a major industry in Britain.

Around this time my dad had managed to get another job, though - he was grafting every hour God sent at Manchester Plastics – and Mum continued to work as a dinner lady at Mellands, a special needs high school in nearby Gorton.

Thousands of miles away, Africa was in the middle of a different kind of crisis – the famine had wiped out millions in Ethiopia – so that same summer Bob Geldof and his mates staged Band Aid, the huge fundraising concert at Wembley that featured the biggest names in music.

Meanwhile, City were still shit and United continued to dominate English football. This wasn't a matter of life and death, of course, but as a Blues'-obsessed teenager it still pissed me off no end.

On my last day at St Alban's I remember walking out the place, watching my fellow pupils streaming out of the school gates, and thinking *Thank God I'll never have to see any of these idiots again.* Other than my mate B, who'd left school two years previously, I wasn't able to count any other student among my friends; I'd just never connected with anyone. It was a shame, really.

'What are you going to do for a job, then?' Mum and Dad had constantly asked as my last day had loomed. We all knew that, while the world of theatre and entertainment had captured my heart, it was a hugely competitive industry in which jobs were scarce, especially while unemployment levels were so high. Realistically, I'd have to set my sights a bit lower if I wanted to earn some money.

The government had not long launched its Youth Training Scheme, which intended to keep school leavers like me out of the Job Centre, instead encouraging them to enter the world of work. I found a YTS placement at a firm in Ardwick as an apprentice joiner, which would pay me £25 per week. That wasn't actually bad in those days, although I'd always give my parents a tenner for board and lodging.

I cycled to my new workplace each day to save the £2 bus fare, and always took a packed lunch (the canteen food was so shit, even the mice took Rennies). In all honesty, I hated every single day of it, and only ever looked forward to my hour-long lunchtime, my two fifteen-minute tea breaks, and my weekly pay packet.

There were a few interesting characters there who helped to break up the monotony, though, including one lad who happily described his carpentry as his 'part-time' job. His 'full-time' job, I soon learned, involved heading out to leafy Cheshire and breaking into wealthy households. Every Monday morning he'd arrive at work with his 'swag bag' – that's what he called it – and would try and sell us whatever he'd nicked that weekend, from Sony Walkmans to video cameras, and from cordless phones to half-bottles of aftershave. He even stole a dog once, but couldn't palm it off on anyone.

Deep down I knew that my YTS job was merely a means to an end, and that my career path would not lie in carpentry. My sights were still firmly set on my first love – my stand-up magic act - and I continued to perform at local venues, keen to learn my trade and gain as much experience as possible. I loved doing my set, though, and no matter how many times I got told to 'Get off, yer SHIT!' I still went back for more.

One Sunday, I was invited to do a gig at the British Legion in Longsight.

'You're on after the bingo,' said the compere when I arrived. I immediately got the impression that everyone in that club that night – a mostly female audience - had turned up for the bingo, not some half-baked comedy magician. Nevertheless, I was getting paid £30 which was good money for half-an-hour and a fiver more than my weekly YTS wage.

Following the final shout of 'HOUSE', I was introduced onto the stage. Despite doing all my best jokes, gags and tricks, I didn't hear a single titter. Not one. One woman seemed to smile among the sea of stony faces, but I reckoned she just had bad wind. After the show I went to the dressing room to get changed, feeling a little sorry for myself. There came a knock on the door, and the club secretary entered.

'Well done lad, very good,' he said, handing me a brown envelope. 'Just wondering whether you're free to do our kids' Christmas party? There'd be forty-five quid in it for you...'

Now this got me all confused.

'Hang on a minute. Nobody laughed, hardly anyone smiled, and you want me back?'

'They liked you out there, I can assure you,' he smiled. 'They didn't start chatting or reading their *Woman's Weekly*, which is always a great sign, young man.'

Much to my irritation, it was back to the YTS grindstone the following Monday, and I remember having to spend the whole day – a whole fucking day - shaving down a long piece of wood with a plane, even though my bosses had machines to cut them to size. Exasperated, I decided to ring Tony at the Contact Theatre to see if Alan needed an apprentice carpenter.

'It's funny you should say that,' he said. 'We've just been sent a form asking us to take on a YTS trainee. We'd get a tax break, apparently. I'll look into it and let you know, Mike.'

Tony rang back, and it was good news. Within a matter of days, I'd handed in my notice at the Ardwick sweat shop, had collected my final wage packet and had switched to a two-year apprenticeship at the Contact. My placement would also include a day-release course in Theatre Studies, which was a massive bonus.

I reported for duty the following Monday and got straight to work with Alan, building the set for the next scheduled play, aided by £100-worth of tools that the theatre had bought me. At the Contact, I was simply in my element. I loved learning how to construct sets and scenery, it stood me in great stead as I am quite good with my hands and saved myself a bit of money on jobs around the house! I loved witnessing how each department came together and probably most of all, I loved watching the actors rehearse. Some, I discovered, were better than others; I remember one actor really struggling to remember his lines, causing Tony to almost tear out his hair in frustration.

'Are you okay?' I asked the actor in the green room, during a tea break.

'I'm fine,' he said, unconvincingly, before explaining that this was his first gig after leaving drama college, and that he'd felt beset with nerves.

'I get nervous all the time when I do my stand-up act,' I said. 'Nerves can sometimes be good for you.' I then advised him to cast his mind back to a time when he felt really assured – an interview, maybe, or a speech - and to keep that mindset locked in his head.

'Thanks, Mike,' he said, before heading back to rehearsals. *I bet he thinks I'm a right fucking smart arse,* I thought. Here was I, a seventeen-year-old budding magician, doling out advice to a drama school graduate.

The next day this lad sought me out and thanked me for my tip, claiming that it had worked. He went on to become quite a well-known TV actor, and I often wondered whether he continued to use the famous 'McClean technique'.

At the Contact, I'd regularly find myself chatting to various performers at lunchtime and would love listening to their funny anecdotes or their bitchy comments. Some of these 'thespians' were a breed apart, I admit. They'd say 'yah' instead of 'yes', would wear cravats and cardigans and would eat weird food like chickpeas, tofu and quails' eggs. They read *The Guardian* and *The Times*, and could quote William Shakespeare at length.

My cultural remit, however, generally extended to sleazy porn mags, the *Daily Star* crossword and a memory bank of Bernard Manning gags. Despite our differences, I'd find myself having great time with these actors, and would often socialise with them at the weekend. They'd invariably ask me to perform my tricks for them, and I was soon given the nickname of 'Magic Mike'. (No ladies not the stripper.)

I recall the late great Rik Mayall once doing a show at the theatre. I was a huge fan of his – I adored *The Young Ones* – and, even though it was a bit uncool to get all starry-eyed over a work colleague, I just had to collar him during a break. He was a real gent, patiently answering all my fan-boy questions and offering up some great insight into a show that changed the face of British comedy. He was quite shy in person, but once he got up on stage he just transformed into this amazing comedy performer. I remember him doing some kind of rap, and bringing the whole house down.

Occasionally I'd find myself hogging the limelight, too. I joined the theatre's youth group, which staged the occasional production, and there were other opportunities to perform, too. This included the staff Christmas party, at which each department did their own sketch on stage. Alan, in his wisdom, had suggested that I dress up as 'SuperCarpenter', donning a cape, a tool belt and my work boots. I'd be attached to a wire and would zoom down whenever something on the stage needed fixing. Inevitably, like many of these best-intended plans, everything went tits up. The wires in the wings got tangled, and I was left dangling beneath the theatre ceiling for thirty minutes. Everyone was pissing themselves, probably thinking that it was all part of the act.

One morning, Alan broke the news that he was leaving the Contact to set up his own exhibition company. I was totally gutted. Alan was a brilliant bloke who had taught me everything about theatre carpentry. His replacement, another guy called Tony, wasn't my cup of tea, sadly. He had the personality and charisma of a gnat, together with a whiny Birmingham accent that properly got my back up.

Goooood moooorning there, young Moychul,' he'd say. 'Let's get staaaarted shall waaaaaay?'

He didn't last long, thankfully. His successor, a Scotsman called Nick, was much easier to work with and proved to be a great teacher. We worked on a production of Raymond Briggs' *The Snowman* and, much to my delight, he let me build the small house that dominated the stage. I worked so hard on it, and was so proud of the end result.

The production made a real impression on me for other reasons, too. Tony the director had kindly let me sit in during *Snowman* rehearsals, enabling me to observe how he communicated his ideas and instructions, and allowing me to see how the actors reacted to his advice and brought their characters to life. I can still picture myself sitting there, absolutely enraptured with the whole creative process.

With my YTS nearing the end of its course, I applied to go to Arden College of Performing Arts in Manchester, and was immediately accepted. While I was absolutely thrilled, I still felt really sad to say goodbye to the Contact Theatre. I'd loved my time there, had made some great friends – especially Alan, Tony and the production manager, Roy - and had experienced something that was truly life-changing. My spell there had given me both a wider and wiser outlook on life, and had given me the confidence to aim high and achieve my dreams.

****

Arden College was based on Sale Road in the Manchester suburb of Northenden. It was an old, run-down place, but grant funding had enabled it to build a brand new theatre and stage its own in-house productions. As it was the first of its kind in the region, *Granada Reports* sent down a camera crew to film the new intake of students. The presenter that day was a very attractive blonde by the name of Judy Finnigan who, together with her partner Richard, was one of the TV station's rising stars. She interviewed me for a few minutes – I think she asked me about my set-building carpentry skills - but my piece to camera ended up being cut. My starring role on that night's *Granada Reports* amounted to me shaving a bit of wood in the background. Typical.

Arden's three-year Theatre and Television course was run by a failed actor called Rob. He wore cravats and tweed jackets. He drove a sports car. He had an ex-pupil as a girlfriend. He was, in fact, the true embodiment of a mid-life crisis.

I remember one of our first lessons involved us being taught how to breathe.

'Why do we need to learn how to breathe?' I asked Rob. 'I've been doing it successfully for the last eighteen years? In fact, I'm so good at it that I can do it in my sleep. And I did it on the bus this morning, too...'

The only person in the class who didn't laugh was Rob.

'I think I can guess your chosen field of acting, Mr McClean,' he said. For some reason he never used our forenames. 'Is it comedy, by any chance?'

Our first production was *To Kill A Mockingbird*. Every student had to audition, and those that didn't get a part had to work backstage. I was among the unlucky ones, and was given the job to construct the set. To say that I was pissed off was an understatement.

Things didn't get any better. The course, to put it mildly, didn't meet my expectations, and proved to be a real disappointment. I'd not signed up to build sets or to learn a musical instrument, I'd signed up because I'd wanted to learn how to act and perform. To be frank, a few of the plays that were staged – *Hamlet*, for example – just went over my head, and some of the classroom exercises were plain ridiculous.

'I want you to imagine that you're a tree, and that you're blowing in the wind,' Rob announced one lesson. As if I was having any of that.

'I'm sorry, Rob, but I'm not being a tree,' I said. 'Not now - not ever - will I be a fucking tree.'

Predictably, he asked me to stay behind at the end of the lesson, and I gave it to him, full barrel. I told him that his course was a load of bollocks, and that I'd had enough of being shoved backstage, and that I just wanted to act. My tutor just stood there in his tweed jacket, his half-mast pants and his loafers, looking like he couldn't give a shit. *So why don't you just leave the course, then..?* he seemed to be saying to me.

****

My college woes meant that I started to live for the weekend. By then Sunday football had become a big part of my life, and I'd begun playing for a pub side in Levenshulme - the Pack Horse, on Stockport Road – that was managed by a friend of my dad's, Mickey Durber. One of my fellow teammates was a lad called Derek Broadhurst, also known as Degs. We didn't like each other when we first met – maybe I was jealous of his amazing goal scoring rate (one season he scored over forty) - but after a while we clicked and he became one of my best mates.

I adored playing football every week, and I loved the social element too. The Pack Horse became my 'local' and after each game we'd all head to the pub for a few drinks, where I'd often hook up with my dad, too. The camaraderie between us all was amazing, and I have really fond memories of sitting on the pub steps with lads like Degs, Dustin, Stevie, Mickey and the Bestie brothers, eating burgers, having a laugh, taking the piss, and generally putting the world to rights.

We were a mixed bunch; Degs worked in a supermarket, Dustin worked in a factory, and Stevie taught art at a girls school in Torquay. When we weren't at the Pack Horse, we spent many a night at the Manor House in Didsbury, where we'd meet up with another group of top lads, including the Bestie brothers, Johnny Worth, Tommy Cox and Steve Swindles.

It was at the Manor House that I remember becoming smitten with a gorgeous-looking girl who I'd regularly spot across the bar. Like me, she went to Arden College, and I'd admired her from afar for ages. I found out from the Bestie brothers, who knew her, that that her name was Lea Riley.

'You'll never pull her, she's well out of your league,' the lads would laugh whenever they saw me staring at her, all misty-eyed.

'Yeah, you're probably right,' I'd say, sadly.

****

I still continued to perform at weekends and evenings, too, with my interest in magic – especially comedy magic - getting stronger all the time. I became good friends with a bunch of fellas at the magic club who would gladly offer me some brilliant advice and guidance, none more so than Peter Woolley, the resident comedy expert. Every Thursday Peter would invite over a select few to his house in order to go through various tricks and routines. He'd often ask me to perform my latest act, and would promptly rip it to shreds.

'Why don't you try this?' he'd say, suggesting I add in a clever aside, or a funny punchline. 'You don't just want to amaze your audience, Mike, you want to entertain them, too.'

Peter knew instinctively what made an act work, and his advice was usually spot on. I'd always accept his constructive criticism, and would learn not to take things personally. He and his acquaintances were great students of magic, too, and had their finger on the pulse as regards the latest up-and-coming talents. Paul Daniels remained the star of the magic world, but among the new kids on the block was a young magician called Wayne Dobson. Wayne was not only a great conjuror, but he was very funny, with some killer lines.

'Keep your eye on him,' said Peter. 'He's good. Very good.'

Back at Arden College, Rob had decided to put on another production and, yet again, I'd failed to secure a part, despite what I'd thought was a decent audition. For me, this was the final straw, as I felt I was being overlooked out of spite, pure and simple. I confronted my tutor, only for him to trot out some feeble excuse and no sign of any constructive feedback which may possibly have encouraged me.

'All I want to do is perform, Rob and you're not giving me a chance,' I said.

'But you are performing, McClean,' he replied. 'You've got your stand-up, haven't you?'

I looked him straight in the eye, and felt my head pound with anger. I know now he was goading me, obviously so much of his own bitterness and a class of worshiping students was the best audience he could work to, so I was a thorn in his tweed clad side.

'You are a complete and utter knob, and you can stick your course right up your thespian arse.'

And with that I grabbed my bag, never to return again. How often when you were younger and full of your own surety did you decided in a moment of hotheadedness to stick it to someone? Mind you, in hindsight it wasn't a bad move seeing what came next…

CHAPTER 6

Stand Up

I continued to visit Peter Woolley's house every Thursday, and he still revelled in his role as the Magic Circle's answer to Simon Cowell.

'That's rubbish,' he'd say, shaking his head, whenever I showcased the latest add-on to my act. 'Go away and think of something funny.'

And that's just what I'd do. For some reason I tried harder for Peter than I ever did for anyone at Arden College.

I remember my mentor telling me that the best way to improve my stand-up was to perform it constantly. Since I didn't have an agent to find me gigs, the only other alternative was to try and secure myself a summer season. I was put in touch with an agent called Paul Bridson, based in Chester, who in turn got me an interview with Joe Rozsich, the manager of Winkups holiday park, located in the North Wales resort of Towyn.

'You must be Mike,' said Joe when I arrived at Winkups one cold February afternoon in 1988. As it was out of season the holiday complex was deathly quiet, with vacant caravans and empty swimming pools. Joe sported a tan, a tight perm and wore a very snazzy grey suit. He also smelt of expensive aftershave and, every time he moved, his jewellery jangled.

For all his flamboyance, however, Joe had a reputation as being a bit of a miserable sod, and I'd been forewarned that it took a great deal to make him laugh ('the solar eclipse happens more often,' people had commented).

'Right, show me what you've got then...' he drawled, taking a sip from his mug of tea as I clambered onto the Winkups stage and commenced my act. I was as nervous as hell – this was a big deal for me – but I decided to do my failsafe 'Dippy Duck' trick, whereby a blindfold wooden duck would choose the correct card, but – in true Tommy Cooper style - it would become clear that all the cards were the same. When I finished it, he laughed. I swear to God, he actually chuckled. Following my routine, he asked me to wait by the bar for a few minutes, and my mind began to race.

I hope I've impressed him, I remember thinking. *This could be my big opening into the world of showbusiness...*

Joe sidled up to me and handed me a glass of Coke.

'Okay, Mike. From what I've just seen, I think you'd be ideal to host the Winkups' kids' club. Games, competitions, that kind of thing,' he said. He then went on to explain that the season ran from June to September, and that he'd be able to pay me £120 a week (not bad considering I'd lied about my age to him to get the job!).

'Not only that,' he continued, 'I'll also give you two half-hour spots per week to do your stand-up act. How does that sound?'

I could hardly hear him speak, my heart was thumping so much. The next thing I knew we were shaking hands, and he was telling me to report for duty in four weeks' time.

Bloody hell, I thought as I sat on the Manchester-bound train. *I've only just gone and got my first professional contract.* Then an element of panic set in as I realised that I didn't have a fucking clue about kids' clubs, games or competitions. But, there again, I knew a man that did. Derek Lever, a lovely guy who I'd met at the magic club, was a second-hand dealer of magicians' equipment, but back in the day, had reached the final of ITV's *New Faces*. He'd worked the holiday camp circuit for decades and knew everything there was to know about these venues. I met up with him a few days later, and he passed on some wise advice.

'Take your time, and don't rush your words,' he said (I tended to do this when I was nervous). 'Don't be so aggressive – you could do with softening your delivery - and make sure you look smart. This is showbiz, remember...'

June arrived quickly enough, and it was time to pack my suitcase and head for Winkups. My good friend Dave McMahon and his wife Terry Ann drove me over to North Wales, and I remember feeling so, so nervous as we approached my home for the next few months. I was immediately shown to my caravan, which I was to share with the compere, a tall lanky guy with a very tight perm (they were all the rage at Winkups).

The next night saw my debut as the camp's host-cum-entertainer. Instead of my usual magician's dinner suit I decided to go for an informal, smart-casual look, sporting a shirt and a pair of trousers. I was introduced to the resident DJ, Mal, who informed me I'd be organising the junior disco dance competition. Before I could ask how it worked or what the rules were, he'd said, 'Ladies and gentleman, your host for this evening is Mike McClean, so please give him a warm Winkups welcome,' before handing me the mic. I honestly didn't have a clue what to do but, despite being thrown in at the deep end, I suddenly grew some enormous bollocks and I just got on with it. Much to my delight, I found myself relishing every single minute.

'Did you enjoy that?' asked Joe at the end of the night.

'Loved it,' I answered.

'Good,' he said, stony-faced, before walking off.

'Don't worry, love, you'll get used to him,' smiled an elderly barmaid who'd been working at Winkups for decades. I'd come to learn that Joe had a gruff, grumpy side to his character and, as such, wasn't universally liked by his staff and the visiting acts.

'What a miserable sod,' they'd say when he told them to calm things down on stage, or turn the music down in their caravans. I got on fine with him, though, probably because I knew how to make him laugh and never caused him any problems. Every Friday morning we'd have a chat and a cuppa while I sorted out all the winners' medals and certificates, and I can honestly say we never exchanged a cross word.

That summer season was an eye-opener for a young lad, to say the least. I wasn't completely naïve you know, but there are things that happen on these holidays camps that you wouldn't believe! For instance during one particular disco night, I distinctly remember Mal furiously beckoning me over to his DJ booth. He was still spinning his discs, but his eyes were rolling around and his speech had gone all strange. *Is he on drugs?* I remember thinking to myself. *Is he having some kind of funny turn?*

All became clear when I went over to check Mal was okay, and discovered a female holidaymaker on her knees, in his booth, giving him a blow job. He gave me a wink and a thumbs up, and I made a sharp exit back to the unsuspecting families on the dance floor. Holiday camp DJs were never short of women, I'd learn, especially those – like Mal - with the gift of the gab and a twinkle in their eye. He was like the Mr Myagi of Winkups and he taught a single lad like me some valuable lessons about summer lovin' at a caravan park.

'Rule One, never sleep with anyone on the first night, Mike, because you'll have to entertain them all week, and they'll think you belong to them,' he said.

'Rule Two. If they're here for a fortnight, never bed them in the first week, as per Rule One. And, if you do fancy shagging someone, get your end away on the Friday as they'll be leaving for home on the Saturday or the Sunday.'

'And as for Rule Three,' he added, 'never give a lass your home phone number or address and *always* tell them that you've got a girlfriend.'

Now I'm not saying his rules were right or his attitude, but it was a different time back then and to be honest the girls were more than up for it, there was never any coercion on anyone's part and it was all above board. Mind you there were sometimes some tears on a Saturday morning at the end of what the girls thought was a summer romance.

Joe allowed me to perform my magic-cum-stand-up act every Wednesday and Friday, the former for the adults, the latter for the kids. I'd often die on my arse on the Wednesday night because I'd tend to do gags about my demanding wife and my troublesome kids (both were non-existent, of course, and I think my audience knew it). My act didn't quite ring true, I guess, and for me it was a lesson learned. Can you imagine sitting watching some teenager trying to pull off gags about life experience he couldn't possibly have? I do cringe looking back at this!

On the other hand, every Friday I'd storm it, across both age groups. I'd make fun of the young 'uns - but always in a gentle, inoffensive way – and would tell the odd risqué gag that would often go straight over the kids' heads, but would be lapped up by their parents.

Life wasn't always laughter-filled at Winkups, though. One week we hosted a group of underprivileged children, many of whom who had been badly mistreated by their families. I'd often find myself chatting to the care workers, who'd tell me heart-rending stories of neglect and abuse. I remember noticing one little girl, aged about six or seven, who continually clung to her helper. She'd suffered no end of cruelty at the hands of her parents, apparently, and this was the first time she'd been away from home.

I decided to make it my mission to give her the best holiday she'd ever had. Midway through the week she'd gained enough confidence to leave the side of her carer, and I remember taking hold of her hand and bringing her onto the stage for a competition. I ensured she won, of course, and made her laugh in the process, which she probably hadn't done for some time.

'Wow,' said her helper after the show. 'That was amazing. She's never responded to anyone like that before.'

From that day on, the little girl turned up to every single kids' event, usually sporting a beautiful big smile. On the group's final evening at Winkups, when it was time to give out all the prizes, let's just say she left with everything on the top shelf. On departure day she drew me a picture and gave me a massive hug and, when her coach chugged off, I'm not ashamed to say that I shed a few tears. Technically I'd just been doing my job – I was paid to bring fun to people's lives, and to make their holiday special – but this lovely little girl had made a profound impression on me. Sometimes I might come across as a bit arrogant but that's not who I am deep down and even then, I hated to see children suffering and being abused. There's just no need for it and I know that throughout my career and with all the work I did with children, I always looked out for those that needed just that little bit extra.

Soon September was upon us, and my stint as a Winkups holiday entertainer had come to a close. Our final evening on site was marked by the annual 'owners' party', to which a top visiting act was always invited. That year I was lucky enough to have the pleasure of watching the legendary Ken Dodd in action. I had fond memories of watching 'Doddy' on TV when I was younger, and that night he didn't disappoint, giving us a first-class lesson in comedy. For two-and-a-half hours he barraged us with gag after gag, knowing exactly when to pause and let the laughter die down before delivering the next punchline. Ken was a true master of his craft and I'm not afraid to admit that I mentally took notes.

The next day I reluctantly headed back to Manchester, feeling sad to leave Winkups but feeling very grateful for the experience. I'd learned so much that summer, not just about the business but about how to handle people.

I'd also saved enough money to pay for driving lessons. I'm not ashamed to say it took three attempts to pass my driving test, but I had a lovely female instructor (for some reason I never took to a bloke teaching me) and she got me through.

Now, however though, I was faced with a choice of either getting a job or living off my savings, I'd used a little of mine already to buy my first car. It was a Ford Fiesta which my friend Macca got for me, as he was and still is, brilliant with cars. A425 CVK - amazing how you never forget your first registration. This also meant that I could get myself to gigs too.

So, like many 'resting' showbiz people, I had to sign on the dole, which I absolutely hated, and had to pay weekly visits to the Job Centre. To amuse myself, I'd make up elaborate job-hunting stories which I'd regale to the staff on the desk.

'So what have you done to gain employment?' they'd ask.

'I'm waiting to hear back from MI5,' I'd answer, causing them to raise their eyebrows. 'Sorry... got that wrong... I mean MFI,' I'd add.

'And, where d'you see yourself in ten years' time, Michael?'

'Probably in Strangeways,' I'd say, straight-faced, 'after murdering someone who asked me stupid questions.'

They'd often accuse me of wasting their time, but it was the only way I could cope with such a dire situation. I know that it helped me afford to carry on building the career that I loved, but they make it so soul destroying (and I know even today that still hasn't changed), not every person wants to be there and many are out on their arse, so having to justify your existence is sometimes just too much to bare. Comedy helped me and I know I took the Mick, but I never took for granted that I couldn't do what I loved without that little bit of help.

I was still doing the odd gig here and there and picking up the odd cash-in-hand job, but nothing massively exciting. At the weekend, I'd still play my football and frequent the Manor House, and it was probably around this time that I finally made a move on Lea. I'd noticed her looking at me a few times and after much ribbing and piss-taking from Degs, Stevie and the lads, I plucked up the courage to go over for a chat. I asked her if she'd like to go out for a drink, we swapped numbers and I said I'd give her a call. As all lads do, I flashed her a smile and coolly sauntered off before getting outside the pub and punching the air.

'Yesssssss!!!' I shouted.

'About fuckin' time...' said Degs.

Lea and I had our first date at a bar in Withington called Bertie's, and we spent all night chatting and laughing (I'd begun to learn that making a girl giggle was half the battle). Lea asked what I did for a living, and when I told her I was a stand-up magician she seriously thought I was taking the piss (she had a proper job with regular wage, working at the banking centre in Manchester). From that night on, though, things progressed nicely and Lea became my first serious girlfriend. We really enjoyed each other's company, and I became incredibly fond of her.

'One day I'm going to be famous,' I'd tell her, as we sipped our drinks in the Manor House, 'and when I do, I'll buy us a nice big house in Didsbury...'

In April 1989, Joe from Winkups rang to ask if I'd like to go back there for another season.

'I'll give you a rise if you do,' he promised, 'so have a think about it.'

A rise? I thought, *that's not like him.* And not only that, I knew it was highly unusual for him to ask anyone back for another year. I went away and discussed things with Lea, and came to the conclusion that I'd only do the job for two hundred quid a week, and not a penny less. I'd impressed Joe the previous summer, and he was obviously keen to see me return, so I reckoned it was the very least I deserved. I called him back, poised to push a hard bargain.

'I'll give you a tenner more, Mike,' said Joe. 'How's that for you?'

'That's fine, Joe,' I replied, without hesitation. I needed the work, didn't I?

June soon arrived, and Lea travelled to Towyn with me, staying at Winkups for the first weekend. And, while I knew I'd probably enjoy this season a bit more - with one stint under my belt, I felt far more relaxed and clued up - I made a pledge to keep away from the women. Now that I had a serious girlfriend there'd be no messing about with female holidaymakers, and certainly no flirting with any magician's assistants.

That was the plan, until Nicky arrived. I'd had to perform alone for the first fortnight – Joe had not yet appointed my helper – but one night this absolutely stunning brunette turned up for her first ever summer season. Like me Nicky was attached but, before long, we were hooking up for some caravan-based action. I felt guilty as hell but Lea never found out, and neither did Nicky's other half. Not that I'm saying that makes it right, but we've all done things we're not totally proud of when we're young and stupid!

Every Thursday, Winkups welcomed an Elvis impersonator, a Scouser by the name of Chris Clayton. He was fabulous – as was his live band – and the theatre would always be packed to the rafters when he was on stage. For a laugh, I'd hand Nicky little notes to give to Chris, telling her that they were song requests from the audience. Instead, I'd write things like 'I want you, love Nicky', or 'I can see the outline of your cock, love Nicky,' or (my personal favourite) 'Come back to mine, Elvis, and make love to me, but keep your blue suede shoes on. Love Nicky.' I'd piss myself as I'd watch Chris reading them, and then see him flashing a smile at a none-the-wiser Nicky.

This continued for most of the season until, one Thursday night, Nicky discovered my ruse, having casually looked at one of the notes and nearly falling off the stage in shock.

'I'll get you back for this,' she grinned, through gritted teeth.

And she did, good and proper. On our final Friday, following the usual prize-giving ceremony, Nicky turned up at my van in floods of tears, announcing that she was pregnant. The baby, she insisted, was definitely mine.

I'm twenty-years-old, I remember thinking as I felt the blood draining from my face. *I'm not ready to be a dad. Shit, what do I tell Lea. And what do I tell my parents? And how the fuck do I change a nappy?*

The little minx kept it going for a good few hours – it's amazing how many thoughts go through your head in those situations – before eventually coming clean.

'That was for Elvis,' she said, giving me a playful whack.

Guys, I'm sure I don't have to tell you the relief I felt in that moment! Ladies, this is a cruel, cruel trick please don't play it!

Nicky and I had to say our goodbyes the next morning. We kissed, and she had a little cry, telling me that she'd had the best time ever and had never laughed so much. We swapped numbers – bang goes Rule Three - and said we'd meet up one weekend for dinner. We never did, though, and I never heard from her again.

As for Joe, well I will always be grateful to him for giving me my first job and we are still great mates to this day.

CHAPTER 7

I'm On The Tele

In September 1989 it was time to audition again, along with a cast of millions, for a role that paid £45 a week. Yep, I was back signing on the dole. Things had gotten serious at the Job Centre, though, and to qualify for my income support money I now had to shelve the M15-MFI jokes and instead keep a written record of my job-seeking.

One Monday morning my number was called out and I found myself sitting in front of a proper battleaxe. No doubt she'd done this mundane job for years, and was probably counting down the days until retirement. Whatever the case, she was in a foul mood as she scanned the list of companies that I'd scrawled onto the back of an envelope.

'So, Mr McClean,' she said, snooty as fuck. 'If I were to ring one of these numbers to enquire if you'd spoken to them about employment, they'd confirm this to be true. Yes?'

I just smiled at her. I hadn't contacted half of those numbers, and Old Mrs Battleaxe knew it. She picked up her phone and dialled, maintaining eye contact with me the whole time.

Fuck.. .which one has she picked? I thought, trying to remember all the places – takeaways, pubs, betting shops – that I'd copied from the *Manchester Evening News,* and all the numbers I'd got by ringing Directory Enquiries.

'Hello,' she said, 'this is Levenshulme Job Centre. Can I just check that a Mike McClean has rung you this week, with regard to gaining employment with your company?'

After a few seconds she put the phone down.

'It seems that Buckingham Palace don't keep records from callers.'

She then asked me what job I'd enquired about. I looked at her, deadpan.

'Butler to the Queen or Prince Philip... I'm not fussy.'

The woman at the next desk along nearly fell off her chair. The battleaxe wasn't amused, however, and continued to go through my list of numbers, speaking to a dog groomer, a mobile hairdresser and an escort agency. After a while she'd had enough, and wearily completed my paperwork.

'Perhaps you'd like to pursue some more realistic options next time, Mr McClean' she said.

****

Each year, the *Manchester Evening News* would host its annual 'Search For A Star' talent show which, in the past, had produced some big winners, including Rochdale-based singer, Lisa Stansfield.

'You should go for it, Mike,' said Peter Woolley one evening. I took his advice, sent in my application form and found myself getting selected for the heats at Salford's legendary Willows Variety Club. Everyone and anyone in showbiz had performed at that venue, and as I arrived that Sunday night I walked down the corridor, passing by a photo gallery that included VIPs like Bob Monkhouse, Bernard Manning, Tommy Cooper and Freddie Starr.

Each act in my heat was given a twelve-minute slot, which allowed the singers to perform three songs and gave the comics plenty of time to establish a rapport with the audience (the sole juggler on the bill might have struggled a bit, though). My gut feeling told me that everything was going to go well for me, and it did. My gig went like a dream, in fact; every trick went down a storm, every gag got a laugh and every ad-lib was spot-on. I could have probably stood there and farted for twelve minutes and still received a standing ovation. I was absolutely buzzing when I came off the stage, with all the applause ringing in my ears.

'Well done, Son,' said the compere, patting me on the back. 'I usually hate magicians, but you were brilliant.'

Backstage, most of the other acts shared the compere's opinion – 'you've won this, hands down...' said the juggler, and soon it was time for the result to be announced.

'Going through to the grand final of *Manchester Evening News'* 'Search For A Star' is... MIKE McCLEAN!'

I received a winners' cheque for fifty quid, which was a nice bonus. As I sat on the bus back home to Levenshulme all I could think about were the brand new, £25 Puma 'Maradona' boots that I'd now be able to buy. I also decided that it would only be fair to give the remainder of my winnings to Mum and Dad.

The next day I found myself in a BBC Radio Manchester studio, being interviewed by a presenter called Susie Mathis, who'd been one of the judges at The Willows.

'Well done, Mike,' she said when the show went on air. 'No comedy magician has ever got through to the final, so you should be really proud of yourself.' I was, in fact super pleased with myself and for the first time, actually thought *I'm not too bad at this comedy lark*.

I then paid a visit to Peter who, together with another magician friend of his called Barry – warned me not to alter my act for the final.

'Stick to the same routine,' they said. 'It'll be a different audience and the judging panel is bound to change.'

The Willows was packed to the gills on the night of the final; in the audience was one of my mentors, Barry but, yet again, my parents had opted to stay at home.

Whilst backstage, I remember striking up a conversation with a blond, male vocalist-cum-pianist from Cheshire who seemed a nice lad and incredibly talented, although his decision to wear white trousers that night had turned out to be an unwise one. After our chat, he'd gone to the loo for a pee, and (well chaps you all know what can happen no matter how much you shake), returned backstage with a yellow-ish stain around his groin area.

'Take my advice, mate: never wear white trousers,' he said. 'It's a bloody good job I'm sitting behind a piano.'

His name, I learned, was Gary Barlow.

It's a lesson I took seriously and I can thank Gary as I've never worn white trousers on stage, in fact I don't think I've ever worn white trousers.

It didn't seem to do him any harm though if his career is anything to go by, but it's funny how you remember people no matter how big they get. Gary is still as down to earth today and as nice a chap as he was then.

My twelve minutes in the spotlight came and went and everything seemed to go to plan, including a great response from the audience. In my opinion, Gary, was undoubtably the star of the show – he was a truly gifted musician – and I fully expected him to win. The compere, however, didn't announce either of our names in third or second place. And he didn't announce them in first place, either. Winning the 1990 'Search for a Star' contest was a rock band – their name still escapes me – who didn't exactly set the music world alight.

The following Monday I received a call from a Granada TV producer, asking if I'd fancy performing some magic on a children's show called *WAC 90*, which at that time was presented by Michaela Strachan and Tommy Boyd. I couldn't believe it, and I couldn't wait to tell my mate Degs since he had a massive crush on Michaela. I don't think I can even begin to express just how excited I was getting the phone call asking if I wanted to come on the show, I mean, this was something huge! I set about sorting out what tricks I was going to do I only had 6 minutes so I thought, "OK 2 tricks, 3 mins each."

I practised like mad for the week leading up to my appearance. Then just a day before I was told it will have to be the following week. I was gutted for a minute I thought maybe they'd changed their minds. That said it gave me another week to practise my routine. Strangely, I actually slept OK the night before but when the car picked me up at 6am the next morning to take me to the iconic Granada Studios in central Manchester my nerves started. I remember looking at my hand and it was shaking fast, I had a panic moment thinking "I need steady hands or I'm going to look like an idiot on National TV, Oh God, did I just say National TV?"

A researcher showed me to my dressing room and, before the rehearsals began, I took the opportunity to have a quick wander around the building. I walked into the set of *Coronation Street*, at one point finding myself by the bar of the Rover's Return.

Mum would have killed to be here... I remember thinking to myself, *but only if they served dry white wine.*

I got changed and went onto the studio floor to rehearse my spot and I was taken aback by how many people worked on the show. When it came to going live I stood next to a roadie of one of the bands, a smallish lad with a mop of dark hair who I'd later discover was a certain Noel Gallagher, he said it was Inspired Carpets (I hadn't heard of them).

Then it was my turn my heart was pounding like an African drum. Before you know it we were live. I did my first spot, and performed a card trick with Michaela, along with a number-related prediction that very nearly went wrong. Both, however, went down brilliantly. I look back on the clip now and it looks like I have Parkinson's I was shaking that much!!

Later in the show I did some more magic, this time with Tommy. He was a bit of a prick, to be honest, and for whatever reason was doing his utmost to sabotage the trick. What he didn't know was that I'd just finished a summer season at a holiday camp, where countless smart-arses in the audience would try to suss you out. I'd learned how to deal with these situations, and – much to my satisfaction – I tied him up in knots.

'I loved what you did, Mike, especially the way you handled Tommy,' said the executive producer, Nick Wilson, after the show. As soon as he said this, I thought I'd strike while the iron was hot.

'How's about having a resident magician on the show every week?' I asked cheekily. 'I could do a couple of tricks and a few running gags. If you get me the gig, Nick, I reckon I could even make a jet plane vanish,' I added with a grin. He said he loved my suggestion and told me to go away and write something up.

'When you've got some ideas together, call my secretary and book in a meeting,' he said.

My first impulse was to ring Peter and Barry.

'Guys, we needed to think fast,' I said, and I hastily arranged a get-together. Barry came up with the nice idea of me working in a magic shop – each week I'd show the presenters a new trick – and I devised a running gag about a duck (long story) which Peter liked a lot.

Disappointingly, and despite countless calls to his secretary, Nick never got back to me. I was gutted – his initial enthusiasm had led me to believe I could be a *WAC 90* regular – and thought that this behaviour was pretty cruel. Much to his embarrassment, I got the chance to remind him of his empty promises when I met him again, a few years later.

****

In June 1990 I finally got myself a proper job as – believe it or not - a private detective. Even Lea thought I was winding her up when I told her that I'd become The Burgess Detective Agency's newest recruit, having answered a Job Centre advert and having coasted through the interview. I was delighted, of course, particularly since I'd be getting my own company car.

The work didn't prove to be as glamorous as I'd hoped, though. I'd fully expected to be working on murder cases or kidnappings (I watched far too much *Magnum PI*) but I spent most of my working week serving divorce papers, handing over winding-up orders and tracking down company directors or mortgage defaulters. I tell you something, if you can front up in those kind of situations, then you can stand on any stage. I never realised at the time the kind of emotions people go through when it comes to divorce and money, wasn't until I went through divorce myself, that I could appreciate why some of those blokes were really angry.

I had a lovely colleague in June, though. A small, sturdy woman in her fifties, she had teeth missing and would smoke so much that, whenever she opened the office door, people would think we were electing a new pope. She liked a good natter, and would often touch type while she spoke, rarely needing to look down at her keyboard.

She occasionally gave me a few mildly exciting assign-ments, including a job that came through from a client who suspected his wife of having an affair. He'd hired us to keep tabs on his house - and his wife - while he was away on some bogus business trip. While undercover, I had to sit outside his big posh Cheshire gaff, 24/7, and record every little coming-

and-going, from the postman delivering a letter to his missus going shopping. Every movement had to be captured in photographs, too.

During one early-hours stakeout I found myself struggling to keep awake, and thought I'd try and stay alert by having a little walk around the house. I climbed over the back garden wall, only to see a light on in the kitchen. Peering more closely, I saw this fella's wife astride some young guy, shagging away like her life depended on it and getting up to all sorts of shenanigans. Yep, she was having an affair, all right. I stayed there a while to take some photos – always pretty difficult with one hand if you know what I mean (hey I was young, don't judge!) – and went back to write a blow-by-blow account, no pun intended.

By the following Monday I'd got my report finished and my photos developed at Prontaprint (taking advantage of their 'buy one set, get one free offer went down a storm with my mates at the pub). Revealing the agency's findings to the wronged husband, and seeing this fully-grown man reduced to a blubbing wreck, was pretty horrible, to be honest.

'Is it definitely her?' I remember him asking me and June. 'Is she honestly cheating on me?'

I had to stop myself from saying *Which bit of your stark naked, wife humping a young stud doesn't ring true, for fuck's sake? D'you think we planted a lookalike for a wind up?*

He settled his bill in cash and left our office a broken man, the poor sod. It was a lesson in love for me and a twinge on my emotions, I would never want to be in that man's shoes. By rights we should have declared this and other cash payments to the agency boss, Ian, but June would often say, 'Let's just keep this to ourselves, eh?' and we'd split the fee. Neither of us liked Ian very much so we weren't exactly consumed with guilt.

My workmate and I would often have long chats, whereby she'd spill the beans about her non-existent sex life, often causing me to spit out my tea, and I'd reveal my dreams of becoming a comedian or a presenter.

'I'm going to make it one day, June,' mark my words,' I'd grin.

A few months later, having had my fill of my increasingly boring PI role, I finally handed in my notice. Shortly after, Ian the boss phoned to ask why I was leaving, and when I outlined my showbiz ambitions he just laughed.

'You need your head testing, Mike. Why are you giving up a job that gives you loads of money and security? Bloody stupid, if you ask me...'

I gave him a bit of a mouthful and called him a dick; I couldn't help myself, yes I was young and cocky but I knew what I wanted to do and no one was going to call me stupid. I handed back my car keys to June in the office and didn't look back.

'I'm offski,' I said, giving her a kiss. 'Thanks for everything. And don't forget to keep your eye out for me on the telly.'

'I won't, Mike love,' she smiled.

****

In October 1990, Lea and I had sadly called it a day. Now that I was a free agent, I decided to fulfil a long-held ambition and spend a gap-year travelling the world. Using the cash I'd accumulated from my PI work, I bought a round-trip ticket that would fly me to the United States, Australia, and back to England.

I announced my plans to my parents at home, over dinner; while my dad was really excited for me – 'that sounds great, Son...' - my mum dissolved into tears. For weeks she'd been nagging me to find my own place, yet here she was, wailing about me getting kidnapped by Mexicans and having one of my lungs sold on the black market.

'Your problem, Mother, is that you watch too many cop shows...' I said, offering her a hug.

When I told my mates that I was going abroad for a year, one of them, Dustin – Stevie's older brother - decided he was coming with me. He'd just received a nice redundancy cheque and felt in the mood for an adventure.

'Be my guest, Dustin,' I said, thinking that it would be quite nice to have a travel companion.

CHAPTER 8

Time To Travel

In February 1991, Dustin and I headed down to Heathrow airport, from where we'd catch our eleven-hour flight to Los Angeles. I'd set off with £1,500-worth of dollars (to last me a year, supposedly), and had decided not to waste my money on costly travel insurance. Unbelievably reckless, in hindsight but in those days it wasn't really deemed that important.

This was going to be my first trip Stateside, and as our jet cruised over the Atlantic I contemplated some big *Hollywood-here-I-come* scenarios. Maybe I'd find myself a cigar-smoking, Cuban heel-wearing agent and crack it in the movies. Perhaps I'd get a stand-up gig in some cool venue, sharing the bill with Bill Cosby and Eddie Murphy. Or, if all else failed, maybe I could clean pools or valet cars for some rich dudes, while sleeping with their beautiful wives.

'Would you like some more snacks, sir?' said the Continental Airlines stewardess, snapping me out of my dreamland.

Upon landing in Los Angeles, Dustin and I headed straight for the youth hostel in the San Pedro district, which would be our base for a fortnight or so. LA seemed so huge and sprawling and, like everyone had warned me, the sidewalks were virtually deserted; absolutely everyone used their Chevrolets or Cadillacs to get about. The hostel was brilliant, with a great vibe, and was teeming with backpackers from all over the world. I remember chatting to a very amusing political journalist from Japan and daft-as-a-brush traveller from

New Zealand, who told us how he funded his travels by cutting the ends off various fingers and toes to get compensation pay outs.

I treated my first couple of weeks like a holiday, seeing all the sights of LA, eating out constantly and visiting swanky department stores. Then I suddenly realised that my cash reserves were dwindling – I was spending money like there was no tomorrow - and knew that, ideally, I'd need some kind of temporary job to pay my way. I got chatting to a guy from Yorkshire who was working as a mechanic, fixing English vehicles.

'Is there any work going around here?' I asked. He shook his head.

'Jobs in LA are really hard to come by, mate. Sorry...'

Naively, perhaps, I decided to try to find an agent to secure me some acting work. I spent a whole day on the phone, ringing various entertainment organisations, but had no joy whatsoever. *Thanks, but no thanks*, was the common response. It was like trying to get a meeting with God Almighty.

'Maybe they don't need a short little funnyman, when they've already got Danny DeVito,' I said to Dustin in the wake of my final snub.

We decided it was time to up sticks from Los Angeles, and plumped for Las Vegas as our next stop. We chose the cheapest travel option – a grotty Greyhound coach – which meant spending four torturous hours with a busload of backpackers and crack addicts. Eventually we arrived at our destination – another youth hostel - and I sauntered into reception wearing my sky blue Manchester City shirt.

'Man City?' said the guy behind the counter in a thick northern accent. 'You can fuck right off, pal. No room for the likes of you in here.'

Then he started laughing and explained that he was a Leeds United fan, and we began bantering about the state of our respective clubs back in England. This lad also told us that, if were prepared to do three hours of work at the hostel per day, we'd be entitled to free accommodation.

'Sounds perfect,' said Dustin, and we started helping out the next day.

It was while I was in Vegas that I visited my first ever lap dancing bar, in the company of a few other hostellers. There seemed to be one on every street, and this particular place was right opposite the hostel. It was manned by two hefty bouncers who checked our ID, took our five dollar bills and waved us in.

'Y'all have a good night, now,' they said.

What? I remember thinking. *When was the last time a bouncer at Wetherspoon's asked me to have a good night?*

We entered the club just as the youth hostel manager was leaving – he gave us a knowing wink – and ordered in some drinks. As I got settled, a dancer came over and started gyrating in front of an American guy sitting next to me. He just looked on, cool as a cucumber, but I could hardly hold my drink properly. Then the girl slowly started to take her clothes off as the music played, giving me a sidelong glance as she did so.

'Eh, lads, I think I'll be getting the next dance,' I said, hopefully.

She then revealed possibly the biggest pair of tits I had ever seen. Bloody hell, they were massive. Plastic surgery was at its peak in America - excuse the pun – and I couldn't believe my eyes. When the song ended she gave her punter a peck on the cheek, put her gear back on and asked me if I'd like a dance.

'Er, yes...' I stuttered, unsure of the etiquette in these places.

'Or,' she said, 'we can go into the private room in the back...'

In my naivety, I honestly thought she was coming on to me, that she genuinely fancied me. *Bloody hell*, I thought. *I've only been in Vegas one day and I'm about to have sex with an American woman. God Bless America!'*

Then she casually mentioned that it would cost me $30 for a private dance, and $20 if I stayed put where I was. I nearly spat out my Diet Coke (I couldn't afford the cocktails). I honestly had no idea you had to pay extra; I thought the $5 entrance fee was all-inclusive. My stricken expression must have amused the lap dancer, because she started to laugh.

'I guess it's your first time here,' she said, before explaining that my most cost-effective option would be to mooch around the tables and stick dollar bills in the knickers of the dancers. I took her advice but, being a broke backpacker, was careful not to dish out too many notes.

Later that evening I got chatting with her again, after she'd clocked off her shift. She was so pleasant and polite, asking me about life in England, before discussing her own circumstances.

'I hate my job, to be honest, but it pays well,' she said. 'I'm a single mom with a daughter to feed so I gotta go where the dollars are.'

Dustin and I returned to the hostel that evening, only to find that someone had stolen his money belt from the bottom of his sleeping bag. He was absolutely fuming.

'That's it,' he announced. 'I've had enough. I'm going back home.'

I was upset that Dustin had decided to return to the UK. He was a great mate, though he could be a grumpy sod at times and wasn't always the easiest person to get along with, he was still my travel mate and I knew it would be harder being away on my own. Of course you do need your glass half-full when you're travelling on a budget, 24/7, so I couldn't be down for long.

I was keen to give my friend a great send-off before he flew home, however, and his last night was certainly one to remember. A crazy chain of events meant that we found ourselves partying on the famous Las Vegas Strip with a fella called Henry Rono, a renowned Kenyan athlete who'd held the 3000 metres steeplechase world record for over a decade, and who'd also been a brilliant 5000-metre runner in his heyday.

Henry was also the president of the Youth Hostel Association and happened to be in Las Vegas to sign a massive sponsorship deal with Adidas. Bizarrely, he'd waived his management's request to stay in swanky hotel accommodation, preferring to doss in our youth hostel for a few days. Dustin and I got chatting to him one evening, and discovered that he was a lovely, down-to-earth person.

He stayed in a dorm on our corridor and would go for a run in the Nevada desert every morning. One day I joked that he should give me a knock on my door so I could join him; he only went and took it literally, waking me up at 5 a.m. the next day, dressed in his running gear. I'd been on a bender the previous night, though, so blearily made my excuses.

On Dustin's last night we all decided to head out for dinner, and out of courtesy asked Henry if he'd like to join us.

'Sure', he said, explaining that he couldn't be out past midnight since he had his big Adidas signing the next day.

So off we popped to the bright lights of Vegas with a world-beating athlete in tow. It soon became abundantly clear, however, that Henry liked a drink. As the night progressed he got absolutely smashed on Long Island Iced Tea (a lethal cocktail of tequila, vodka, rum, triple sec and gin) and proceeded to perform African dances on tables and run around various bars with his top off. In fact, Dustin and I were enjoying his company so much that we totally forgot we had to have him back in the hostel by midnight. We all finally staggered in at sunrise, with a paralytic Henry collapsing onto our dormitory floor since he was physically incapable of walking to his own room.

Four hours' later I awoke to hear a huge commotion outside in the corridor. Henry's management company, it seemed, had turned up to the hostel – along with some big cheese from

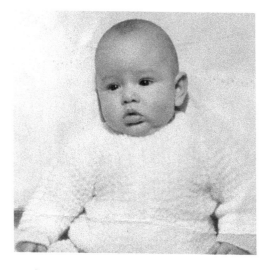

My first publicity photo. How big are my lips?

With Mum & Dad

Obviously, Dad wasn't as funny as me…

With Aurora and mum

My lovely sister now (excuse her nose)

My old school St Albans RC High School in Gorton
Manchester

Mum & Dad in their twenties

My Mum and Dad still married still in love and still to-gether. Not bad after 55 years together

My world in my arms Carter 2 & Cooper 6 months

Future Man City stars, or so they tell me

My boys, my best mates, whom I love so much.

With Carter & Cooper in Florida

My girlfriend and best mate Kate

My lucky Man City shirt always
wearing my lucky number

Me being a cock

The legend that is Mike McClean with George
Forman (see what I did there)

Adidas, and a host of PR and press guys – and were banging on his door, trying to rouse their client.

'You won't find him in there,' I explained as I popped my head out of the door, 'because he's kipping on my floor.'

Cue absolute mayhem. Henry's management barged into our dorm, took one look at their comatose athlete and threatened to sue me for taking someone who had 'serious alcohol issues' out on the town.

'You've ruined our PR campaign,' one guy wailed. 'If he doesn't sign this contract then I will personally issue a law suit against you.'

As if I was going to stand for that.

'Hang on a minute,' I said. 'Why all the blame? If it wasn't for me, you wouldn't have Henry here today, full stop.'

'Care to explain?' he asked.

'Last night my mate and I spotted Henry, pissed up, wandering around the casinos, and we knew he needed help,' I said, before outlining how we'd actually stopped him getting into a fight, thus avoiding any negative publicity that would have reflected badly on Adidas and their client.

'Then we took it upon ourselves to bring him back,' I continued – I was on a roll - 'but he'd lost his key, so we let him sleep in our room, and Dustin and I took it in turns to check him so he didn't choke on his vomit or anything.' Henry's entourage looked across at Dustin, who just nodded.

'And now *you're* threatening *me* with a lawsuit?' I yelled. 'By rights I should be contacting the press about how you failed to protect a world famous athlete...'

Suddenly their whole mood changed, and an apology followed.

'We're so sorry, sir,' the PR guy said. 'If there's anything we can do...'

There certainly was. As a result of my rant, I got mine and Dustin's accommodation paid for, and managed to wangle a few food vouchers, too. One thing I'd learned very quickly about Americans is that they hated bad publicity, and here was a case in point.

Not long afterwards Dustin left the US for the UK, and I decided to continue on to Australia. I loved my time Down Under – I visited Melbourne, the New South Wales town of Liverpool and, finally, the amazing Sydney – but after a few months I was ready to return to Manchester. I hardly had a cent to rub together and, having been away for over three months, I was also feeling increasingly homesick. By May I was back on British soil.

I travelled straight from Heathrow Airport to Maine Road – City were playing Middlesbrough at home – and following the full-time whistle I headed across to Levenshulme to surprise my parents. Mum couldn't believe it when I walked in - she immediately grabbed me close and began to cry, in her Spanish way – whereas Dad gave me a pat on the back before telling me to sit down and shurrup because *Noel's House Party* had just started.

The first thing Mum wanted to do was cook for me – no surprise there – and that night I had the best Spanish soup – *lentejas con chorizo* - followed by a warm, comfy sleep in my very own bed. Paradise.

When I awoke the next day, however, the reality of my situation began to bite. Here I was, back in Manchester, single, broke and jobless. After enjoying a home-cooked full English breakfast I got onto my agent Paul Bridson and, as luck would have it, he came up trumps.

'D'you fancy a summer season in Cornwall, Mike?' he asked, informing me that I'd be working for Haven Holidays as a compere, at a resort called St Minver, near Bodmin. 'They're offering £200 per week. Is that okay with you?'

'I'll take it,' I said.

So, I set off for Cornwall in April 1991, unsure quite what to expect as I'd never been to that neck of the woods before. I was immediately captivated. St Minver was beautiful – so quiet, clean and breathtakingly scenic - and I instantly fell in love with the place.

The complex's entertainments' manager was called Caroline Jones, and our friendship would become one of the best I ever had during a summer season. She was a great girl – very, very funny and truly excellent at her job – and we clicked straight away. It was all very platonic, though (my only significant romance that summer was with a stunningly gorgeous dancer from Essex called Charlie). I happened to get on really well with Caroline's boyfriend, too; Craig was part of a very funny double act called Collinson and Wright, and we bonded over our love of comedy. He is a diamond of a bloke and helped me out no end at St Minver, forever donating gags and suggesting routines.

In October 1991, it was time to return to Manchester, so I chugged back up north in my little red Fiesta. I was more excited than usual to head home; that summer my sister had given birth to a baby girl, so I was now a proud uncle to the lovely Nicole. By this time Aurora had settled down having mixed with the wrong crowd for a while and had trained to be a hairdresser. I always got her to cut my hair and this didn't change until it was time for it all to come off (but that's a long way off to be fair…).

I'd also signed up with a new agency, Pan Artists, who supplied walk-on 'extra' parts for northern-based shows like *Coronation Street*, *Emmerdale*, *Brookside* and *Heartbeat*. In order to be eligible for work, however, I needed to apply for an Equity card to become a member of the actors' union. Unfortunately for me, to satisfy their criteria I needed to show evidence of recent TV, stage or film contracts, which I obviously hadn't got. Any hopes of being able to wing it were dashed when I received a call from the Pan Artists office.

'Next time you come into the offices, Mike, can you bring three photos, your CV and your Equity card?'

With the help of a bottle of Tipp-Ex and my old pal Peter Woolley (he had a printing firm) I managed to supply a convincing list of contracts which secured my Equity card as well as my agency representation. I registered myself as 'Steve Peters' (Steve and Peter are my middle names) since I'd been advised by many performers not to use my real name. Casting directors rarely gave extras the opportunity to audition for proper roles but, by having another persona, you could easily disassociate yourself from your 'bit-part' alter-ego.

I vividly remember my first job on *Coronation Street*. It was a Friday, and I was asked to bring along three changes of clothing since it was a multi-episode, meaning that I'd be filmed drinking in the Rovers Return or walking down the famous cobbles on three separate occasions. I'd earn £120 for these extended sessions, instead of the regulation £70 for a single episode. Even better, I could legitimately sign on the dole, too, since I was working under twenty-seven hours per week.

My walk-on parts became more frequent, much to the delight of my *Corrie*-loving mother, although my appearances could be so fleeting that I'd have to pause the VHS for her and point myself out.

'Oh jes...' she'd say, squinting at the screen. 'Is dew!'

Not everyone was enamoured, though, in particular the existing clique of extras who seemed to despise the arrival of any fresh new faces. This close-knit group was largely made up of old 'turns' in their fifties and sixties – ex-cabaret singers, dancers, magicians, ventriloquists – who were all convinced that their big showbiz break was going to happen on *Coronation Street*. Being given some spoken dialogue, no matter how brief, was the Holy Grail, and they'd all fight tooth and nail to get a line here or a line there. I wasn't really that passionate about it, I didn't think I was going to be discovered there and become the next Ena Sharples; I just wanted to do the job and get home in time for my dinner.

One afternoon all hell broke loose, though. The *Corrie* director needed someone to ride a bike down Rosamund Street, and all the extras put themselves forward, desperate for added exposure on prime time telly. Except me, that is, since I wasn't remotely arsed.

I was sitting in the corner of the green room reading a paper, having a brew and minding my own business, when the third assistant director walked in and singled me out.

'Hey, Steve, can you ride a bike?' he asked (I never quite got used to them using my Equity name).

'Er, yeah,' I replied, citing my cycling proficiency certificate from 1981.

'You'll do, then,' he said. 'We need someone young. Follow me.'

Well, you could have heard a pin drop in that green room, and the stares I got from my fellow extras couldn't have been filthier. You'd have thought I'd been given the leading role in *The Sweeney*.

'He's only been here five minutes,' I heard someone hiss. 'I knew it wouldn't take long until he got too big for his boots...'

I straddled the bike, followed the director's instructions to hit my mark on time, and that was that. Easy-peasy. I then returned to the green room to wait for the next scene and, a few moments later, the third assistant director came over and asked me to sign a document.

'What's this? I enquired.

'The payment form. You get an extra fifty quid for riding a bike. It's classed as a special skill,' he said. That, as you can imagine, went down like a lead balloon with my bit-part buddies.

'Ideas above his station, that lad...' I heard one of them moan.

You really have no idea of just how cutthroat those sods could be…

CHAPTER 9

It's Behind You…

Pan Artists continued to keep me busy with a variety of walk-on parts. I think they liked the fact that, unlike some of my contemporaries, I was always punctual, I never complained and I was very professional. During filming, I'd make it my priority to make a director's life easy by maintaining eye-lines, hitting my mark, and picking up the right shots and I don't think it went unnoticed.

My extra roles increased as a result and, as well as supping fake beer in the Rovers (which is a vile mix), I found myself walking through a busy *Emmerdale* village, masquerading as a doctor or a dying patient on *Medics* and being all manner of policemen, firemen and criminals in a whole host of other soaps and dramas.

'I saw you dealing drugs on *Brookside* last night,' my mates would laugh. They loved taking the piss whenever I popped up on their TV screens.

That said, I'd often purposely avoid being in shot. I was ever-mindful of the fact that my status as an extra might deter casting directors from giving me meatier roles and, as such, was more than happy for 'Steve Peters' to remain firmly in the background.

Slowly but surely, I became accepted by the cliques of old-timers who'd been performing walk-on roles since the Dark Ages. Lost in their little showbiz world, they'd sit me down and regale me with rambling tales of which programmes they'd appeared in, and would give me little insights into all the actors they'd worked with.

'Ever since we worked together in Birmingham, Paul Henry and I still exchange Christmas cards,' one old dear once bragged, in true luvvie-style. 'He's such a darling, such a wonderful, wonderful friend...'

'She means Benny from *Crossroads*,' whispered another extra, raising her eyebrows.

I rubbed shoulders with some well-known stars myself, most notably during the week I spent on the set of *The Darling Buds of May*. David Jason was starring as Pop Larkin, alongside an up-and-coming actress by the name of Catherine Zeta Jones who played the role of his daughter, Mariette. I was given two parts; firstly, as a member of the local council who had to nod briefly at Mariette, and secondly, as a poet's friend with a three-word line of 'See you later'. Not exactly BAFTA-winning fodder, but I was just happy to be getting a weeks'-worth of money. As it happened, you couldn't even hear my solitary line when the episode finally came out, but I really wasn't bothered. I'd got paid for my troubles, and that was paramount.

I can tell you that Catherine Zeta Jones was a stunning-looking woman, who not only had real star quality (she was clearly destined for bigger things) but who also seemed refreshingly grounded. She was the first leading actress I'd met who'd taken the time out to chat to the extras and make us feel welcome, it might not sound much but personally I think it says a great deal about a person.

Other than the occasional brush with celebrities, life as an extra wasn't as glamorous as most people assumed. Most of your day would be spent either hanging around waiting for your 'moment', or killing time by reading newspapers (this was long before the days of Wi-Fi and iPhones, of course).

Sometimes, however, you'd meet a character who'd reduce the boredom. The legendary 'Silver Fox' was one such person. He'd been working as an extra for years – hence his nickname - and one day he'd become so fed up with the daily grind that he'd decided to devote much of his time to winding people up.

His most notorious prank, I remember, involved an inexperienced young extra who was filming a scene outside *Emmerdale*'s Woolpack pub. The director had told this lad to merely walk out of the pub and then out of shot, to coincide with one of the main characters, Joe Sugden, getting into his car and driving off towards the farmhouse.

That was it, pure and simple. Nothing more, and nothing less. But then the Silver Fox set to task and, a few minutes before the scene was due to be filmed, he took the young extra to one side for a quiet word.

'You do realise that the director *loves* it if you improvise and throw in your own lines, don't you?' he said.

'Really?' said the young lad, all wide-eyed.

'Yeah, definitely,' continued the Silver Fox. 'Anyone who uses their imagination gets serious brownie points. Some even earn themselves a proper acting role.'

'Wow,' said his fellow extra. 'Thanks for the heads-up. Really kind of you.'

Before long, the director was ready to film the take, and a hush descended upon the *Emmerdale* set.

'And... ACTION! he shouted.

The lad exited the pub as instructed. However, with the Silver Fox's advice fresh in his mind, just as Joe Sugden climbed into his car he sidled over and shoehorned in his improv.

'Hey, Joe, any chance of a lift, mate?'

The director went absolutely ballistic.

'*CUT...CUT...CUT*,' he bellowed. 'Who in God's fuckin' name is HE? Get him out of here. NOW!'

The hapless extra was banished from the set and never graced *Emmerdale* again. It was both cruel and funny, like much of the showbiz world, I suppose.

****

I loved the fact my mother was Spanish, whilst she hadn't taught me the language, once I'd learnt it from my Spanish family she'd chatter away to me (particularly if she didn't want my friends to know what she was saying!) and I treasured my cultural heritage - but boy, it was sometimes frustrating. Relaying telephone messages was a case in point. Even though she'd spent three decades in the UK, Mum's English was pretty terrible, having worked full time and brought us up there'd never seemed time for her to learn to read or write English, so of course this meant that taking down names and numbers was often problematic.

'Okay, I will tell 'im dew called, goodbye...' she'd say whenever anyone rang for me, before abruptly slamming down the receiver and failing to note anything down. Then I'd get home and, in passing, she'd mention that day's call.

'Say, Michael du friend he a-phoney for dew,' she'd say as she prepared my dinner.

'What was his name, Mum?' I'd ask, wondering whether it was a routine social call from my mate or a vital business call from my agent.

'Oh, I can no remember,' she'd say, absent-mindedly. 'Say a few names and I tell dew...'

This would happen all the time, and it would do my head in. One of these calls, it transpired, had come in from my old mucker from St Minver, Craig Collinson who, luckily, tried to call me again that same evening, in November 1991.

'Mike, d'you fancy doing a panto in Tunbridge Wells?' he'd asked when he finally got hold of me, explaining that a juggler called Pete Mathews had been due to play the roles of the Chinese Policeman and the Genie of the Lamp in *Aladdin*, but that appendicitis had caused him to pull out.

I accepted straight away. I'd adored pantomimes as a child, and couldn't believe I was about to star in one as a professional. Not only that, it was being produced by Dave Lee, whose company – Pantoni Productions – was among the most renowned of its kind in the country. I gave Dave a call, and he told me that I'd come highly recommended by Craig, and that he could offer me £350 per week, plus subsistence and holiday pay. Rehearsals would commence in November, and performances would start on 5th December and finish on 11th January.

Aladdin, I learned, would also star kids' TV presenter Dave Benson-Phillips, and legendary ballet dancer Wayne Sleep. Top of the bill, however, was none other than Jon Pertwee. Yep, only Doctor-bloody-Who and Worzel-bloody-Gummidge himself. To say that I was thrilled to be in the same cast as this acting legend was an understatement, and I began to count the days until rehearsals.

In the meantime, I continued with my bit-part work, including a memorable day spent on the set of BBC's *Crimewatch*. I remember attending the audition at the TV studios on Oxford Road, Manchester, where I was briefed by the director.

'We're need to stage a reconstruction of a bank robbery in Oldham,' he said, 'and we'd like to see you take on the role of one of the attackers.'

I had a similar height and build to one of these hoodlums, apparently; he was a particularly violent individual, by all accounts, who had traumatised some poor bank clerk during the hold up.

'We're looking for authenticity, for credibility,' said the director.

'I'll do my best,' I replied.

I stood outside the mocked-up bank foyer and waited for my cue. Once I heard 'ACTION' I took a deep breath and burst into the room.

'PUT YOUR FUCKING HANDS IN THE AIR,' I screamed, my face contorted with rage, 'AND THEN GET ON THE FUCKING FLOOR.'

The actor playing the bank clerk looked genuinely petrified. This was method acting at its finest. Marlon Brando would have been proud.

'DO IT NOW,' I shouted, wielding my imaginary shotgun, 'DO IT FUCKING NOW, YOU BASTARD. I'M NOT FUCKING ABOUT, BELIEVE ME...'

'...and, CUT,' said the director, whose jaw had dropped at the sight of this Mancunian maniac.

'I think we can safely say the job's yours,' he smiled. 'Maybe just curb the language next time.'

I was delighted. To me, this felt like my first proper acting job, a high-profile role that could fully test my wide-ranging drama skills. *I can't wait to tell my mates,* I thought to myself and, in the pub that night, bragged for Britain about my big break.

The *Crimewatch* shoot took place a few days' later. As soon as I arrived I was taken to see the BBC's wardrobe assistant. I got dressed into the dark clothing that she'd handed me, and awaited my make-up session.

'Here you are,' she said, handing me a black woollen balaclava.

'What's this?' I asked.

'All the robbers wore masks,' she replied. 'As you know, reconstructions have to be as accurate as possible...'

I was crestfallen. I'd told everyone about my starring role, and now – with this sodding balaclava on - I wasn't even going to be seen. I could have been anybody. And what's more, when the show finally got broadcast a few Tuesdays later, I was on screen for all of five seconds.

My friends in the Pack Horse found this hilarious, of course.

'Mike, don't have nightmares,' they laughed on the night of transmission, before loudly singing the *Crimewatch* theme tune. The funny fuckers.

In November 1991, with my car packed to the gills, I drove down to Kent for my first panto season. I'd never been away over Christmas before, and my poor mum was inconsolable.

'My boy, he not going to be here for Christmas... I am going to miss dew...' she wailed, amid a sea of tears. Unsurprisingly, Dad was far more composed.

'Enjoy yourself, Michael,' he said. 'Just make sure you stay away from those dancers.'

My first port of call 'dahn sahf' was the Beck Theatre in Hayes, Middlesex. There, I watched my mates Craig and Martin (a.k.a Collinson and Wright) starring in their panto – another version of *Aladdin* - which was already up and running. Also in among the cast was Ted Rogers, a veteran comedian whose *3-2-1* game show had been a big hit in the 1980s, and had been memorable for its 'Dusty Bin' booby prize.

The panto itself was awesome, with every gag being delivered perfectly and every comedy routine getting laughs. I sat there, my adrenalin pumping, feeling so excited about my up-coming stint in Tunbridge Wells. Craig and Martin introduced me to Ted after the show – what a lovely man – before inviting me back to their digs, along with the rest of the cast.

I remember my eyes nearly popping out of my head when I saw a famous female *Neighbours* star rolling a joint; that same week I'd watched her promoting the panto on a kids' TV show, all sweetness and light, yet here she was in Craig's flat, getting high as a kite.

'D'you want a toke, Mike?' she smiled.

'No thanks, love,' I replied. I'd never been into drugs and, other than once getting stoned on a hash muffin with Degs in Amsterdam, I had generally shied away from any funny stuff.

I said my goodbyes the next morning and headed off to Tunbridge Wells (or 'Royal' Tunbridge Wells as many of the locals pointed out to me). It was one of the most beautiful places I'd ever visited in the UK; the town centre was full of well-dressed people with very posh accents and most build-ings seemed to have tables and chairs outside, on the pave-ment. In Kent, that usually signified a café. In Manchester, that usually meant an eviction.

I was totally shitting myself when I arrived at the theatre the next morning for the first day of rehearsals. Not only had I never been in a full professional panto before, I'd also be performing with celebrities that I'd grown up watching on TV. Wayne Sleep and John Benson-Smith were pretty well-estab-lished in showbiz-land, but the biggest star of them all had to be Jon Pertwee. The man had a real presence about him and, as he said a booming 'Hello' and shook my hand, I remember thinking *"that's Doctor Who, that is..."* If like me you grew up with Dr Who and kids TV then I'm sure you'll know exactly how I felt at that moment.

We all assembled on the main stage where the director, Brian Marshall, asked everyone to sit down and introduce themselves.

'Tell everyone your name and what part you're playing,' he said, but when it came to my turn I completely froze.

'Hello I'm...erm...erm...erm...' I said, blushing from head to toe.

Everyone laughed – they clearly thought I was joking - but for those few seconds, with all these famous faces staring at me, I literally forgot my fucking name.

'It's Mike McClean, yes?' smiled Brian. 'Our Chinese Policeman? Our Genie of the Lamp?'

'That's it!' I said, amid more gales of laughter.

'What a clever way to break the ice,' remarked an actor called Simon Gregory during the coffee break.

He was playing the Emperor of China – he was an excellent performer, a proper panto past-master – and over the next couple of months we'd strike up a great friendship. I shared a dressing room with Simon (and Dave) and it was non-stop laughter from start to finish. He had a wicked sense of humour, did Simon, and we'd spend our time telling each other stories, taking the piss out of cast members and leering at the dancers. He made no secret of the fact that he preferred the four muscle-bound males, as opposed to the six gorgeous girls that had caught my attention.

Our company's star dancer, Wayne Sleep, became a complete pain in the neck, though. During rehearsals he'd often come up to me and try to grab my bollocks; at first it was mildly amusing but after a while it started to piss me right off. He once lunged at me when I was in the midst of a telephone call, and I snapped.

'Will you FUCK OFF?' I yelled, as he scuttled off, laughing.

'He must like you,' said the dance captain, a very talented and attractive girl called Sue Eastwood who'd starred in nearly every show on the West End.

'Just ignore him; he'll probably go away,' she added, before walking away, turning around, and flashing me a big smile.

I might be daft but I'd had a few summer seasons under my belt by then and even I could tell that I was on to a winner. Within days we'd started seeing each other, and regardless of anything else this did me a massive favour as Wayne promptly stopped tweaking my testicles. I hadn't considered that I might have been giving off the wrong vibes!! Sue and I quickly realised that we had a lot in common; having had dancing jobs in Spain, she spoke the language perfectly and had even worked in La Coruna, my family's home city. Unusually for panto romances, we carried on seeing each other for a while after the run ended, disproving the old theatre-land adage that 'dancers were just for Christmas, not for life...'

With all the rehearsals done and dusted, *Aladdin* at the Assembly Room Theatre was up and running. It was a decent little show – really quite funny in places – and the director even gave me a little window to do a brief magic routine. Jon

Pertwee entered into the spirit of things in his role as the villainous Abanazar and we shared quite a lot of stage time together. Before and after shows, however, he'd make a point of taking me aside and offering me snippets of advice, telling me how to deliver a line, how to time myself, or where I should be standing.

At first I appreciated this – the bloke was an acting legend, after all – but as time went on, his constant tips and pointers began to grate on me. I felt he was implying that I wasn't good enough, and that I had much room for improvement. My mate Simon disagreed, however, and believed that Jon's intentions were well-placed.

'You're the only cast member he gives any time to, Mike,' he explained. 'I honestly think he likes you a lot, and I think he's genuinely trying to help you.'

As the weeks went by, I came to realise that Simon was probably right, and I started to appreciate Jon's words of wisdom. Occasionally he'd even invite me into his dressing room where we'd watch old episodes of *Doctor Who* together, during which he'd offer his insight, like a director's commentary before they became all the rage. I ended up getting on really well with him, and that's despite the memorable night when he committed on-stage robbery.

During every performance, there came a point in the panto where a scheming Abanazar would rub the magic lamp, prompting a crew member to activate the smoke machine, thus providing me with the cue to jump on stage as the Genie. On this particular night, however, the machine became jammed and the smoke wouldn't stop belching out, meaning that Jon and I could hardly see a thing.

Jon decided to go with an ad-lib - 'Where the hell are you, Genie?' - which got a laugh, since panto audiences enjoy - and expect - the occasional mishap. I waited for the titters to subside before unleashing my own off-the-cuff remark.

'Sorry, master, I am having Kwik-Fit repair the fog lamps in the morning,' I said, which got an even bigger laugh, together with a round of applause. Jon looked at me and winked, which filled me with pride and satisfaction.

'An excellent ad-lib, young Michael,' he said as we came off stage. 'Well done.'

As bad luck would have it, the smoke machine jammed again during the next day's matinee performance and, as the mist shrouded the stage once more, I psyched myself up for my tried-and-tested ad-lib. Then Jon opened his mouth.

'Where the hell are you, Genie?' he boomed. 'Make sure you have Kwik-Fit repair the fog lamps in the morning...'

What the fuck? The cheeky bastard had only gone and stolen my fucking ad-lib. To say I was furious was an understatement.

'Hope you don't mind, old boy, but it's a great one,' he said as the curtains went down. 'Better if I have it, don't you think?'

The words that went thought my head were '*Actually Jon, yes I do mind you having my funny ad-lib, you thieving fucker, it's not as if you don't have many lines in the whole fucking show, is it?*'

But what actually came out of my mouth was 'That's fine Jon, not a problem,' I was resigned to the fact that he was the master, and I was his apprentice. In fairness it was a compliment and payment for all the great advice he'd given me. Ego though is an easily bruised thing and I was still learning the ropes.

We parted on great terms, though. After our final performance Jon shook my hand, told me how much he'd enjoyed working with me, and handed me a signed picture of himself in his *Doctor Who* guise.

To my good student and friend, all the best, Jon Pertwee he wrote. It still has pride of place on the wall of my Bog of Fame (which is not as much of an insult as it might sound.. I spend a fair amount of time in there and it's a great place to contemplate!)

'It's been a pleasure, Jon,' I said to him, and I meant every single word. Working with Jon, Simon, Dave – and even Wayne the gonad grabber – had been one of the best experiences of my life.

As the panto season neared its end, I'd approached the director, Brian, to ask if he'd consider representing me in the future, whether for pantomimes or other TV and theatre roles. He worked for a huge talent agency, Qdos, who looked after some of the biggest acts on television.

'Send a letter to my office and I'll see what I can do,' said Brian, somewhat ambivalently, before offering me a wet lettuce handshake.

A really shitty and sarky response arrived in the post a few weeks later, along the lines of 'when I next need a comedy genius I'll be in touch...'

Just you wait and see, you dick, I thought as I digested his words, wondering quite what I'd done to offend him.

Revenge, as it happened, would be sweet, and would occur just a few years down the line.

CHAPTER 10

Nickelodeon

In January 1995 I'd found myself a new agent who specialised in castings for television, theatre and commercials. One day he phoned to tell me that new kids' satellite TV channel, Nickelodeon, was due to be launched in the UK, and that they were seeking fresh new presenters. He didn't exactly fill me with confidence, though.

'I'll send in your CV, Mike, but wouldn't hold much hope of an audition,' he said, explaining that it would be the usual scenario of TV executives plumping for middle-class, university-educated, London-based candidates. He had a point, I suppose; few children's TV presenters were working class with regional accents, and I probably wouldn't fit their mould. Deep down he must have thought I was totally wasting my time, though, because a few weeks' later he sent back all my publicity photos, along with a curt letter informing me that he could no longer represent me.

'I suggest you contact Nickelodeon direct if you want to chase things up,' he said.

Sod you, I thought, screwing up his letter and aiming it into a waste bin.

By this time, I'd had my fill of agents, and decided to represent myself, inventing an alter-ego. Adopting a very posh Home Counties accent, I rang the Nickelodeon office and asked to speak to the head of live TV, David Rose.

'Oh, hello David,' I said, like some hammy old actor. 'This is Steve Peters, Mike McClean's agent. Just wondering whether you managed to have a look at my client's CV.'

'I have, in fact,' he replied, explaining that there'd been a setback regarding the audition process, hence his delay in replying.

'Oh, I see,' I replied, trying to stay in character. 'It's just that Mike's very keen to see you, David. He's such a talented young man. A super stand up, an excellent magician and so wonderful with children and adults. It'd be such a damn shame if he slipped through your net.'

'I'll be in touch soon, I can promise you that,' he said.

Job done. Who needed a bloody agent anyway?

The following week my mobile phone rang. It was the Nickelodeon number. I took a deep breath and pressed the green button.

'Hello, Blue Heaven Management, Steve speaking...' I said, blurting out the first company name that entered my head.

'Hi Steve, it's David Rose. Just wondering whether your client Mike would like to come down to London for an audition?'

'I'm sure he'd be delighted, David,' I replied, before requesting a few more details about the new channel. He happily outlined all their plans, which sounded terrific. It was hard to rein in my excitement and conceal my Manc accent, but I think I just about managed it.

'Sounds like it could be quite big, David.'

'Big? It's going to be massive,' he said, adding that his secretary would be in touch shortly.

I waited and I waited for that call back, but for weeks I heard nothing. In the meantime, I had no option but to take a summer season job at Reighton Sands holiday park in Scarborough (£350 per week plus my own caravan). I was going to be the compere in the family room, working six days per week from 7 p.m. until 10 p.m. at the earliest.

Just before the season started, however, my mobile rang. It was David Rose's secretary.

'Steve, could Mike meet us at Spitfire TV in London? He'll need to prepare four links to camera, one for ten seconds, one for thirty seconds, one for a minute and the last for two minutes.' I hoped she hadn't heard the gulp at the other end of the line.

'I'll send you the info through the post, Steve,' she added, 'so I'll need your office address.'

Shit. What do I say?

'Can you send them direct to Mike, please, as I'll be in New York with a client,' I said, giving her my Levenshulme address.

A few days' later the details arrived via Mum and Dad's, and my preparation began in earnest. I studied BBC children's presenters on TV, watching how they linked in and out of programmes, how they back-referenced what they'd just seen, and how they offered teasers for upcoming features. For my audition, I decided to read out some letters and - don't ask - make a dog out of balloons. I wrote a little script for myself, reciting it over and over again until I was word perfect.

The night before, I drove down to London. I had barely enough money for petrol, so had no option but to sleep in my car at a service station, which wasn't exactly ideal. I drove to the Spitfire studios the next morning, feeling sick with nerves. A runner came to collect me and introduced me to David Rose, who was nothing like I'd imagined. He wore jeans and a leather jacket and he looked far more casual than most television executives. He also had a twitch in his right eye.

'Lovely to meet you, Mike' he said, extending his hand. 'You come highly recommended by your agent.'

I smiled. 'That's very kind of Steve to say.'

Accompanying David was his right-hand man, a guy called Malcolm Bird who produced as well as presented. I could tell by his limp handshake and his arrogant attitude that he wasn't keen on me at all.

'Hi,' he said, looking down his nose at me, before proceeding to talk to David as if I wasn't there.

In the green room, I found all the other candidates lounging around and loudly chatting. I immediately noticed *Eastenders'* actor James Gilbey, as well as a presenter called Lucy Alexander and a petite former ballerina called Sarah Cawood. In the corner were two curly-haired brunettes who I'd assumed were twins but who, judging by their conversations, were best mates called Mounya and Yiolanda who worked together in a shoe shop. I got talking to a Bournemouth-based local radio DJ called Rick Adams, a bespectacled, geeky-looking guy.

'You've done stand-up, then? You'll be absolutely fine,' he assured me.

Despite this vote of confidence, I remember sitting there and feeling really intimidated, convinced that all these super-sassy people were shoo-ins for these coveted Nickelodeon gigs. To calm my nerves, I grabbed myself a cup of strong tea – such a typical northerner - before revising my script.

The floor manager called in each candidate, one by one. Soon it was my turn.

'Mike McClean, please...'

I wiped my clammy hands on my trousers, and took a deep breath.

'Just relax and enjoy yourself,' said David Rose as I entered the studio. First up was my ten-second link to camera.

'Coming to you in ten...nine...eight...' said the floor manager.

Come on, Mike, don't fuck this up, I thought as my mouth got drier by the second.

'Seven...six...five...

Shit, this was it. My time to shine and get the gig of a lifetime.

'Four...three...two...one...' I heard, and I was cued up.

'Hi, I'm Mike McClean,' I grinned, staring straight down the camera lens. 'Coming up in today's show I'll be reading your letters, and there'll be music from our studio guests, 911. And then I'll be showing you how to make a dog with a balloon. It's all coming up on Nickelodeon...'

My first TV link, done and dusted. Then the production team threw in a curve ball, asking me to stand up and talk about myself for a minute.

Hang on a minute, you crafty bastards, this wasn't part of the drill...

It's amazing at how many people go blank after twenty seconds, but not me; David and his pals would have needed a gun to shut me up. After that I did my other links, which seemed to go really well; I pretended to back-reference a *Rugrats* cartoon, before reading out my fake letters (including one asking me to make my balloon dog). I was flying, I felt confident and, before I knew it, my studio time was up.

'Mike, that was brilliant,' said David. 'You're a natural. Are you free for the next couple of months?'

I couldn't believe my ears.

'I'm more free than John Inman,' came my reply and, much to my delight, David said he'd be in touch. I left Spitfire TV and drove back to Scarborough, feeling thrilled that things had gone so well. A week later my phone rang. It was Malcolm Bird from Nickelodeon.

'How are you, Malcolm?' I said, as my heart pounded.

'Yeah, good, Mike,' he replied, before pausing for a moment. I'd learned that a pause was never a good sign in these situations. 'As you know,' he continued, 'we saw a lot of people at the audition. You were certainly one of the better ones, but unfortunately we've decided that you're not right for us on this occasion.'

Then he thanked me for my time, and told me he'd keep my details on file. I managed to squeak out a little 'no worries' and 'thanks' but I felt devastated. I must have stood with the phone in my hand for about five minutes, with his damning words - *You're not right for us* – looping around my head.

David Rose rang the next day, asking to speak to Steve (I'd almost forgotten about my agent alter-ego). I put on my cut-glass accent and tried to sound as rational as I could.

'Hello there, David...'

'I had to ring you. Just to say that we thought Mike was brilliant. He came well prepared, he was funny, and he hit every link on time. We honestly couldn't fault him.'

'So why not offer him a job, then?'

'We were looking to take on four or five presenters and we just felt Mike wasn't quite right for us yet,' he said, before going on to explain that Nickelodeon was planning to open a mini-studio in the Museum of the Moving Image in Bradford, and that there was a tour guide job up for grabs if I wanted it.

'Oh, I'll let him know,' I said, when I really wanted to tell him to stick his museum job up his arse. I ended the conversation, furious that - yet again - I'd done everything right but it still wasn't enough.

In the middle of June, with my summer season going well, I received a phone call from the new Executive Producer at Nickelodeon, Catherine Kirkwood.

'One of our presenters has had to attend a funeral next week,' she said. 'Any chance you could cover for them?'

I said yes, of course, and walked around the camp with a massive spring in my step. In the meantime, I decided to take a peek at the channel to get a feel for it. I couldn't believe my eyes when I tuned in. There on the screen were none other than the two shoe shop girls - Mounya and Yiolanda – along with the actor James Gilbey, the DJ Rick Adams and producer-cum-presenter Malcolm bloody Bird. As I watched I could see why they chose the two girls, and perhaps Rick, but I honestly didn't think James would get the gig because he was more of a luvvie actor than a children's presenter, and wasn't particularly natural on screen. And as for Malcolm, he didn't have much warmth as a host; he was far too cock-sure for his own good, and was often really condescending towards the kids who phoned in. Of course, that was just my opinion and I was only going on my experience working with kids throughout the summer.

Nickelodeon was broadcast out of The Trocadero, an entertainment complex-cum-shopping centre in the middle of London. I arrived for my big debut to find a pretty basic studio comprising of a camera, a sofa and a backdrop of shoppers gawping through the glass walls, no doubt in an attempt to get on TV. There I met Paul Heron - the director, cameraman and general jack-of-all-trades - who handed me a running order of the three-hours-worth of programming that I was to link into.

'Is there a script?' I asked.

'Nah,' he replied in his Geordie accent. 'That's basically it.'

I watched on as Sarah Cawood finished the presenting stint before mine, and marvelled at how professional and natural she was. Then it was my turn.

'On air in two minutes, Mike,' said Paul, before wishing me luck.

Looking back, I have no idea how I got through it all, but somehow, I did. Working in my favour was the fact that Nickelodeon as a channel was in its infancy, and with a cameraman doubling up as a producer, there was no big team calling the shots or telling me what to do. I was left to my own devices, really and as a consequence I got away with plenty; it was guerrilla TV at its finest. My shift finished, and I handed over to James Gilbey.

'Will you be doing this again?' asked Paul as I returned my ear piece to him.

'Not that I know of, mate, but I'd be more than happy to,' I said, and he told me he'd put in a good word. I couldn't stop smiling as I caught my train back to Scarborough, particularly when David Rose called me up, telling me that he'd enjoyed what he'd seen, and to invoice him £100.

I received even better news the week later, when Catherine rang to ask me if I could cover the 10 a.m. to 1 p.m. shift for a whole week.

'Oh, thank you,' she gushed when I said I could oblige. *Thank me?* I remember laughing to myself. *I should be kissing your feet, love...*

All this positivity did make me wonder why they hadn't used me in the first place, especially when my audition had seemingly gone so well. It wasn't long before Catherine revealed the true reason. Malcolm Bird, the guy who'd told me I 'wasn't quite right' for Nickelodeon, had since left the channel. It turned out that he'd always billed himself as 'the funny one' and, by all accounts, had felt threatened and intimidated by my audition. To stop me stepping on his toes, he'd convinced David Rose not to hire me, and had apparently gone ballistic when he discovered I'd done a cover shift.

'McClean must NEVER present on this channel again,' he'd stormed, yet thankfully he'd soon have no say in the matter, because he was out on his arse. That was to be the start of a lot of in pressure I discovered around TV. Some people had clout and an ego to match and would throw their weight around potentially blocking someone's career, out of nothing more than their own insecurity. Throughout my time on TV I was to come up against this over and again and it never failed to make me see red. If someone has a talent it should be shared and promoted, you never know who you're going to work with that can, in fact, bounce well off you and improve your own performance and I loved the chance of working with new talent.

CHAPTER 11

Sign On The Dotted Line

I was on the up, it seemed, so much so that Catherine from Nickelodeon asked me to provide presenter cover during their summer holidays. To say I was delighted was an understatement, particularly as I could fit it around my season in Scarborough.

Shortly after, however, David Rose asked if we could meet up. It all sounded a bit ominous to me. *Shit, what have I done wrong?* I remember thinking.

We met at an Italian cafe, just near his offices on Oxford Street.

'Would you like a mocha?' he asked, to which I said yes, despite the fact that I'd hadn't a fucking Scooby Doo what a 'mocha' was. We were still drinking Maxwell House and Mellow Birds in Manchester.

'Mike, I'm sorry, but I can't keep on paying your expenses,' he said. 'It's just costing the company too much.'

My heart sank, and I contemplated asking him to drop my fee instead, or to use National Express instead of Virgin Trains.

'What if I offered you a three-month contract?' he continued, 'with a view to it being extended for another six months if things go well?'

I nearly spat out my mocha. This was the news I'd been waiting to hear for weeks. We went back to his offices to sort everything out, and I learned that my fee would be £600 a week, along with £100 per month clothing allowance and all expenses paid. Not only that, David finally decided upon a six-month retainer, which meant that, even if the channel didn't require my services, I'd still be getting paid.

'Who's your agent?' asked David's secretary, Natalie.

'You're looking at him,' I replied. Not only was it time to consign my Steve Peters alter-ego to history, it was also time to mentally flick the V's to the agent who'd dumped me a few months' earlier, and was now missing out on some decent commission.

Natalie advised me to get a proper agent at some point. I wasn't keen to give anybody ten per cent of my earnings, but I sought the advice of David Hahn, an agent I'd met a few years earlier and who represented javelin star Tessa Sanderson. He gave my Nickelodeon contract the once-over, telling me it was a pretty standard document, and that all seemed above board.

'If you need an agent I'd be more than happy to represent you,' he said.

'I'll think about it,' I replied.

Finally, after all those years of knocking on doors and having them slammed in my face, one of them had finally opened and, once I'd said my thankyous and goodbyes to my colleagues in Scarborough, I was able to head down to the London studio to start this brand new chapter in my career. I sorted myself out with some digs, too, staying with my mate

Rob, who I'd done panto with at the Kenneth More Theatre in Ilford. Rob was an amazing guy, and I loved living with him. He was a single gay man (I used to call him my gay mum) and was one of the most laid-back people I'd ever met.

The following Monday, I was asked to report to Nickelodeon HQ at 5.30 a.m., to observe a new summertime programme called *Rise and Shine* that I was due to be co-presenting. The show comprised cartoons, competitions, phone-ins, and celebrity guests, all packed into two hours. It was fascinating to sit in the gallery and watch all the behind-the-scenes mayhem. Once everything went live, however, the presenters - Rick Adams and Sarah Cawood - were calm personified and made it look so easy. I was crapping myself.

I'm not sure I can do this... I told myself. *What if I run out of things to say or I go dry?*

At the end of the show, the producer – another woman called Catherine Head- came over.

'So tomorrow you'll be presenting between seven and nine with Sarah, Mike,' she said, 'so just be funny, okay?'

The next day, I caught the 5 a.m. train from Ilford to central London and, as I made my way from the station to the studio, I spotted the same producer getting out of a car.

'Why are you walking, Mike?' she asked, bemused, before explaining that Nickelodeon had sent a car for me. I hadn't expected this sort of thing – this was a whole new world to me – and it turned out some irate cabbie had woken Rob up at dawn, banging on the front door. As I prepared myself in the studio, the floor manager fitted me with an earpiece.

'D'you want your talk-back open or closed?' he asked. I didn't have a clue what he was referring to; this was all new to me. 'Open', I learned, meant you could hear everything behind the scenes, including comments from the vision mixer, camera calls from the director and observations from the producer. 'Closed' meant that you just heard the counts into the break, and notes from the producer. As a presenter you just had to choose which was right for you. Throughout my whole career I chose to have my earpiece open – unlike many of my colleagues - because I just liked to listen to everything going on in the background. It's not as easy as you think, but over time I'd become quite skilled in talking to the camera while people nattered away in my ear.

Soon, it was time to go live.

'Just be funny,' said Catherine – again – and before I knew it Sarah was introducing the show and I was linking into my first programme.

'But right now,' I smiled, 'it's time for *Rugrats*.' This cartoon was massive, and was one of many top shows brought over from America – all completely new to British audiences - that included *Doug, Kenan and Kel* and *Sabrina the Teenage Witch*.

My style was cheeky, but never rude; thanks to my summer season training, I was able to tell jokes that the kids at home got, but that the adults got, too. I'd pretend that I was bored as hell with certain calls – I'd yawn and roll my eyes as some poor seven-year-old chatted away – and would cut them off. It was great to hear people in my earpiece laughing out loud; they'd never had a presenter being this cheeky to the kids, but it seemed the TV audience loved it.

So I took care of the funny segments and, because she loved musicians, Sarah took care of our special guests. That morning we welcomed the latest boyband sensations, 911, although to call them 'musicians' was probably pushing it; let's face it, the only instrument they'd ever played was a Kleenex box with an elastic band around it.

The show finished and Catherine came and gave me a massive hug.

'Well done, Mike,' she said. 'Honestly, you were brilliant.'

It appeared the big bosses had loved it as well, although David Rose warned me about the importance of striking the right balance between cheekiness and rudeness, which I totally took on board.

It had been a busy, if not chaotic show, not unlike the channel itself. Nickelodeon, despite being the new kid on the block, was starting to make name for itself as the 'must-watch' children's TV channel, and was being talked about by school-kids across the UK. Not only that, it was ably competing with the likes of BBC and ITV, often beating them hands down in the ratings. In fact, we were hearing whispers that our competitors were in awe of the channel, due to the way that it's fresh, new, live-to-air approach appeared to be changing the face of kids' TV.

****

I'm just going to stop here and reflect for a minute. All of those times that I'd put "TV Presenter" as an occupation on an application form, believing in myself was now happening. The times I'd been told to "get a proper job" and the arguments I'd had with Mum and Dad about not having a "real job", were going to be a thing of the past. This WAS my real job and I WAS a TV presenter. I know that during the time it seemed to happen in a flash but I will never forget the occasions I doubted myself, the times lying in bed wondering if I was ever going to do more than summer camp. I think, looking back, I can credit the determination my Dad had when he came to this country, in showing me that if you want something hard enough and are prepared to work, you can make it happen.

****

A few weeks later David convened a talent meeting, comprising myself, James, Sarah, Rick, Lucy Alexander and Mounya and Yiolanda. Also, there were fellow presenters Helen Chamberlain and Nigel Mitchell, as well as our resident puppets, Bogey and Rude, who were operated by two amazing puppeteers, Dave and Craig. David announced the new presenters' schedule: the breakfast show would be hosted by Rick and Lucy, Mounya and Yiolanda would do the afternoon shift, and Sarah would take care of the evenings. I'd be tasked with the Saturday and Sunday breakfast shows, with Nigel, Helen and James occupying the rest of the weekend roster (Bogey and Rude would fit in wherever and whenever).

Helen, sadly, would soon leave Nickelodeon for pastures new. I'd never known a woman so enthusiastic about her football – she was a diehard Torquay United fan – and it came as no surprise when a sports network came to snap her up.

'D'you reckon I should go for it, Mike?' she asked after she'd been offered a presenting role with Sky Sports' new Saturday morning show, *Soccer AM*.

'Course you should,' I said, trying to mask my jealousy (it was a dream of a role for anyone who, like me, loved football as much as they loved TV). Helen went on to do a sterling job and, as I write, she's sadly left the *Soccer AM* sofa.

Around the same time that Helen left, we learned that the Trocadero studios would be closing, and that all our shows would be broadcast from two new studios at Rathbone Place. I was sad to say goodbye to the Trocadero; I'd had great fun working there and it left me with some great memories. I also discovered that Nickelodeon had commissioned a new show, called *Fish and Chips*, that would be filmed from an amusements arcade in Leeds. It would be produced by Yorkshire Television, would be directed by a guy called Sebastian Light, and would star at least one Nickelodeon presenter. To my delight, I received a call from Yorkshire TV, who'd earmarked me for a role, and who wanted to offer me £300 per show.

'We need a funnyman, and you fit the bill,' the executive said. He also mentioned that, as the show would be scripted, I'd have to learn lines. I generally hated working without an autocue - the only time I committed things to memory was during panto, and most of those lines were gags that I had written – so the thought of a proper acting role over twenty-six shows filled me with apprehension.

Every week I'd travel to Leeds, check in at a hotel with the rest of the cast and spend four days filming five shows. It was hard work, not helped by the fact that Sebastian – a posh boy with a real superiority complex - was one of the rudest directors I'd ever worked with. This comes back to my earlier comment of over inflated egos and inferiority complexes!

One evening, as the cast and production team had dinner at the hotel, I remember making my excuses that I needed an early night.

'I'm going to bed to learn my lines,' I said, when what I *really* wanted to do was get away from that fool of a director before I killed him. As I got into bed, the hotel receptionist rang, telling me that Sebastian had requested that I come back downstairs. As I re-entered the restaurant, the cast was still sitting around the table.

'Sorry about this, Mike,' he said, 'but we've all had a chat and we're a bit worried that you're not going to be able to deliver the goods required for this show.'

My colleagues looked mortified as he continued to tear into me, in front of everyone. It was toe-curling. I don't know if you've ever been embarrassed like that in public? I never had been before and as you may have gathered by now, I'm not one to mince my words when riled (although strangely Aurora is known as the fiery one in the family..)

'If I wasn't good enough, Nickelodeon wouldn't have put me for the job,' I countered, before accusing him of being unprofessional, and suggesting that we continue our conversation in private, at the bar. I was fucking fuming that this posh little prick had dared to speak to me like that. Who the hell did he think he was? I stayed calm, though, and just asked him what he'd like to drink.

'Oh, a red wine, please, Mike,' said Sebastian. As the waitress turned her back I put my arm around him.

'If you ever, EVER fucking speak to me like that again, I will fucking kill you,' I hissed, I handed him his glass. 'Enjoy your wine, and good luck with your show as I will not be fucking doing it. Goodnight'.

My phone rang constantly for the rest of the evening, but I never answered it. Instead, I called my agent friend David Hahn to relate that night's events. David was relieved that I hadn't hit him, but he told me not to be silly, to go to bed, and to get up in the morning and act as if nothing has happened.

'Just be polite,' he said. 'Don't let him get you down.'

Bollocks to that, I thought. *Let him fucking stew.*

I received similar advice from a Yorkshire TV sound man known as Daisy, who'd also worked with me on *The Darling Buds of May.* He also told me to maintain my professionalism and just do my job, which is exactly what I did.

You come to realise over time that the people behind the cameras have their heads screwed on and have seen it all, listening to their advice is often the right thing to do.

One day Sebastian had needed a little kid for a walk-on role, just to play on an arcade machine in the background. To save any faffing around finding a suitably 'licensed' child actor, I suggested to the producer that my dad could bring over my niece Nicole.

'That's great, Mike. I'm ever so grateful,' she said. 'You've saved us a lot of bother, there.'

An hour-or-so later, Dad and Nicole arrived. I gave her a handful of tokens to play on the machines, telling her that I'd give her a shout when we were ready to roll. However, when it came to filming the scene, Sebastian decided that he no longer wanted a child in the shot, despite knowing full well that my dad and my niece had come all the way from Manchester. I went ballistic but that was the measure of the man.

Fish and Chips, as it happened, was a huge success, so much so that Nickelodeon commissioned another twenty-six shows. *You can count me out*, I remember thinking. *No fucking way am I working with that twat again.*

'Such a shame I won't be able to do the next series,' I said during our last day of filming, 'but I really can't turn down panto...'

'How long for?' asked Sebastian. 'We can always get someone to step in for a couple of shows in December and January.'

He hadn't got the message. Even when I told him I was going on holiday, he wanted to know its duration.

'However long it takes to film the next series,' came my reply, as the crew tried to stifle their laughter. 'I don't think you're getting my drift, Sebastian. There's no way I'll be doing the second series if you're involved.'

He started ranting on about having to re-shoot new opening titles, which would cost him a fortune. As if I gave a shit. Part of me hoped someone from a bit higher up would ask why, maybe I was cutting my nose off to spite my face but I think I was better off not working with him as I doubt I'd have managed another serious without an assault charge!

CHAPTER 12

Onwards And Upwards Michael

My next Christmas pantomime – *Sleeping Beauty* - took place in the Kent town of Gravesend in December 1995. Starring *Bread* actress Pam Powers and Sixties' singer Craig Douglas, the show was going to be produced by panto past-master John Spiller. John had recruited me the previous year in Scunthorpe - I'd starred as Wishee Washee, with ex-*Grange Hill* and *This Life* actress Luisa Bradshaw-White as Aladdin – but my career had soared in the intervening twelve months. With my star in the ascendancy, I decided to haggle with my producer for a larger fee.

'I'm on the telly now, John,' I said.

'You cheeky sod,' he replied. 'How does five hundred per week sound?'

'Not as good as six hundred sounds.'

'Five-fifty, then.'

'Job's a good 'un, John...'

It was on the very first day of rehearsals that I met the woman I'd later have two children with. Andrea – she was a third-year dance student at Brian Rogers' Dance College – and after a couple of weeks we started seeing each other. Again I didn't remember the "Dancers are for Christmas" motto.. Looking back, I probably could have saved myself a lot of heartache if I had, but at least I have the boys.

Doing the panto was a killer, and not just because I had to juggle it with my Nickelodeon duties. Every single night I struggled to get laughs, and after a while it really started to get me down. I knew my performance was funny, and *Sleeping Beauty* was earning great reviews in the media, but for some reason the Gravesend audiences weren't having me at all. Maybe they just didn't like my cheeky Northern schtick. I began to dread every night on stage, and I vowed to never do another panto in the town again.

Not long after I finished *Sleeping Beauty* (thank the Lord) I discovered that some big changes had been made at Nickelodeon. David Rose had left – I never found out why – and a new Head of Live had arrived, an American called Niels Schuurmans, as well as Managing Director Janie Grace. Nickelodeon was fast becoming the number one kids' channel in the UK – mums, dads and kids were raving about it - and these two TV bigwigs had been brought in to take full advantage. Niels and Janie were great, to be fair; she was a real go-getting northerner, and his energy and creativity was infectious. Soon, posters promoting our shows and presenters were emblazoned in bus stations, newspapers, magazines and cereal boxes, and there was even a Nickelodeon ride at Alton Towers. The channel set up a dedicated press office, resulting in me being asked to do more photo shoots, interviews and public appearances.

Now it's funny that when you're on telly, everyone wants a piece of you… You're asked to "Guest" on TV shows, you get invites to parties and you get new "friends". You even get new clothes, I remember one well known clothing company who shall remain nameless inviting me in to their offices with my agent, putting 5 catalogues in front of me and saying just pick what you want and we will send it to you. All they wanted was for you to wear it on the tele or in a few photos. Now I'm not knocking it and I will admit to using it to my advantage and getting my true mates into VIP areas in nightclubs or to Premiers with me. To me though, it was more about staying grounded than getting swept up in the hype which again I think comes from my humble Manchester beginnings.

But there was going to be more and more hype as, under Niels and Janie's watch, the channel became more streamlined and professional. Each programme team had its own producer, researcher, junior researcher and runner, also we were to have regular Friday boardroom meetings.

Soon, Niels announced that he wanted to meet all the presenters individually for a chat about our Nickelodeon aims and objectives, which immediately got us all worried about our future. He did release Lucy Alexander from her contract, as it happened, but luckily mine was renewed for a year. Phew. I'd half-prepared myself for this good thing to end, but I always knew I had the safety net of my stand-up act to rely on if necessary.

Janie handed me my contract, pointing out that I'd earned myself a £2,000 annual pay rise along with an extra fifty quid's clothing allowance. She told me to take the paperwork away before reading it, signing it, and returning it. Many presenters would have taken it straight to their agents and demanded more money, but I wanted to avoid any mercenary messiness.

'It's not about the money, it's about me doing the job I love,' I said, and I meant it. The next day I bought Janie some chocolates and left them on her desk with a little thank you note. Like my dad always said, it doesn't take five minutes to say thanks and be nice. I was so grateful, though. Securing my Nickelodeon role for a year – with the added guarantee of panto income – came as a great relief to a freelancer like me. It was a huge weight off my mind.

Around this time, my flat-mate Rob began a serious relationship with a guy called Neil whom he later married and after 22 years are still married today (love you two). I thought it best if I moved out of his place and found my own gaff, so I began a search for a suitable flat.

****

A production manager at Nickelodeon, a Brummie called Jackie Moore, soon became my agent. Jackie was brilliant at dealing with contracts and producers; she took no prisoners, she didn't fuck about one bit, and I loved her for it. Unlike other agents I'd dealt with, I got on really well with her, and knew that she had my best interests at heart.

Within a month she'd sorted out a meeting with Michael Forte and David Mercer, who headed up children's TV at Carlton Television. The duo had launched a Saturday morning programme – *Scratchy & Co*, presented by Mark Speight and Gail Porter – in order to rival the BBC's *Alive and Kicking*. Michael and David were looking for someone to present a segment of the show called *It's Not Fair*, based around fairground games.

Jackie and I went to meet them at ITV's HQ. David and Michael both knew about me - they liked the way I presented - and discussed their plans for *Scratchy & Co*. Jackie played a blinder - she knew what to say, when to say it and how to say it – and the meeting couldn't have gone any better.

'You've got this, I promise you...' she said confidently as we walked into the lift. She wasn't wrong. A few days later, a call came in to offer me the show, and Jackie met me over lunch to discuss the fine detail.

'It's five hundred per show, Mike, and there's going to be sixteen episodes,' she said, explaining that it would take a week to film, with three shows per day. I quickly did the maths. Eight thousand pounds for a weeks' work. I was blown away. I'd only been with Jackie a couple of months and she'd already landed me a game show on kids' Saturday morning television, on ITV no less. Nickelodeon very kindly granted me a week's leave, deeming it good to have 'one of theirs' presenting a show on terrestrial TV.

It's Not Fair was a great little show. It was filmed at Carlton's Nottingham studios and was produced by a top guy called Martin Fox, and directed by another lovely fella called Richard Bradley. Those studios had helped create some iconic shows – *Crossroads*, *Celebrity Squares*, *Auf Wiedersehen, Pet* and *Family Fortunes* to name but a few – and I considered it an honour to work there.

I was the Ringmaster, and I had two assistants - Candy and Floss – who marshalled three teams as they tackled various games, quizzes and physical challenges. Michael Forte and David Mercer came to the recording and, as (bad) luck would have it, after the first days' filming I began to lose my voice. Luckily, the intervention of a good doctor, some antibiotics and a vow of silence in my hotel room did the trick, and I was good to go.

The production team and crew were a great laugh and hugely professional; and the whole thing was a completely different experience than *Fish and Chips*, with the awful Sebastian.

'It's not going to be the last that ITV see of you, Mike,' said Michael as we wrapped up the filming, which chuffed me to bits, particularly since I knew that he had a great track record of discovering new talent.

It was at this point that Martin, the producer told me of some of the issues he was having with Gail Porter. She presented a segment of the show called *Wish TV*, which aimed to make kids' dreams come true. He felt Gail was difficult to work with, he said she was always late for shoots and was reluctant to mix with the families, so Martin asked me if I fancied doing the rest of the series. I jumped at the chance, and became involved in the whole *Wish TV* process, helping with all the scripts and gags. I loved the whole experience, particularly when a little kid expressed a desire to become a Butlin's Redcoat. We took him to the camp in Brighton, and had a whale of a time on stage, making sure that I looked like an idiot and he shone like a star.

Back at Nickelodeon, Sarah, Rick and myself were asked to present the advertising night at the Shepherd's Bush Empire, an annual event which saw Nickelodeon inviting various ad agencies to have a sneak preview of our new schedule. It was designed to tempt them into spending some serious money with us, of course. We planned a budget-busting show comprising lots of fun and games, much of it based around Chris Evans' very clever *Don't Forget Your Toothbrush* show.

The prizes were amazing; all the invitees had to bring their passports with them, just in case they won a trip to Paris, New

York or Australia. The advertisers, however, were clearly there for the free-flowing booze, and I knew that this was going to be a hard gig. Rick opened the show with the first on-stage game, and promptly died on his arse since the pissed-up audience weren't interested in the slightest, and he'd failed to grab their attention. Sarah hosted game number two, and didn't have a great time of it either.

I, however, was used to this kind of crowd. I'd had to deal with drunken pricks like this throughout my career, whether it was in working men's clubs or holiday camps. I had one problem, though. I'd been told explicitly that, since this was an event to promote child-orientated Nickelodeon, I wasn't allowed to swear.

Sod that for a lark, I thought, as I prepared for my opening gambit.

'Right, you lot. I've been told I'm not allowed to swear tonight, so if there are any words you don't think I should say, just shout them out now...'

Cue an avalanche of *fucks, twats, bastards and wankers*, which got everyone laughing and lightened up the atmosphere. Thankfully it had been the right thing to do despite it being a bit of a gamble. My on-stage game went brilliantly, and after I finished I got a massive cheer. I had a moment of panic when the Nickelodeon hierarchy came over but they actually gave me the thumbs up. I think I'd surprised many of my colleagues - they'd never seen me in doing any live stuff, in stand-up mode – and for the next week I was the talk of Nickelodeon. All those summer seasons, from Winkups to Reighton, had paid off brilliantly.

With the good news came some bad, however. Jackie informed me that she was leaving Nickelodeon to pursue other projects, and therefore wouldn't have time to represent me. While was gutted, I was so grateful for all her help. I then decided to turn to David Hahn and his company, Celeb Agents. He'd recently secured comedian Mike Reid an amazing £130,000 deal for a Sky TV advert, which had really impressed me.

'I'll do my best to get you some great gigs,' he said. I had my concerns, though. I really loved Dave as a person, but I'd seen at first hand the way he worked - he could be a bit slapdash - and I'd find myself getting wound up when he didn't return my calls. I agreed to have a trial six-month period with David, on the condition that I negotiated all my Nickelodeon and panto contracts myself, and that his role involved securing me some lucrative television and corporate work. He asked for twenty per cent commission - a fair old whack - but I agreed, and we shook hands.

Not long afterwards, I received a call from a former Nickelodeon producer, Trudy Dance, who was now working on *The Big Breakfast*. She told me the shock news that Chris Evans was leaving, and that they were actively seeking a new presenter.

'You'd be brilliant,' she said. 'Get your showreel over to the executive producer as soon as you can.'

I phoned David, asking him to sort this out, pronto.

'I'm onto it,' he said. 'I'll get it biked over today.'

Rick Adams had already been screen tested, so I knew that I already had some stiff competition. He had energy, he was fresh and he was a damned good presenter with a style not dissimilar to Evans's. That Friday, however, Trudy called me, asking why I hadn't sent in my showreel; her boss, a big cheese called Charlie Parsons, had definitely not received it. I rang David and went fucking ballistic. He claimed he'd sent the package over, but I smelled bullshit. In the end I had to organise it myself, but to no avail. It arrived too late. The production team had already trawled through hundreds of showreels and had already made their choice.

I don't think I'd ever felt so angry and pissed off. *The Big Breakfast* was one of the finest shows on TV – everyone watched it – and, as far as I was concerned, I'd missed a dream opportunity. I loved David – and I still do – but on this occasion he couldn't have infuriated me more.

A few days' later, rumours began to fly that Rick Adams was going to be leaving Nickelodeon, and I reckoned I knew exactly why. As I'd suspected, he'd been given *The Big Breakfast* gig. I was delighted for him, he is a great guy, but I was gutted for me; all I could think about was what might have happened if David had sent in my showreel promptly.

With that cloud came a silver lining, though. Over lunch, Niels offered me the Nickelodeon Breakfast Show and sorted me a new contract amounting to £40,000 a year. I nearly choked on my starter (grilled prawns with a garlic sauce, incidentally, but nowhere near as good as my Mum's). I'd never earned that amount of money in my life before and, not only that, I was to be the new presenter of the channel's flagship show.

'You didn't have to buy me lunch to offer me the position, Niels,' I said, 'but I'll have the Steak Diane with mushroom sauce and a glass of the house red, thank you very much...'

'Have what you want,' he said, 'because I actually reckon you should be paying.'

And I did.

For a while I had to keep the news secret, since Niels' reshuffle was going to lead to the departures of presenters including James Gilbey and Sarah Cawood (the latter of whom went off to present *The Girlie Show* on Channel 4).

This was going to give me a chance to get creative and I couldn't wait.

The breakfast show witnessed the birth of one of my best-ever creations: step forward Michaelangelo De La Toon. I'd been begging to showcase some daft characters for ages; I'd always been a huge fan of Harry Enfield, Paul Whitehouse and the *Little Britain* guys, all of whom had created a legion of funny and memorable caricatures over the years.

The Nickelodeon office was always deluged with drawings that kids had crayoned and painted, so I came up with the idea of introducing an art critic to appraise them all and take the piss, basically. As a kid, I remembered sending in my own rubbish drawing to Tony Hart's gallery on *Vision On*, so I took that idea, turned it on its head, and created Mr De La Toon.

Getting this character right was a serious business, though, and after much consideration, I made him into a camp old oddball. He wore glasses, had buck teeth (I had specially-made prosthetic gnashers) and a mop of curly black hair. He also dressed very extravagantly – lots of gaudy suits and garish shirts - and even had his own dresser to come in and choose his outfits. He lived in a massive mansion (which we'd occasionally film in) and he had a cat, a butler called Sailor and a whole host of staff, all played by me and the producers.

'I don't like white,' became his all-important catchphrase. 'OOOH, TOO MUCH WHITE...' he'd bellow as he slagged off some poor four-year-old's snowman painting. 'Remember, I don't like white...'

Michaelangelo De La Toon had to be funny of course but, in order to be credible, he had to have an exceptional knowledge of art. I studied academic textbooks so that I could become familiar with famous painters and arty expressions. In fact, I'd come up with so much pretentious crap that often it would go straight over the kids' heads, however it gave me respect from the parents, well at least those with an education...

He became a massive hit. The mums and dads ended up loving him as much as their sons and daughters, and the staff and the top brass at Nickelodeon thought he was fabulous, too. Almost instantly, the volume of mail tripled; the post room had never seen anything like it as thousands of kids sent their drawings into our gallery, to be appraised (or annihilated) by De La Toon.

We'd often film his segments as a scripted two-way, so that it became a conversation between Mike the presenter and Michaelangelo the art critic. The kids would get totally thrown by this, as they weren't sure whether the host and the character were the same person.

Nickelodeon soon realised that the kids loved a good caricature, and asked me to come up with some more. I created an American fitness guy, Kenny Sweat ('Kenny Sweat? Yes, he can...') and a Spanish chef, Cook-a-Lotta (inspired by my mum) who had long hair and a massive moustache (the chef, not my mum!). This chef was clearly shit at cooking, but no matter what he put in the oven, it came out looking amazing. There was also Peppa Ratzi, who had all the latest gossip on the *Rugrats* and other shows, as well as Fat Cop, who solved crimes, never uttered a word, and who ate lots of doughnuts.

While I loved them all, it was De La Toon whose popularity soared. Soon the big bosses wanted him in every show but I refused, worried that he'd suffer from overkill.

'The secret is to leave the audience wanting more, not less,' I argued.

They did, however, devise Saturday morning show called *ToonTastic*, which they used as a vehicle to showcase all my characters as they linked into various cartoons. For me, though, that meant filming straight after Friday's breakfast show - I'd often work fifteen-hour days – and led to me appearing on Nickelodeon *and* ITV every Saturday morning. Even I got fed up of seeing myself on the box. I remember staying at Andrea's parents one weekend and, while we had breakfast, flicking through the channels and spotting my face at least twice.

****

Perhaps the finest pre-school presenter at Nickelodeon was Dave Benson-Phillips, who I'd worked with in panto. He was also still represented by Brian Marshall, the producer/agent who'd written me that snotty 'comedy genius' let-ter a few years' previously. One day I learned that Brian was in the building to negotiate Dave's contract, and I couldn't get up the stairs to the office quick enough. There he was, was sitting with an executive called Vanessa, who was well aware of our history. I walked into the office and pretended not to notice him.

'Have you met Mr Marshall, Mike? He's Dave's agent.'

Brian looked up.

'Hello Mike, what the hell you doing here?'

Before I could reply, Vanessa told him how I was their number one presenter and how I was smashing the Breakfast Show.

'...and not forgetting *It's Not Fair* on ITV every Saturday,' I added with a wink.

'Who's your agent?' he enquired.

'I don't have one, Brian,' I replied. He then fished out his wallet and handed me his card.

'Mike, if you need an agent I'd be happy to represent you,' he said earnestly.

'I tell you what, Brian, when I need a 'top agent' I'll give you a bell,' I said, before flashing him a smile and floating down the stairs.

OK OK so it was petty…but I always believe what goes around comes around, he could have taken a risk on me and helped a struggling performer get on the ladder rather than think he knew better and be a tit!

CHAPTER 13

Nick On The Road

By March 1996, the Nickelodeon breakfast show was winning the ratings war, regularly attracting more viewers than *The Big Breakfast*. I felt a bit sorry for Rick over on Channel 4, to be fair. His show had undergone a serious revamp; the house had been redesigned, the opening titles had changed and Sharron Davies had been installed as a co-host. The hiring of the former Olympic swimmer proved to be a huge mistake; a morning show needed someone with zest, but I felt she seemed devoid of personality. The embattled Rick was getting compared unfavourably to Chris Evans - this was totally unfair, since he had his own presenting style - and was also getting hounded by the press.

'They're camped outside my house, taking photos every time I go out,' he once moaned to me.

'You're lucky,' I said. No fucker's ever outside my house, and I've given them my address, times that I'll be in, everything... '

Seriously, with hindsight I was pleased I never got *The Big Breakfast* gig at that time. I don't think I'd have been ready for that exposure, and I still had plenty to learn (probably still have!).

With Nickelodeon riding the crest of a wave, Niels called me into a meeting to tell me that I'd been asked to attend the company's *Kids' Choice TV Awards* in Los Angeles. It was a huge event – attended by big-name film stars – and I was to file a Stateside report as Michaelangelo De La Toon, spending a whole week there. Unlike my last visit to America, this time I'd have money in my pockets, and would be staying in a posh hotel. Niels then gave me some more good news, offering me a two-year deal to sign there and then. I did so without hesitation. I adored working for him – I loved the way he got the best out of me, and gave me the license to do what I wanted – and it was all a bit of a no-brainer.

I also thought I'd strike while the iron was hot by requesting a fortnight's holiday. I really need the break - I was working constantly and hardly took a day off – and, much to my gratitude, he agreed. So, that summer I headed off to Greece with Degs, Dustin, Stevie and Les for a traditional lads' holiday. I don't think I've never laughed so much as I did then, from a pissed-up Degs trying to turn off my air supply while I was diving, to us all mooning at pleasure boats full of romantic couples. You know, there's a lot to be said for down time with genuine people.

When I returned to work, I was shocked to discover that Niels was leaving Nickelodeon UK and was returning to America. I was gobsmacked. I'd agreed my new contract largely because of him, yet it looked like the sneaky fucker had got me to sign on the dotted line in the full knowledge that he was departing. Feeling both furious and upset, I went to see him in his office.

'What are you pissing off for?' I asked, devastated that such a positive, proactive person was leaving us. 'I signed that contract because of you...'

I told him the place would never be the same without him and, if I'm honest, it never was.

Luckily, I got on well with Niels' replacement, Howard Litton, despite him being a massive Manchester United fan and looking a bit like Mick Hucknall. He worked in tandem with a guy called Steve Shannon; both were nice enough guys but were never going to compare with Niels. Howard was a huge Michaelangelo De La Toon fan, so much so that every time I went to see him he'd always speak to me in my character's camp voice. After a while it started to grate, though, and I'd be thinking *can you just be you, please?*

Just prior to my LA trip Howard called me into his office. I thought it was going to be a pep talk about the *Kids' Choice TV Awards*, but it was anything but.

'I'll cut to the chase,' he said. 'We've been asked by Nickelodeon Australia if they can copy De La Toon and a few of your other characters, because they want to use them when they're in LA, too. I've said yes, of course. I hope that's not a problem.'

I couldn't believe what I was hearing.

'So let me get this right, Howard. You're letting Nick Australia steal my characters and ideas, yes?'

'Yes,' he smiled. 'We're all working for the same company, aren't we?'

Cue a massive rant from yours truly, pointing out that these were *my* characters, and that I'd worked so hard to bring them to life. He then offered me an extra two grand in my wage packet; By now I hope you're coming to realise that I've never been financially motivated and have always worked because I love it, but let's face it two grand is a lot of money and contractually I didn't have a leg to stand on, so I pocketed the cash which went towards a flat in Ilford. From that day on, however, any contracts I signed had to stipulate that any characters I devised belonged to me and me only. Many entertainment contracts, as I'd found to my cost, tended to state the exact opposite.

When I bought my first flat I couldn't believe it. I was 26 and I just remember getting the keys and sitting in this empty flat thinking *wow I have just bought this and its mine*. I figured that if the Nickelodeon contract wasn't renewed after the year, I could always rent it out. I was lucky enough to buy it just before the London property boom which set me in good stead for the future. I phoned my parents who were really pleased for me then I spent my first night on a bed-settee watching a small coloured TV. It was mine and I loved it.

So, at this point in my life, I now had my own place, whilst I was yet to settle down I really felt as though things were coming together for me. I'd always lived with other people so having my own place was a new experience. I'm quite the home bod anyway and I do like my home to be tidy and organised. I'm seriously not one for a lot of mess! Sorry no wild parties at Chez McClean. I had a brilliant set of friends, my family were happy and healthy and life in short was good. It might sound boring and certainly not rock & roll but I'd got into a great routine, being up early in the morning for work, having time in the afternoon to come up with new ideas and weekends to relax with friends. It was a simple but fun and at times, tiring.

In March 1996 I flew out to LA for the *Kids' Choice TV Awards*. My colleagues Justine and Jonathan were to direct all the links; Justine was one of my morning directors, who also happened to be married to Niels (they'd got together at a staff

Christmas party). As for Jonathan Bosley, he was very chilled out and never lost his temper (unlike me). He taught me how to perfect the 'Yes' technique with our bosses; whenever a TV bigwig told you not to do this, or not to do that, Jonathan would just nod and say 'yeah, sure,' before doing it anyway, regardless.

I'd imagined the *Kids' Choice* event taking place at a small theatre, with a few celebrity guests, and not much more. How wrong I was. We arrived at this massive arena (imagine Wembley Stadium, but bigger) which was swarming with hundreds of people wearing headsets and donning clipboards. Before long, I was ushered to my trailer.

My trailer?

'All the talent has trailers,' said Justine, noting my quizzical expression.

This was as far removed from a Winkups caravan as you could get. It had everything: TV, hi-fi, Playstation, posh toiletries, fluffy Egyptian cotton towels... you name it. In the adjacent trailer were a boyband called Hanson, three blond all-American brothers who, due to their *Mmmm-Bop* hit single, had gained worldwide fame.

'Hi there, we're your neighbours, they grinned as I unpacked my belongings.

'That's great,' I told them, deadpan, 'but just keep the noise down, eh?' That made them laugh, as it was just the sort of thing my 'character' would say,

On the other side – I kid you not – was none other than Madonna. One night I remember getting dressed as De La

Toon – flared trousers, tweed jacket and chunky platform shoes - and almost bumping into the Queen of Pop as we simultaneously left our trailers.

'Nice outfit,' she said, doing a double take.

'Oooh, Papa don't preach... where you going, on a holiday?' I replied, thinking on my feet.

She looked at me and chuckled. 'You're funny,' she said, before an army of bodyguards bundled her into a big black limo which drove her all of twenty metres to the backstage area. The lazy bitch. Mind you given the chance I'd have loved arriving in style like that. These moments seem quite surreal when I think back.

The no-expense-spared awards ceremony itself was like nothing I'd seen before. It was mayhem. The audience were crazy, lapping it up when hugely famous Hollywood stars like Will Smith and Billy Zane picked up their trophies before being gunged by the presenters. Following the event, all the 'talent' and production teams were invited to an exclusive after-show party, where the VIP guests went home with goody bags that included portable CD players, designer clothes and gourmet food.

Pitched next to our tent were the Nickelodeon Australia crew who, as Howard had outlined, had brought over their version of De La Toon. At one point, a producer came across to introduce himself and the Aussie De La Toon (I was grateful to Justine, who was only too happy to point out to them that I was the character's originator). It was all a bit weird and awkward, to be fair; I'd seen their version in action, and just wanted to yell 'YOU'RE DOING IT WRONG, DICK-HEADS...' However contrary to popular belief I can be a grown up and so I just ignored it as best I could.

My 'entourage' comprised of one cameraman, one sound man, my director and a runner. We filmed all my links from the backstage area before heading back to our Nickelodeon UK tent, from where all our special guests were interviewed by the channel's famous art critic. Famous visitors included the rock band Aerosmith, known for their big hair and massive stage persona, I remember pissing myself laughing when all their makeup artists piled in before the cameras rolled, powdering their faces and combing their chest hair.

I could tell by their faces that Aerosmith weren't sure whether De La Toon was a real-life eccentric or some daft, made-up character so, just before the interview got under way, we did our best to convince them that it was the former, and that he was a massive star in England. Whether they believed us or not is debatable but, like most Americans, they were a PR dream and gave us an awesome interview.

All the household-names from Nickelodeon came through, too, including Kenan and Kel and Melissa Joan Hart, the star of *Sabrina the Teenage Witch*. The only downer for me was that they then visited the Aussie De La Toon which, for me, took some of the shine off us, and made it quite obvious that the whole thing was a piss-take.

We were just about to pack up for the day when a publicist popped her head into the tent, asking if we'd like to interview the actor Martin Landau. Now this man was a true legend. Not only did I remember him from the iconic *Space 1999*, I'd also seen him in countless Hollywood movies. It turned out that he was promoting a new film, due to be released in England later that year, which meant we'd be securing the very first interview.

'Get him over,' we said.

In walked a frail-looking bloke who appeared to be wearing a hairpiece. I was transfixed, though. His face had beamed out of our telly when I was a kid in Levenshulme and here I was, meeting this real-life movie star in the flesh. He was such a nice man – a proper gentleman – and, despite not getting half of our daft gags, he was a total professional and was a joy to interview.

'*Space 1999* was one of my favourite programmes,' I excitedly told him following the interview, explaining how I'd watched him every Sunday afternoon. For some reason I continued to speak to Landau as my De La Toon character, though, and no doubt he went away thinking I was some insane English man!

Once we'd wrapped up all the interviews, I headed back to the trailer where I just happened to walk into the path of my old pal Madonna. Sod it, I thought. I'm going to speak to her like I'd speak to anyone else.

'Hello neighbour,' I said. 'You had a busy day, love?'

'Yes, thank you,' she smiled, before disappearing into her trailer. She was a woman of few words, albeit polite ones. I'm convinced I heard her screaming 'I'VE JUST MET MICHAEL ANGELO DE LA TOON' at the top of her voice, though, and wouldn't be convinced otherwise.

****

Soon after our return to England, I began to feel that the breakfast show was getting a little stale and needed freshening up. I came up with the idea of taking the programme into viewers' homes, and filming the whole thing from their houses. The PR team put out an advert asking for willing kids and families for a new concept, *Nick AM on the Road*. It had never been done before and little did I know how massive it would become.

We got thousands of kids wanting to take part, and decided to film it a fortnight in advance, meaning that another presenter, Matt Brown, would sit in for me on the breakfast show while *Nick AM on the Road* was filmed and edited. Around this time, I was told that Jonathan Bosley – who'd accompanied us to LA – had been recruited by Disney. I knew he was going places, but didn't think he'd be going to our rivals, and I certainly didn't expect him to poach my fellow presenter, Nigel Mitchell. Nigel's replacement arrived in the form of Simon Amstell, an interesting choice of Nickelodeon presenter since, I didn't get the feeling he liked kids very much. Nevertheless, he came in and I thought, did a decent enough job although I don't think his heart was in it. I also learned that the new director for *Nick AM on the Road* was to be Dino Charalambous, a tall, good looking lad of Greek heritage.

Dino and I had worked together at Nickelodeon before, covering Euro '96 in England (a perfect gig, since we both adored football, him being a diehard Arsenal fan). We visited every ground in the tournament - including Elland Road, St James' Park, Anfield, and the old Wembley – and loved catching up with loads of ex-pros. One day we were due to film at Manchester United's ground but for some reason they refused permission, incurring the wrath of Euro '96 sponsors,

McDonalds. I phoned up my contact at Manchester City, the lovely Liz Douglas, who put me in touch with Chris Bird, the club's head of media.

'United aren't letting us film, Chris,' I said, explaining that it would be great if City could instead let us capture some footage at Maine Road, which might prompt the media to run a positive story (although *The Theatre of Ruined Dreams'* or *'Mean United say No'* would have been my editorial take on things). United got wind of this, however, and suddenly we received a call from them, informing us that they'd performed an about-turn, and filming would now be permitted. I have absolutely no idea which City-supporting TV presenter tipped them off. No idea at all. Shame really as I'd have loved to film on my favourite ground.

The sponsors had allocated a pair of Euro '96 final tickets to Dino and I, but as England progressed through the tournament, the value of these sought-after items was soaring. A friend of Dino's offered us £1,000 for each ticket but, when England beat Holland – and became favourites to lift the trophy - this soared to £2,000.

'There's some serious money to be made here,' I whispered to Dino over lunch.

'Yeah... maybe we could sell them and just watch the match at my flat, he suggested, before spending the next half-an-hour discussing the pros and cons with me.

'But what if England win it?' I said. 'We'd be able to tell our kids and our grandkids that we were there at Wembley...'

'Yeah, good point,' conceded Dino.

'Nah, sod it, let's sell 'em,' I laughed.

That became the plan, until we dropped by Nickelodeon HQ on the day of the semi-final, that is. We were pulled by Stuart Atwood, one of the channel's marketing executives.

'You've both still got your Wembley final tickets, haven't you?'

'Of course... why?' we answered, sheepishly.

'Phew, thank God for that,' he said, before revealing how some colleagues had been caught selling theirs on the black market, causing McDonalds to go apeshit.

'Nope, that's not our style, Stuart,' I lied. 'We can't wait for the game, can we Dino?'

England went and got beaten by Germany in the semi, prompting a Germany versus Czech Republic final. You can only imagine how delighted my pal and I were to watch Jurgen Klinsmann's boys triumph, both of us having missed out on a £2,000 windfall. That's not to say that we didn't enjoy watching some class football, nor did we really take for granted the fantastic opportunity we'd been given. Those are memories I'll always keep with me and know how fortunate I was to have them.

****

Nick AM on the Road was a huge project. Helping us to get everything off the ground was a decent crew, including Doug the floor manager (a chilled-out dude who watched far too much telly) and Nadine the researcher (a single, self-assured thirtysomething who was extremely good at her job).

The show was a roaring success, with every household offering us a warm welcome. Ireland in particular was amazing. Most of the families we visited wouldn't let us leave until we'd sampled 'Dublin's best sausages'; we didn't have the heart to tell them that we'd already eaten them with another family the day before, and the day before that.

I was gutted when Dino announced he was quitting the show, particularly since Nadine was to be his replacement. While I liked her, to me she wasn't ideal director material; her people skills weren't great, and she appeared to have no idea about comedy, or what made things funny. Two new staff also came on board; a down-to-earth Mancunian researcher called Vicky Harrison and production manager Tash Roslin (cousin of TV presenter Gabby). Tash was great, and became the victim of one of my finest wind-ups.

She liked to party after a day's filming and, during a week the crew spent in a Torquay hotel, would often go to bed a bit worse for wear. My hotel room was next to hers, and one night, while she was out gallivanting, I noticed her bedroom window was ajar. I climbed onto the balcony, crept into her room and ever-so-slightly moved things around in her room. I put her bag on her bed, turned her TV on and rearranged the toiletries, really subtle little things.

'I must have been really pissed last night,' she said as we sat around the breakfast table next morning, explaining how she simply hadn't remembered turning on her TV and messing around with bathroom items.

The next night I did the same thing, but this time made it far more obvious, like moving her suitcase next to her bed, and taking the laces out of her trainers before hanging them in her bathroom. Yet again, the following morning Tash came downstairs totally freaked out with all the weirdness going on in her room. It became her topic of conversation for the rest of the day – she was convinced her excessive partying was affecting her memory - and it became hard for me and the crew to keep a straight face.

On our last night in Torquay I really went to town. I set her bedside alarm for 2 a.m., I set her TV alarm for 3 a.m. and I ordered an early morning call for 5 a.m. with a full breakfast. I then packed her case and moved all sorts of furniture in her room. When we got back from dinner she went up to her room and yelled in horror.

'This room's bloody haunted, Mike.'

'Don't be daft,' Tash, I told her, trying to maintain my composure. 'There'll be some explanation. Go to bed and we'll have a chat in the morning.'

From my adjacent room, I heard both the early-hours alarms going off, followed by the premature arrival of breakfast.

That morning, Tash was beside herself. She was convinced there was a ghost in her room and was ready to draft in a priest. I knew then that it was time to own up and confess. Tash chased me all around the hotel and promised that she'd get her own back. I'm not sure I ever topped that wind up but I still laugh now when I think about the look on her face.

For me, being on the road was always about having a laugh. Whenever I stopped laughing, I knew it was a sign to quit the job.

CHAPTER 14

Mad For It

It soon became clear that *Nick AM on the Road* was far exceeding Nickelodeon's budget, and it became inevitable that I'd end up back in the studio. In the meantime, the channel had undergone lots of change, and not necessarily for the better. Simon Amstell was now doing the afternoon shift, Matt Brown was presenting on Saturday and Sunday mornings, and Mo and Yo were doing weekdays.

I was back doing the breakfast show but, yet again, it felt ripe for a change. We decided to do some links from some schools with Michaelangelo De La Toon, and it succeeded in breathing new life into proceedings. It often felt like the show was on a ventilator; every time we thought it had died we'd come in with the paddles, we'd stand back and - *ZAP* – we'd revive it.

I did have the sinking feeling that my time at Nick was coming to an end, despite the fact that in 1996 I'd been nominated for a 'Satellite TV Presenter of the Year' award and – according to our PR department – I was favourite to win it. My bosses even bought me a new suit for the ceremony, which was due to take place at the swanky Grosvenor House hotel in London. However, when I received the invitation I realised it clashed with Manchester City versus Manchester United at Maine Road. I'd never missed a home derby, and this wasn't going to be any different. Daft, I know, but I'd supported my team since I was five, and they meant more to me than an awards ceremony, even if there was a possibility I'd win. Unless you're a huge fan I don't suppose that'll make sense, but like money having awards wasn't what I was in it for and after all the Blues have always been my first love.

'I've got a problem, Sal,' I told Nickelodeon's head of publicity, who nearly fainted in disbelief when I told him the reason behind my non-attendance. In the end, he went on my behalf, while I cheered on my beloved Blues at Maine Road. As it happened, some guy called Sacha Baron Cohen won the Best Presenter award. I've no idea what ever became of him but I heard he was replaced soon after by Ali G.

Not long afterwards, Howard and Steve called me into their office to discuss a Nickelodeon project called the *Red Hot Lobster Tour*. A live show for kids and families comprising gunge-related games, it had gone down a storm in America.

'D'you fancy hosting it, Mike?' they asked. 'You're the only presenter with any live experience, and we want it to have the same impact in England as they've had in America...'

Most of the year I'd be able to dovetail it with the breakfast show, then in the summer months I'd be taken off air to join the *Red Hot Lobster Tour*, full time. I was really excited; not only was this right up my street – I loved working live, on location - it would enable me to get off air for twelve weeks. I flew out to Los Angeles to meet with the producers and watch the show; while I thought it would be received well in the UK, I knew that we'd have to work extra hard for two big reasons. Firstly, we couldn't rely on the Great British weather for our outdoor activities – it was something we'd have to work around – and secondly, our hometown audiences probably wouldn't get as fired-up and frenzied as they did across the pond.

Rehearsals soon started back in London – some producers flew over from the States - and I soon realised how great Americans were at putting on an extravaganza like this. The set basically comprised two massive trucks at the back of the stage, as well as gunge tanks, water cannons and all sorts of games equipment, which would be manned by a huge crew of staff. It was to be one of the biggest projects that Nickelodeon had ever undertaken, and I felt honoured to be its presenter. Producer Sally Wallwork would be in charge of the entire project, and the tour manager would be a great mate of mine, a former DJ from Manchester called Chris Pearson.

Chris had once hired me when I did my magic act; he'd spun the discs and I'd provided the entertainment. I remember one disastrous gig he organised, for a fruit machine company called Barcrest. These punters had been drinking all day, and the last thing they wanted was a magician doing bloody tricks. I was dying a horrible death on stage, and I can recall him laughing his head off, while filming my misery for posterity. He's still got the video, apparently.

'Get ready for the tour of your life,' I said to Chris when I learned he'd got on board.

The *Red Hot Lobster Tour* visited twenty-two towns, spanned three years, and gave me some of the best times of my life. With the extra money I earned, I finally bought my much-wanted flat for £41,000, putting down fifteen grand and securing a small mortgage, just prior to the property boom.

****

By now I was without an agent – I'd agreed to part company with David Hahn after the Big Breakfast palaver, though we remained great friends – but was still trying to find another route into terrestrial TV. During our final *Red Hot Lobster* tour, I'd received a call from Michael Forte and David Mercer, requesting a meeting at ITV. It seemed the Commissioning Editor of children's ITV, Nigel Pickard, was looking at creating a new live show. Ant and Dec had just been given a new Saturday morning vehicle - *SMTV Live* - and he wanted to broadcast a similar midweek offering.

'Have you got any ideas?' asked Michael.

'I have, as a matter of fact,' I replied. 'Give me a few days and I'll write something up for you.'

I hadn't, of course. But by the end of the week, I had. I burned the midnight oil for days, racking my brains and writing up my new programme. I was keen for it to be wild and pacy like Nickelodeon, and crazy and funny like *Tiswas*. It also needed be aired live, in front of a studio audience. I suggested little segments like a talent show, a kids' version of *Blind Date* and a gunge cage, as well as a multitude of competitions and games. I also thought there should be some sort of outside broadcast, coming live from a viewer's house. Before long, my new show idea was conceived.

Michael and David loved my pitch, fortunately, and asked me to have lunch with the rest of the ITV kids' team, including Nigel Pickard and his colleague Mick Robertson. Mick used to present a 1970s children's TV show called *Magpie* – it was the commercial channel's equivalent of *Blue Peter*, I suppose - and when he walked into the restaurant I instantly recognised him. You could have blown me down with a feather when he gave me a big smile and told me he was a fan of mine. It turned out he was a massive Portsmouth FC supporter, and he knew that I was firmly in the Manchester City camp.

After lunch, we headed back to ITV, where the assembled executives discussed my big idea. I was introduced to all and sundry as 'one of ITV's up and coming talents,' which as you can imagine, pleased me no end. For the next hour-or-so they fired questions at me about my concept and I found myself in the surreal situation of telling the Commissioning Editor of children's ITV how to make a successful TV programme. Some people around the table registered concerns about my junior version of *Blind Date*, but I assured them the segment would work.

'I did stuff like that in holiday camps for years,' I smiled. 'Trust me, it always went down a storm.'

'All right,' said Nigel, after some thought. 'I like the sound of this show of yours, Mike. I'm going to commission twenty-six weeks of it.'

I nearly fell off my chair.

'What's the programme going to be called?' one of his colleagues then asked. I paused for a moment, before revealing its name in a loud and proud Manc accent.

'*Mad For It*,' I grinned.

The phrase had been coined by Oasis' Gallagher brothers - who by then had become superstars – and had since become a common saying among kids and adults alike.

'*Mad For It* is, then,' nodded Nigel.

Afterwards, Michael offered me his congratulations and asked me to invoice him for £2,000 for my troubles. *Not bad for two days' work*, I thought.

'One question, though, Mike...' he added, with a glint in his eye. 'Who's going to present it?'

'I've no idea which girl you're going to get, but I'm damned sure which guy is doing it,' I smiled. I'd written it and pitched it, and I wasn't going to let anyone else present it.

For the next few days, as the *Red Hot Lobster Tour* hit Scotland, I had to keep everything hush-hush. I knew that, if I was definitely going to present *Mad For It*, my Nickelodeon days would be over. I'd have to travel to the Carlton TV studios in Nottingham on the Tuesday for rehearsals, before doing the live show on Wednesday, and I doubted very much that they'd give me leave of absence.

I had a big decision to make, therefore, and - as I often did when I needed good advice - I chatted with my former agent David Hahn, and my old mentor Peter Woolley. David reckoned I should chance my arm and juggle both networks. Peter told me just to be truthful with Nickelodeon, and see what they said. I veered towards Peter's advice, and visited Howard and Janie. The upshot, as I'd suspected, was that I couldn't do both jobs. It was decided that I'd quietly move over to ITV, without any fuss, perhaps returning to Nick when *Mad For It* finished.

Within days I'd signed the ITV contract, and had met the production team and crew at Carlton TV's studios in Nottingham. This included the director, Peter Leslie. Within seconds I knew we weren't going to get along - he spoke to me like I'd got my head zipped up at the back - and I had a feeling that he and I would clash. Peter had previously worked with Dave Benson Phillips, so I rang my old pal to get the lowdown. Dave never badmouthed anyone, but his reply spoke volumes.

'I wish you luck there, Mike.'

I found Peter to be a deeply unpleasant and obnoxious man. He was full of his own self-importance, constantly banging on about how he'd made stars out of Trevor and Simon, the comedy 'swing yer pants' duo who'd featured in BBC's Saturday morning *Live and Kicking* show.

Michael was desperate for ex-*Byker Grove* actress Donna Air to co-present, but for whatever reason, things didn't work out. I suggested Yiolanda from Nickelodeon; Michael and David met her, liked her and offered her the job. During our many *Mad For It* production meetings, Peter tried to stamp his authority all over the programme, which pissed me right off. It soon drifted off from the show I had written, and became far too safe and far too congested. When I mentioned my reservations to him, he just gave me an icy stare.

'Let us produce the show, Mike. You just need to look the part and present it.'

I was fuming but, since the Sebastian-related issues in Leeds, I'd learned to keep my cool and not fly off the handle. I took a deep breath and just smiled; no scowls, no flippant remarks, nothing.

Other than Peter, we had a great team. Producer Rob Taverna, who I'd worked with at Nick, was on board; Rachel looked after the bands and the music; Justin and another girl called Rachel produced, and an excellent production manager, Jane, oversaw everything. We also had a brilliant props woman called Annie who was well past retirement age, but still loved working on a day-to-day basis. We used to take the mickey out of each other something rotten.

'What are you looking at, you old bag? Not long now for you...' I'd say when I arrived at the studio.

'Ooooh, here he comes, Mr Talentless,' she'd retort.

In fact, all the crew were great, from the camera operators to the sound and lighting guys. Michael and David had put together a brilliant team; it was just a shame the head of it was a complete tit.

Ant and Dec had successfully kicked off the new look kids ITV with the brilliant *SMTV Live* (and other shows like *The Top Ten of Everything* and *Pump It Up*) and now it was down to us to carry the baton and run with it. It was so important for the first show to go well and, thank goodness, programme one of *Mad For It* was a resounding hit.

'Everyone at school was talking about it, Uncle Mike,' said my niece Nicole the following day, which was good enough for me. She also told me that she was getting deluged with autograph requests from her classmates, so I gave her a load of stickers and signed photos to dole out. I later learned that she sold them for a profit, which made me laugh. I'd taught her well.

One Tuesday afternoon I invited Nicole and her friend Laura to watch our rehearsals, which they loved; my niece even got the chance to pull the lever that released all the gunge, and she became the talk of the school.

Mad For It finished its first-season run, having averaged over 2.5 million viewers, which back then was a hell of a lot. It won a BAFTA too, albeit for its opening titles (look, a BAFTA's a BAFTA). I was so proud of it, but was really disappointed when, following the second series, ITV decided to axe it. Season two was a mess from start to finish, to be honest, including the hiring of Simon Amstell for the show's outside broadcasts (he got fired after just two shows). The only saving grace about that run was that Peter Leslie hadn't directed it.

****

In 1998, *Blue Peter* presenter Richard Bacon found himself getting busted by the *News of the World*. He was caught snorting cocaine during a night out with friends, and it turned out that his so-called best mate had set him up, allegedly selling his story for £25,000. The paper was of course notorious for its many 'exclusives' that often exposed celebrities behaving badly, whether it was getting laid or getting high. Around that time, tabloid journalists appeared to be gunning for kids' TV presenters and - as well as Richard - had targeted others including Mark Speight from *Scratchy and Co*, who'd also been snapped taking drugs. Never in a million years did I ever think they'd come looking for me. But they did.

In December 1998 I'd been doing another panto – *Cinderella*, in Scunthorpe - and the cast had included a 22-year-old actor, playing Prince Charming, who was fresh out of drama college and was as green as grass. He made the mistake of, during the run up to his birthday, admitting that he was still a virgin.

'You're going to have a birthday to remember, lad' I announced.

The following Friday, after the show had finished, two dolled-up lap dancers appeared at the theatre, with their blonde hair, big boobs and false tans. They were pointed in this lad's direction, with orders to 'ruin him.'

'Oh, we will,' said the first girl.

'Hey, aren't you the guy from *Mad For It?*' said the other.

To cut a very long story short, following a night on the tiles in Scunthorpe, I ended up in bed with the second lap dancer. But guess what: I couldn't perform. The beer had worked its way to my brain, and had told my penis to forget any ideas about sex. Any blood circulation in my nether regions was shut down and, much to my embarrassment, I couldn't rise to the occasion. No matter how hard this poor girl tried - 'hard' not being the ideal choice of word - nothing was happening. At one point I thought she was going to call time of death on it. I was mortified.

A few weeks later, the same girl rang to say that she'd been watching *Mad For It*, and told me that we had some unfinished business. I agreed, but explained that I was filming in Nottingham, and was nowhere near Scunthorpe.

'I don't believe it!' she exclaimed. 'I'm working in Nottingham tonight, too. I'm probably staying around the corner from you.'

Wow, what are the chances of that happening, I thought, none the wiser.

I walked into the hotel foyer, and found this girl reclining on a sofa in the bar area. The place was virtually empty, with loads of free seats, yet sitting on a nearby sofa were a man and a woman. I sat down beside her, and she ordered a couple of drinks. We chit-chatted for a few minutes, and it didn't take her long to get down to business.

'What would you like to do to me?' she whispered.

Wow, this girl is really forward, I thought to myself.

'I dunno,' I replied, unsure exactly what to say. 'Wear suspenders, heels, that kind of thing?'

Then, without any hesitation – and before I'd even finished my drink – she gestured for me to follow her to her room. As we did so, the couple in the bar got up, too. I remember thinking it was slightly odd, but my brain was too busy telling me to prepare for some fun, and I stupidly ignored that nagging voice of doubt.

We entered the room, had a little kiss, and then she told me to strip off. She clearly wasn't into foreplay.

'Go on, get your pants off,' she said.

'Aren't you going to get undressed too?' I asked. 'Shouldn't both of us be naked?'

She shook her head, and I could only assume that she was going to use me as some kind of sex slave. *Ah, just go for it,* I thought.

The next thing I knew her phone started to ring – 'Yep, I'm in my room now,' she said - and moments later she was telling me to get my clothes back on.

'My agent's arrived,' she said, 'and he's coming up to my room. You'd better go...'

'What the fuck?' I said, looking down at myself. 'I can't leave the room with this, love, I'll have someone's eye out.'

I couldn't believe it. Five minutes ago we'd been under starters orders, and now I was back in the paddock.

'I'll ring you later,' she said when I asked her what the hell was going on.

I hastily got my kit back on and went back to my hotel. To say I was pissed off was an understatement.

A fortnight later I'd be even angrier, though, I landed at Gatwick airport having been on a great holiday with Degs and Les and we went to Tesco to get some shopping. Les was reading the papers and I suddenly heard... *'Mickey you're in the paper'* he held up the News Of The World. I bought a copy and took it home to read it, I was mortified. 'NOT SO CLEAN McCLEAN. KIDS TV PRESENTER SLEEPS WITH LAP DANCER.' I had to phone parents and my dad had already read it as he got the paper delivered, to my horror and annoyance he'd read it to my mum as she doesn't read English. It said I made love to her 5 times in 4 hours . I remember thinking actually *that's not too bad really… She didn't say I had a small penis*, it was basically all bullshit. That morning my phone didn't stop ringing and I recalled my conversation with Rick wishing I'd had the press at my door! Andy Leach who is a comic rang me up and said *what a great bit of publicity*. I thought what? He then pointed out that I was in one of the biggest selling newspapers, as he said all publicity is good publicity.

The lads were pissing themselves laughing at the 5 times in 4 hours saying *'now we all know that's not true.'* An old girlfriend rang me up and said *'Bloody hell, why didn't I get the 5 times in 4 hours?'* After I had cooled off I actually thought about what Andy had said and he was right. My good friend Dino Charalambous rang me, as he had been working with Frank Bough, who had got done a month earlier in a story about him in a sex dungeon . He said *'Mike whatever you do if the reporters ring and they will, don't answer any of their questions.'* The next day the phone rang and it was the reporters from the News of the World.

Did you see the article? The hack asked.

'Yes' I said

'What did you think?'

I said *'It was great thanks, ooh and thanks for spelling my name right. Have a lovely day.'*

I was due to go on tour with Nickelodeon and I had to go into a meeting with them and the head of publicity, I was pretty nervous to be honest but they were cool they said that by the time the tour starts no one will remember it. I was also due to do panto that year in Weymouth and the theatre were concerned, the producer John Spillers just told them to stop being silly *'Come December no one will give a shit'* he said. *'I was just gutted it wasn't in the paper in December, as it would have been great publicity for the panto.'*

The head of Kids ITV were great, they said had it been drugs it would have been hard to get out of, if you had been gay so what.? But you have slept with a lap dancer? So where is the story?

If I am totally honest I never lost anything from it, in fact, if anything, I now had a reputation as being a great lover! I have to be honest even to this day I have NEVER done it 5 times in 4 hours. The only time I want to do it twice is before I've done it once!

****

It's a fact of life that every comic dies on their arse at some stage in their career (even my good mate Gerry Kaye, one of the best comedians I've ever gigged with). Some would say it's good to 'die', though, because you never fail to learn from the experience. I've worked with brilliant funnymen and women who've taken the roof off a venue yet, a couple of days later, at the very same place, have had an absolute stinker. Most of the time it's not the comic's fault, though; if you have a decent act, and you know it works, then it's often your audience that has the problem.

I remember once compering at The Hob in London, a lovely little comedy club run by a couple called Ron and Emma. If it was the first Saturday of the month, the place would always be quiet and subdued and, as a result, the acts could hardly raise a titter. On the other hand, if it was the last Saturday of the month, The Hob would be busy and buzzing, and the laughs would come thick and fast. Why? Because the punters had just received their pay packet and had enough money to buy drinks. It was often as simple as that.

By the spring of 1999 I'd secured the services of Nick Ranceford-Hadley, an agent working for Noel Gay Artists who looked after some huge showbiz names. He was a very charming man - very well-educated and well-spoken - and would always book the most exclusive London restaurants for our meetings, the kinds of places that didn't take too kindly to Mancunians sporting jeans, trainers and sunglasses.

Not long after I hired him, Nick secured me a great corporate gig – worth £5,000 for just one night's work - to host and present the annual Advertising Agency Awards at a glitzy hotel in central London. My brief was a ten-minute spot of stand-up, before presenting the awards themselves. Associations like these would often ask gobby comedians or poised presenters to host these kinds of events, as they could handle crowds and were able to ad-lib. To me, it sounded like a nice, well-paid easy booking. How wrong I was.

'Everyone's really up for it... they've been drinking all afternoon,' smiled the organiser when I arrived at the venue. By rights, when he said that I should have just grabbed my hat and coat and got the hell out of there fast, but instead I thought *Cool, they've loosened up and will be up for some laughs*. Scanning the room, I reckoned they were a similar kind of advertising crowd that I'd faced during my Nickelodeon days.

Within minutes of going on stage I realised this was going to be one shit night. I began with a few gags about being a Mancunian in London that I thought might raise a few giggles. Nothing. Tumbleweed. Some bloke shouted out 'Sorry mate, I don't speak northern,' though, and they all bloody pissed their sides at that.

'I'm sorry, I don't understand dickhead,' was my immediate response – unlike Jimmy Carr, I didn't specialise in withering put-downs - which proved to be a big mistake. Bobby Big Bollocks in row C now thought he was hilarious, and wouldn't shut up.

'Mate if you keep heckling I'll stop getting punters for your sister,' I countered, which prompted some shocked 'ooooohs', before someone else shouted out 'Oi, he's called your sister a slaaag...'

Things were fast getting out of hand. Out of desperation I tried to do some different gags, but nothing worked. In the end I abandoned the stand-up and went straight into the awards. Please don't let that mouthy idiot win anything, I thought to myself, but guess what? Yeah he did. Three times. When he first mounted the stage I went to shake his hand, only for the wanker to pull it away and smooth his hair with it. *I'll shove this award up your arse, you twat...* I recall thinking to myself.

Usually, following corporate gigs, the organisers make a beeline for you to offer their thanks and congratulations. They didn't that night, however, and I thought it best to collect my belongings and make a sharp exit. I didn't sleep a wink that night. I relived the whole evening, blaming myself for being unable to handle a challenging crowd, wondering how I could have done things differently, and speculating how I'd have disposed of the chief heckler's corpse. I'd let myself and the organisers down badly, and I was devastated.

'I hear you had a tough night,' said Nick when he called me the next day. As I'd suspected, the organisers were not best pleased with my hosting skills, but still paid up.

'Don't let it get you down,' added Nick, which was very easy for him to say. I was mortified that I'd bombed, and my confidence was now shot to bits.

Looking back, Nick was never going to be the right agent for me. In similar circumstances, David Hahn would have given me a pep talk, would have made me feel ten feet tall again, and would have rung the organisers to bollock them for allowing these people to get so pissed, so early. Then he'd have got me another corporate gig straight away, telling me to keep the faith, regain my confidence and get back on that horse again. After that fateful night, however, I vowed never to do any more stand-up. It was a decision that I'd come to deeply regret.

As it happened, I got offered plenty more corporate gigs, but I chickened out every time. This was so out of character for me - maybe I 'd become a southern softie – but the thought of reliving the whole nightmare made me feel physically sick.

CHAPTER 15

The Big Breakfast

I was becoming increasingly frustrated with my agent, Nick. He was hardly sending me to any castings or auditions, having initially pledged to get me meetings with the heads of ITV and BBC, not to mention Sky TV.

Meanwhile, Trudy Dance was still working on *The Big Breakfast* and, one day, in June 2001, she phoned to tell me that Richard Bacon - who presented the show's outside broadcasts and occasionally sat in for main host Johnny Vaughan - was busy doing some filming for the BBC.

'We need someone to cover for him, Mike, and I've suggested you, if you don't mind,' said Trudy, explaining that I'd been invited to attend an audition in Canary Wharf. I couldn't believe it. The *Big Breakfast* was right up my street and suited my style of presenting, and I'd always longed to make amends for the showreel catastrophe. I relayed the good news to Nick; despite my issues with him, this was too big a deal to handle myself.

I was nervous as hell as I headed to the audition; I wanted this so much, but I was also fully aware that the transition from kids' TV to adults' TV was notoriously difficult. The executive producer, Richard Hopkins, had been tasked with overseeing a new-look *Big Breakfast*, which was to be relaunched with three new presenters, Donna Air, Amanda Byram and Paul Tonkinson (Paul being a comic from Scarborough who I'd met many times on the circuit).

In the meantime, the outgoing host, Johnny Vaughan, would continue to man the show most mornings, sitting alongside female presenters like Kelly Brook and, for a second stint, his old mucker Denise Van Outen. Johnny and Denise had struck up one of the best TV partnerships on British telly, but for some reason the chemistry hadn't quite worked when they reunited, which was a shame.

That morning I was shown around the set by Trudy, who really put me at ease. She introduced me to the producer, Paul Connolly, who was going to take me outside to film a short outside broadcast, as if I was actually doing the show. With him was a runner, a tiny Asian girl. Paul was big Northern Irishman and, to be honest, seemed a bit stand-offish when I met him, like he couldn't be arsed faffing around with this pretend OB. As we got to work, however, he loosened up a bit and made a few little comments and asides that made me laugh. He seemed to love his comedy, and made it clear that he liked working with presenters who could ad-lib and bring some humour to proceedings. *Something tells me I'm going to get on with this fella*, I remember thinking to myself.

My OB would involve me reporting on dogs in the docklands. Paul explained that I was to knock on residents' doors and interview them about their dogs and, if they didn't have one, knock on another door until we found someone that did. It had to be shot as live, which meant that I'd have to cope with any old men telling me to eff off or psychos taking me hostage.

'We want to see how you can deal with live situations,' said Paul.

The broadcast comprised three links. The first was a minute's tease, the second was the knock itself, and third was the actual hit – the main interaction - which was to be of five minutes' duration (that's a long time in live outdoor broadcasting, trust me). Having watched the *Big Breakfast* on numerous occasions, I knew these OB's could be a bit hit and miss, but I was determined to make mine a good 'un.

The Gods must have been looking down at me that day, because the first door I rapped on was answered by a complete oddball whose dog was nearly as big as him. I knew instantly I'd struck gold with this one. I handed back to the studio as if it were live, then got ready for the crucial five-minute segment. I interacted with this mad dog owner and dropped in some funny gags and, as I did so, I noticed that Paul was laughing. And, before I could say 'Gizza job,' it was a wrap, and my audition was done and dusted.

As I headed back to the offices I saw my ex-Nickelodeon colleague, Matt Brown preparing for his own audition, and my heart sank. Matt was a great guy and a brilliant presenter, and I was pretty damned sure he'd get this gig over me. For some stupid reason, I stopped to chat and I gave him the heads up about what to expect. *Duh.*

All I could do now was wait, and pray. That afternoon, my agent Nick phoned.

'Mike, the *Big Breakfast* team have been in touch,' he said, and my heart began to pound. 'They did say you were a bit old school...'

Oh, shit...

'...but it turns out they like a bit of old school. They loved you, and want to know which dates you can cover.'

The first thing I did was phone my old mentor, Peter Woolley, to tell him the good news, and he was as excited and elated as me. Later that night Nick rang again, telling me that the producers wanted me to do my first one-off OB in two days' time.

'D'you think you might be free?' he said.

'Might I be free?' I laughed. 'Has Judith Chalmers got a passport?'

A couple of days later, I met up with another producer, John Donaldson, to go through my first proper *Big Breakfast* OB script. It was going to have a Harry Potter angle - it had just been announced that Daniel Radcliffe was going to play Harry in the movie – and I would be tasked with finding a better candidate on a street in Reading.

The next morning, I arrived at reception at 5 a.m., my feelings a swirl of nerves and excitement as I went through the script and looked at my cue cards. Before long we were coming live from Berkshire, and Richard Bacon – sitting next to Donna Air in the studio, was doing the show's run-down.

'...and today we've got new boy Mike McClean live in Reading, finding our very own Harry Potter,' he said, as I smiled and waved at the camera.

'How's your first day going, Mike? How's everyone treating you?'

'Yeah all good, Richard,' I grinned. 'I've found my own peg for my coat, I've got name tags in all my clothes...' – by now could hear people laughing in the studio – '...and my Mum's packed me some sandwiches...'

Accompanying me that morning was the same female runner who'd been with Paul during my screen test, and who gamely became the butt of some of my jokes.

'Morning Richard,' I said as I did my first link, 'today I'm in Reeding...' (I'd mis-pronounced it to get a laugh, and the runner purposely came into shot, pretending to whisper in my ear).

'Reading? Are you sure?' I said, at which she nodded and darted back behind the camera. 'Okay, I'm in *Reading*,' I continued, 'where we're looking for more Harry Potters, and more wizards that can do tricks. It's just a shame my sister's not here, 'cause she does tricks...' Cue more guffawing back at the *Big Breakfast* house.

Two hours' later, my big debut was over.

'Mike McClean, everyone...' I heard Richard say, 'who, I'm sure you'll all agree, has done a great job on his first day,' at which the crew all cheered. I was on such a high, and I wanted to do it all over again.

We headed back to the hotel for a bite to eat, and the feedback started to flood in from the *Big Breakfast* big cheeses who, by all accounts, were delighted with my contribution, including the top boss, Ed Forsdick. John the producer told me that they'd had accomplished, well-known comedians on the show who'd buckled or frozen, and who'd never done an OB like mine. In fact, they were so chuffed they asked me to do the show for the rest of the week.

I immediately phoned my parents, who were delighted for me.

'You looked like you'd been doing it for years, Mike,' said Dad. 'You should be so proud of yourself.' After all the years of performing, hearing my Dad say that really meant something. I was proud of all the years I never gave up and of all the hard work I'd put in.

The *Big Breakfast* headed north for the following day's OB, which was to take place at a barber's in Northampton. Our theme always related to current news stories – that day we'd read that men were spending more time grooming themselves - so each morning the production team would pore over the tabloids and broadsheets before coming up with ideas. Filming went as well as the day before; I relished being out and about, I loved knocking on people's doors and I loved doing ridiculous things to camera. I think Richard was as equally happy to see me covering the OBs, too; he clearly loved covering for Johnny and, apparently, had become a little bored with his usual outdoors role.

Whenever we descended on a particular street for an OB, the residents would always say the same thing: 'Why pick our street, Mike?'

I'd tell them it was all pretty random, but that wasn't quite accurate. We'd normally ring up the local taxi company to ask them to pinpoint the roughest area, before driving over for a recce the night before to check that it wasn't a total no-go area. We discovered that, time after time, the nicest people and the funniest characters came from the working class areas. They'd always answer their door, they loved being on telly and they were invariably up for the daft stunts we devised. Conversely, the middle-class households would rarely entertain us, often refusing to answer their doors and sometimes reluctant to participate in our games. I think that's quite a reflection on society as a whole really. The higher socially you climb, the more you take yourself seriously.

I covered for Richard in October, too, but this time I was partnered with another producer, Dan Whitehead. We headed up to Scotland together to film a piece about the Loch Ness monster, which had been reportedly sighted again; we arranged for an expert to turn up and went out looking for it on a boat.

As we drove north, I happened to find Richard Bacon's passport in the crew car – complete with a really dodgy photo - and told Dan that we should do something funny with it. He disagreed - he wasn't really into comedy, was Dan – but I ensured that I shoe-horned in a gag, though, at the tail end of the OB.

'Well if Nessie ever does rear her head, I'm sure this will frighten her away,' I said, as the camera zoomed into Richard's scary passport photo. Everyone in the house pissed themselves laughing, and Richard himself was gobsmacked.

'Mike McClean, how on earth did you get that?' he asked, going full Alan Partridge. 'That's theft and I shall be reporting you to the authorities...'

Afterwards, Dan grudgingly admitted that my little postscript was funny, but still moaned that I should have given him prior warning.

I looked at him quite quizzically and asked him why 'I've done comedy long enough to know what's funny and what's not funny, Dan, I really would trust me...'

****

Later that year, I received a call from Nick, informing me he'd sourced a panto for me, namely *Peter Pan* at Stoke's Regent Theatre. Starring on the bill were Paul '*Just Good Friends*' Nicholas and Linda '*Birds of a Feather*' Robson. Linda was a lovely person, and was a joy to work with. Paul, on the other hand, was not. He was a complete pain in the arse during rehearsals (he was playing the role of Captain Hook and I was Smee, his comedy sidekick). One minute he wanted me on his left-hand side, yet the next minute he wanted me on his right-hand side, and he really started to piss me off. Also, I was meant to be the comic on the stage, yet he kept using me as a feed before delivering the gags himself. After three days of this I'd had enough, and I rang Nick to tell him that I wanted out.

'Mike, don't be silly, they've printed the posters and everything,' he said.

'I couldn't give a shit if they've had hand-painted them, Nick, I cannot work with this dickhead.'

OK so my people management had taken a back seat at this point but I wasn't the "apprentice" anymore and I felt as though I should have been afforded a little more respect.

That night the company manager, Neil, phoned me, explaining that he'd worked with Paul before, and implying that he resented others stealing his limelight.

Limelight? It's bloody panto, not *Platoon*,' I replied.

'Please stick with it,' implored Neil, and I promised – somewhat reluctantly - that I would.

During rehearsals Paul was at it again, though, with all his *stand here*'s and *stand there*'s. In the end I snapped.

'Look, Paul, where the hell do you want me to stand, because – I'll be honest with you, mate – you're beginning to piss me right off.'

Everyone went quiet – I felt the whole cast staring at me – but I didn't give a shit. I'd had enough.

'Well done for standing up for yourself,' said Linda once everything had calmed down.

'I'm from Manchester Linda, if we don't stand up for ourselves no one does. We tell it how it is.'

From that day onwards, Paul kept his distance and kept out of my face. He barely said a word to me during the rest of the run, apart from one particular night when he totally fucked things up. For some reason he'd turned down the speaker in his dressing room, and as a result hadn't heard his cue. I had to ad-lib with the pirates on stage - luckily I had a few gags up my sleeve – while someone dashed to Paul's dressing room where, apparently, he was busy on the phone ordering a potter's wheel for his wife. As you do.

Paul was shooed out of his room was ushered onto the stage. Unfortunately, in the midst of all the panic, he rushed on without his hook, something that I spotted straightaway. *Time to make the audience laugh*, I thought

'Ah, Captain, I see your hand's got better,' I said, which brought the house down, both in the stalls and behind the scenes. Only one person failed to see the funny side. After the curtain went down the cast exited to a massive round of applause, and Paul came storming over.

'YOU MUST RESPECT HOOK,' he shouted, while for some reason grabbing my nose. Who does that?

'And you must remember to wear your fucking hook,' I replied, not wanting any more hassle and feeling I'd made my point, I headed back to the dressing room.

****

In December 1999 I sold my flat for a tidy profit - and bought a three-bedroomed house in sunny Grays, Essex. It came with a garden. To me this was something special and I loved the garden. I never had a garden when I was a kid growing up so it meant a lot to me.

 By now I'm a long way from Levenshulme but I'm still far from a soft, shandy drinking southerner! I've always been careful when it came to money and I knew that investing in property was the way to go, bricks and mortar made far more sense than any investment schemes and it give me a sense that I was doing "alright"

I continued to do the OBs on the *Big Breakfast*, and I was by then considered a regular rather than a stand-in. Johnny, Kelly and Denise had since departed the show, to be replaced by Paul, Donna and Amanda. Ed Forsdick remained the editor, but we had a new producer, Richard Hopkins.

Unfortunately, the relaunch didn't go to plan. The dynamic was all wrong between Paul and his co-hosts – he struggled to get a word in edgeways with Donna and Amanda, who didn't quite get his comedy – but I kept well out of the brewing discontentment, which was pretty easy to do away from the studio.

It wasn't until I'd worked on the show for a good few months that I actually visited the house itself, on a day that I wasn't out on location. As I walked onto the famous set, Paul came over to give me a hug, thanking me for some great OBs, and Amanda and Donna came over to say hi, too (Donna remembered me from *Mad For It*). I sat as a guest and watched them present the show at close quarters, which was a pretty surreal experience, having watched it myself on the TV for years. It wasn't hard to tell that things weren't going well in front of the camera.

One of our most memorable OBs, produced by Dan Whitehead, took place in France. British lorries had been blockaded in Calais – there was some dispute with the ferry companies - so he'd decided that we should head over to France and stop the natives from going to work until our British lorry drivers were 'released'. We planned for a satellite truck to follow us to a street, where we'd set up our own blockade. The editor, Ed, had suggested I dress as a Beefeater.

We drove over to France, checked into a hotel and, at 5 a.m. the next morning, we arrived in the Calais street where I got dressed into my costume. The first voice I heard down my earpiece was Ed's, who was watching proceedings from London.

'Mike, what the *fuck* are you wearing?'

'I don't know Ed, Dan gave it me...' I said, adjusting my black, bearskin headpiece.

'I asked for a Beefeater, Mike, not a Grenadier fucking guard,' he said, and I could hear the whole studio creasing up. Richard made a big deal of it when the cameras rolled, too, but messing things up was often what made the show great.

The OB went down a storm. As I tried to stop French motorists from going to work, a soundtrack of patriotic British songs and hymns blared out from our broadcast van. Eventually the *gendarmerie* arrived, and I was seen being escorted into a car before getting myself 'arrested'.

Well that's how it appeared to *Big Breakfast* viewers, anyway. In reality, we *did* let people go to work – most of the French commuters happily played along with my daft Grenadier guard act - and, when the police arrived on the scene, we actually asked them to pretend to arrest me. When all was said and done, it was a brilliant OB, possibly one of the best in the programme's entire history.

Being a regular presenter on one of the UK's most popular shows had its pros and cons. It was great to get recognition from viewers and others in the industry, and it was nice to receive invitations to film premieres and glitzy events. And, although I was by no means an A-list celeb, I started to get all sorts of women throwing themselves at me. I'm guessing the previous headlines had given me a reputation I didn't deserve and I could have probably had a different girl every night. Truth be told I was too tired, so I cut it down to one every other night lol. In all seriousness, most of my nights out had to finish by 7.30 p.m. since I had to be up at the crack of dawn. Often, my 'socialising' just meant staying in and watching TV, or going to the cinema.

Weirdly, when I did go out on the town, I got less hassle in Essex than I did in Manchester. My mates from Levenshulme – like Degs, Les and Stevie - were really chuffed that I was doing okay for myself, but there were plenty of Mancs who seemed to be jealous or resentful. I remember going out to the Comedy Store in my home city with Manchester City midfielder, Kevin Horlock and his wife Karen. I'd struck up a great friendship with Kevin who, as well as being a great player, was probably one of the funniest footballers I'd ever met.

That particular Saturday, the Blues had been thrashed 4-0. Later, as the four of us propped up the bar, fans were coming over to Kev and saying 'shame about the score, but well played, Kev', or 'what happened there, Kev, eh?' All pretty civil and respectful. As for me, however, I got no end of shit from some fellow drinkers.

'Hey, you're that guy from the *Big Breakfast*,' some bloke would sneer. 'God, that show's shit...' Then someone else would get into my face to tell me that I wasn't remotely funny, or that I was a big-time Charlie.

Kev and I had to laugh – it was comical that no one seemed to like a local boy doing well - but I wasn't too chuffed when he pointed out that some dirty sod in the Comedy Store had spat on my back, and that a slug-trail of gob was running down my jacket. It's that kind of behaviour that gives us a bad name and I just don't see the need for it.

Back in London, things were going rapidly downhill at the *Big Breakfast* house. The best segments of the show became mine or Richard's OBs, and that really shouldn't have been the case. I re-watched the whole transmission one day, and it was patently obvious that having three presenters, all of whom thought they were the captain of the ship, just wasn't working. You could see Paul getting frustrated during the newspaper review because the girls would often interrupt him as he neared his punchline, ruining his gag completely.

'How's it going?' I'd ask him every time I visited the studio. He'd always give me a look and shake his head as if to say *I'm struggling with these two...*

Richard Hopkin had also noticed the tension between the presenters, which didn't bode well. Something had to change.

CHAPTER 16

You're In The House Squeaky

Much to my regret, I continued to turn down corporate gigs and stand-up shows. As a presenter on the *Big Breakfast* I should have been making hay while the sun shone, and embarking on a money-spinning tour. Paul Tonkinson couldn't understand my mindset; he was still gigging all over the place and earning as much in the evenings as he was in the mornings.

Around the same time, I'd heard whispers that Richard Bacon was probably not going to come back to the show – he'd got another gig on the BBC, apparently - and if that was the case then the OB gig would be mine, full-time. I took that with a pitch of salt, though. There were all sorts of rumours about personnel flying around, many of them negative, with tabloid gossip columns suggesting that the magic of the show had been lost, and that it needed to be recaptured, pronto.

One afternoon, my colleague John Donaldson picked up the crew and I, since we had to drive up to Liverpool prior to Grand National weekend (we were planning to turn up to an estate and get locals to take part in a donkey version of the famous horse race). On the M25, however, John received a phone call from the office asking where we were, and for us to head to the nearest hotel and wait for the production team, who needed to meet us urgently. At the hotel, we chatted over some lunch, and all agreed that something didn't feel right.

'Maybe they want us to do a different OB,' I said, hoping that this wasn't the case as I'd planned to stay over in Manchester to watch City play.

We waited and waited, and there was still no sign of anyone. Then John's phone rang again; it was the editor, Ed.

'Is Mike with you?' he asked.

'Yes, he is, Ed.'

'Tell him we're sending a car for him now. Paul Tonkinson's been fired and we want Mike to present the show tomorrow, from the house.'

John relayed the news, and I was utterly gobsmacked.

'Seems it's all down to you, buddy...' he said.

Shaking with shock and nerves, I immediately rang my sounding board, David Hahn, who was as positive as ever.

'If I thought you couldn't do the show I'd tell you,' he said. 'I'm made up for you, Mike, and you need to grab this opportunity with both hands.'

I then rang my mum and dad who both wished me all the best, as did my very excited sister. My phone then started to buzz non-stop, including a call from the Friday producer, Sarah Clarke, who told me how delighted she was to have me in the studio, and how confident she was that I could do a decent job. I then went onto the *Big Breakfast* website (not always a good idea) to gauge the reaction to Paul's sacking on the viewers' forum. Somehow they already knew that I'd be presenting the show the next day – I can only presume the news had been leaked, since I'd only just found out myself – and the reaction to this was largely positive, other than a few naysayers. There were also suggestions that Richard Hopkins had been fired, too, and that the original producer, Ben Rigden, had been re-instated.

I got home, had a cuppa, and took my dog Ben out for a walk. As I contemplated what lay ahead of me, I took some deep breaths, and tried to clear my head. I couldn't quite grasp the fact that I was going to be emulating the likes of Chris Evans, Mark Little, Peter Kay and the great Bob Monkhouse, who'd all occupied that famous *Big Breakfast* chair (which, sadly, had now been replaced with a sofa).

A few hours' later, at 4 a.m, my bedside alarm went off, and within a few minutes I was washed, dressed and jumping into a waiting car. Rod, my driver, handed me a copy of that morning's script, as well as every daily newspaper. It was my job to trawl through the pages and highlight some funny stories for the paper review which, thanks to Johnny Vaughan, had become an iconic part of the show.

Upon arriving at the studio, I went straight into the script meeting, where Ben Rigden welcomed me (the rumours were true, then). He told everyone that things were going to change and we were going to make the *Big Breakfast* great again. He gave a great motivational speech, like a football manager before a crucial game.

'Just enjoy it, okay?' were his only words of advice to me; he was basically giving me carte blanche to get on with it, and be myself. Ten minutes' later the opening credits were rolling, and I was being counted in.

I was introduced by Amanda and Donna, and opened with a quick gag. Then the girls started chatting, and I said 'Do

I have to roll a dice to get a six to speak here, or what?', which went down well with the crew, who knew what they were like.

By the first ad break, I'd taken off and felt that I was cruising at a good speed. Then it was time for the four-minute paper review, which was the most nerve-wracking part of the show for me. Bearing this in mind, I'd done some prep work with a brilliant writer-cum-stand-up called Simon Evans, and had distilled his fairly long-winded stories into quick, punchy gags and one-liners. I was well aware that some viewers would have thought them a bit 'old school' but I didn't give a toss; they were funny no matter what school they came from. I managed to get through the review, though, and jokingly made a point of asking the girls not to interrupt – something that had always hampered my predecessor, Paul - and this again got a huge cheer.

Later in the show I did an interview with the British canoeing champion, insisting that we spoke to each other while sitting in canoes, in the outdoor swimming pool. At the end of the piece, it all got a bit silly and I threw a floor assistant called Chris into the water. Luckily he was cool with it, and it actually became a running joke; every time we filmed from the pool the poor lad would get chucked in.

During the after-show debrief, and after announcing that we were going to revive the original opening titles and return to two chairs instead of a sofa, Ben asked everyone to give me a round of applause.

'Welcome to the *Big Breakfast* house family, Mike,' he said, and I felt really touched.

My first Nickelodeon photo

My old Nickelodeon colleagues. Never a dull moment with this lot

The Nickelodeon crew. What a great tour

My Big Breakfast crew, Richard, Lisa and Amanda

The last Big Breakfast ever
and the famous gnome

My last ever Big Breakfast
script and phone card

Big pants in Panto

Back in panto with Natasha
Hamilton, Ritchie Neville and
from Towie, Dan Osbourne

With Larry Lamb in Hook

Marcus Collins one of the funniest pantos ever. This guy has an awesome voice.

The Office Christmas Special, with Ricky Gervais. One of the nicest men I've ever worked with.

Me with Gazza and Lee Sharp, `Gazza told me some great stories

Walking out with Brian Robson behind me . Captain of the celebrity football team, Brian wasn't happy when I was given the captains arm band!

Winning the celeb soccer sixes at St James Park with. Peter Beardsley, Michael Greco, Paul Hardcastle, Dean Gaffney, Jezz Edwards, some tall guy and me

At the Oscars with my Winnie

Britney flirting with me . Not long after this she
shaved her head. She couldn't take rejection ha! ha!

Performing at the Hob. One of the best comedy clubs in London

In Sydney Australia having performed on that big ship behind me

Headliner

Panto flyer with the lovely Bonnie
Langford and the odd Robert Powell

My stand-up show at the regent theatre

Later that day, having gone home for a kip, I awoke to my phone buzzing with voicemail messages, including one from Nick telling me to phone him as soon as possible.

'Good news, Mike,' he said. 'They want to offer you a contract, on £3,500 a week,' adding that Ben had arranged lunch for us all at Canary Wharf to discuss things.

Ben gave me the low down. While they were delighted with my first stint as a presenter, Richard was going to continue in the hot seat – contrary to all the rumours of his departure - and I would cover for him when necessary. I'd also continue with my usual OBs, and would occasionally be dispatched abroad for premieres or celebrity interviews. Amanda and Donna would carry on as co-presenters, and Melanie Sykes, an up-and-coming former model from Manchester, would be doing some on-location VTs for the show, including the Oscars (I was jealous as hell about that). I'd also have a new production team to work with, too, comprising Paul Connolly – who I'd met at the audition - Paul Moore and an intern called Gareth Cornick. I had no inkling then about how much influence Paul C and Gareth would have on my career, and how many laughs we'd share in the process. I was about to embark on the best two years of my life, alongside two amazing people.

I don't think I'd ever felt happier after that contract-signing meeting. I drove up to Manchester (City were playing the following day) and took my family out for dinner at the Living Room restaurant to celebrate.

Paul and Gaz proved to be fantastic people to work with, and were ridiculously talented; I used to call them the Messi and Neymar of breakfast TV. Paul especially understood me

as a person and a presenter and, like any good football manager, played to my strengths. We didn't agree on everything –
professionally we had our ups and downs, and we clashed a
bit - but the three of us just wanted what was best for the
programme.

As for the show itself, Ben kept to his word and brought
back the opening titles and the two chairs, as well as previously
popular items that had since been shelved, like Wonga, Family
of the Week and the Friday song. Zig and Zag, arguably the
Big Breakfast's most famous presenters, were also reinstated
due to public demand. Ben, however, had another battle on
his hands. Richard Bacon was a brilliant presenter, but there
was no chemistry whatsoever between him and Amanda
Byram when they hosted together, and at times you could de-
tect an underlying dislike. Building a rapport between the presenters was crucial for a successful breakfast show, and I
sensed trouble looming.

Around that time, David asked me to play in a charity
football match, which was definitely one of the perks of being
fairly well-known. Despite being five foot seven I always
played centre-half for the celebrity team – Showbiz XI - and,
if I had a bigger centre-half next to me (especially if it was an
ex-pro) I'd just drop back, act as a sweeper and clean up. I
used to love rubbing shoulders with former players, politi-
cians, musicians and other famous faces (I remember once lining up with the Eddie the Eagle, of ski-jumping fame).

During this particular game I went for the ball, and one
of the opposing players slid in with a two-footed tackle, taking
me right out. I was in so much pain I could hardly move, and
an ambulance was called to rush me to hospital. I soon received the diagnosis that I'd snapped my cruciate ligament,

which was possibly the worst football injury in the book. I was gutted and worried that I wouldn't be able to play properly again.

On my behalf, David Hahn rang the match organiser - a guy called Jess Conrad, a 1960s one-hit wonder who still walked around like he was a superstar – and threatened to sue him ('I hope you've got insurance,' he said). David was furious that someone could sustain such a bad injury in a so-called charity game, whereupon a player had taken it upon himself to smash me as hard as he could. I told David to forget it, it was just one of those things, but in reality, he was right.

As it happened, the promised insurance money never materialised and, despite pledging to stage a special game to raise the funds for my op (which was performed privately, to the cost of £4,500), Jess Conrad never came up with the goods. Neither he nor his set-up asked how I was or sent me a get well card, so that's how much they cared. It took six months for me to start running again, and to this day my knee is still a mess. I should have listened to David, and sued them there and then.

My *Big Breakfast* bosses weren't overly impressed when I told them I'd busted my knee, and that I was going to be on crutches for weeks. I should have asked for permission first, they said, and as far as they were concerned it was my own fault. They probably had a point. My first post-op OB began with me coming down the stairs in a Stannah stair lift, which brought the house down.

A few weeks' later, Paul Connolly and I attended the Leicester Square premiere of *Bridget Jones' Diary*, with our film crew in tow. This was my first ever movie premiere, and I remember feeling really excited as I hovered near the red carpet. The stars arrived thick and fast – like actors Jim Broadbent and James Faulkner - and I was really enjoying having a laugh with them. Paul had written up a brilliant script, which encouraged me to be quite cheeky to the celebs, asking them why they were here how much they were getting for the gig. There was certainly going to be no arse-licking from our direction.

At one point I delved into my pocket to get my 'notes' and fished out my shopping list instead.

'Could you get me a pint of milk, five pounds of potatoes and some Findus Crispy Pancakes?' I asked Colin Firth who, to his credit, laughed his head off.

The stars kept on arriving, and we pounced on as many as we could.

'What the hell you doing here?' I asked boxer Chris Eubank when he came over. 'I've watched this film and I never saw you in it.'

'I know you,' he replied, narrowing his eyes.

'Well let's hope somebody knows *you*...' I said, quick as a flash.

'Keep it up,' said Paul.

I had to rein it in with some of the bigger stars, but most of them – apart from a humourless Hugh Grant - were good sports. Bridget Jones herself, actress Renee Zellweger, came over and I made out that we were bosom buddies, and that I'd not seen her for ages. She played up to it – fair play to her –

and walked away saying 'Who was that guy,' as I looked to the camera and said 'Who the hell was she?'

The report went down a storm the next morning, and Ben phoned me afterwards to congratulate me.

'Mate, thank Paul,' I said. 'He wrote it and put it all together.' It's easy to take the credit and I hated it if anyone did that to me, so I always made a point of ensuring the right people got a mention.

Elsa Sharp – a very good-looking Italian woman - was the VT producer and, following our red-carpet performance, requested that I do all the celeb interviews. It was hard work, but I bloody loved it. I'd finish my morning stint, before jumping on a Virgin bike, rushing through the streets of London and arriving at Heathrow to catch a flight to New York.

My first visit to the Big Apple – to interview Julia Roberts about her new film, *America's Sweethearts'* - was produced by Colin Paterson, who's now the senior showbiz reporter for BBC 5 Live. Apart from my fleeting conversations with Madonna at the *Kids' Choice TV Awards*, I'd never met a full-blown superstar like Julia, and I was so keen to do a good job. I did hours of research, watching her film frame-by-frame and going through all the questions with Colin.

I entered the interview room for our six-minute chat, only for Julia to apologise and tell me that she needed the toilet. This made me laugh, and the first question on my list was duly amended.

'Julia, ever so nice to meet you, do you feel better now you've had your wee?'

She promptly collapsed into a fit of giggles, clearly taken aback at being asked such a brazen question by a cheeky little Manc. The rest of the interview went brilliantly; I wasn't fazed by her at all, and found myself chatting to her like a mate. At one point she mentioned her love of knitting and, with mock surprise, I told her I was just about to ask her about that myself.

'You must be psychic, like me,' I said.

'Really?' she replied.

'Yep, I'm a medium,' I smiled. 'It says so in my underpants.'

I pulled out the 'Medium' tag on my pants – an ancient gag, to be fair - but she creased up. She'd probably become bored with answering serious questions about the film all day, and I think I came as a refreshing change.

'I like you,' she said after our six minutes was up. 'I hope we see each other again soon.'

'Julia, I have a girlfriend,' I replied, 'but thank you anyway.'

I was starting to make a name for myself as an interviewer, and I became flavour of the month with my *Big Breakfast* bosses. And that was despite Ben receiving a call from a *News of the World* journalist, informing him that they were going to re-run the lap dancer story, but this time with the updated headline of '*Big Breakfast* Presenter's Affair With Lap Dancer.'

Ben was asked for a comment but just brushed it off, telling the reporter that his main presenter Richard had done much worse, and that it was all in the past. The paper never re-ran the story, thank God, but John Mann – one of the show's writers – got wind of it and jokily dubbed me 'Not So Squeaky McClean'. This was pounced upon by Patrick Kielty when he stood in for Richard one morning, and the 'Squeaky McClean' nickname stuck fast. It was even used in the show's interview segments (*Squeaky McClean Meets...*) and people began to shout it at me in the street.

Paul, Gaz and myself continued to work brilliantly as a team, and most OBs we produced were TV gold. The fact that we socialised outside work was key to our successful partnership, because our camaraderie translated onto the screen. There was also no doubting that comedy was the glue that gelled us all together; the three of us had the same taste in jokes, gags and comedians, and it made for some madcap moments in a variety of UK towns.

In Northampton, a McDonalds restaurant had refused to serve a girl because her thong was showing. We decided to pitch up there dressed as military men, only when the camera pulled away Paul, Gaz and myself were seen to be wearing camouflage jackets with just a G-string on underneath. As we handed back to the house we saluted and turned around so they could see our bare backsides, before marching off. What's more, we'd got a load of girls to walk in wearing jeans with their G-strings showing, and the poor McDonalds manager didn't know what to do with himself.

One morning, Ben asked me if I fancied the presenting gig every Friday, since Richard had requested a regular day off.

'I think you'll work really well with Amanda, he said.

So it was confirmed: Fridays would feature Amanda and me in the hot seat. She made it very clear she wanted to be seen as the main presenter, but I also made it equally clear that I didn't give a shit. The newspaper review continued to be the most challenging part of the show for me, so I asked Ben if I could get help from another writer. He agreed, on condition that I'd pay this guy myself, and that all our material would have to be okayed by a script editor – the excellent Richard Turner - to ensure we weren't slandering anyone.

I secured the services of one of the best topical gag writers around – Tim Maloney – and, by 5 a.m on the first Friday, he'd faxed over a stack of brilliant gags. Looking back, I should have employed Tim and Richard to write a whole stand-up set for me, but at that time – for my sins - I was still shying away from gigs.

Just prior to Christmas 2002 I was asked to interview Cher, who was in London to publicise her new album. I did my research as per usual, going through the questions with my colleague Elsa, who told me that orders from high had dictated that in no circumstances must we talk about her famous collection of wigs. As soon as Cher came into the room, wearing a glum expression, my heart sank. I knew immediately that she just didn't want to be there, and my suspicions were confirmed when she gave me a can't-be-arsed limp handshake.

Yeah, I bet you'd much rather be shopping for cheap glittery clothes in Oxford Street Primark, I thought to myself.

I took a deep breath, prepared for the worst, and began the interview with some fluffy questions. I then ramped it up with a few funnies, which seemed to make her smile, and appeared to loosen her up.

'D'you mind considering a new show we'd like you to be part of?' I asked, before pitching *The Mike and Cher Show*, which was clearly all about me, not her. She got the gag and played along, bless her. I'd got her on side, thank God, so I thought I'd take our chat to the next level.

'So Cher, let's talk about your wigs,' I said, and Elsa nearly spontaneously combusted. 'How many have you actually got?'

She answered good-humouredly, which then prompted me to pull out the selection of cheap wigs that I'd smuggled in.

'Let's try some on, shall we, eh?' I grinned.

Her manager's face was a picture – if looks could have killed - but I just winked at her and carried on. After the cameras stopped rolling, Cher was charm personified and happily posed for a picture with me, sporting one of my moth-eaten wigs.

It just goes to show that underneath it all, the "Stars" are still real people and often don't want to be mollycoddled. There are of course the exceptions to this rule but I'll mention them later..

CHAPTER 17

Mixing With The Stars

One Monday morning, Paul, Gaz and I found ourselves preparing an outside broadcast at yet another council estate, blissfully unaware that, a few months' later, it would end up in fifth place in *TV's Most Embarrassing Moments*.

That day's theme was antiques, and to reflect this we had expert Lauren Harries in tow. Lauren had shot to fame in the 1980s when – before her gender reassignment - was commonly known as James Harries and had made a few eccentric appearances on *Wogan*. Gaz was dressed as TV antiques sleuth Lovejoy (famously played by Ian McShane) and Paul was togged up like a toff, in a white jacket. The whole premise was to encourage punters to bring out their antiques so that Lauren could value them.

She and I were told to run down the street and knock on the punters doors, doing our utmost to get into their front rooms as soon as possible so we could have a quick look at their ornaments and knick-knacks before persuading them to get them valued. We struck gold at the last house we visited. The owner proudly led us to a jardinière vase which commemorated the 1981 marriage of Prince Charles to Lady Diana Spencer. *Bingo.*

Only five hundred had been made, we were told, with one of them ending up at Buckingham Palace, apparently, and another 250 having been shipped to America.

'Definitely the most valuable thing we've seen all morning...' I remember Lauren whispering to me just before I linked with Richard Bacon back in the studio.

'We'll be back shortly with Lauren and a whole host of antiques,' I smiled to the camera, delighted that we'd found a gem among the tat and trinkets collected from other residents.

During the ad break, we manoeuvred five or so willing punters into position for our big hit. Paul would bring each individual and their respective 'antiques' to the table, before asking Lauren to assess the items and estimate their worth. We'd then planned for me to tempt the owners with a wad of cash in an attempt to prise their precious items from them.

It was all going pretty well – Lauren had valued a tankard and a plate – and then it was time to welcome the final candidate to the table. The owner of the Royal Wedding vase came and sat in front of Lauren, all expectant, and Paul brought over the item. As he grasped the lid, however, it came away from the base which promptly smashed onto the floor, shattering into tiny pieces. There was a shocked pause before the woman – her face like thunder – finally spoke.

'My fucking vase,' she said.

I looked at Lauren, trying desperately to suppress my laughter.

'What's your expert opinion, then?' I asked, assessing the remains of the vase.

'Well, it's not going to be worth much now, is it?' she replied.

'Cut to a break now, Mike. *Quickly...*' ordered the voice down my earpiece as Paul swiftly ushered the fuming woman out of shot, muffling her mouth with his hand.

I was laughing so much I had to retire to the OB truck to calm down. When I got there everyone else was in bits, too, tears of mirth running down their faces. The team back at the *Big Breakfast* house were falling about too, apparently. At one point, Ben the editor phoned Paul to ascertain exactly what had happened.

'What d'you fucking think happened, Ben?' he said in his broad Northern Irish accent. 'I've just broken this woman's antique fucking vase. How was I to know it was stuck together with fucking Blu-Tack?'

As we went back on air, we did another link to reassure the viewers that everything was okay, and that we'd ensure the antique was repaired. Towards the end of the show we did our usual 'bye-bye' wave, and the vase owner even joined in, bless her. *BIG BREAKFAST* BREAKS ANTIQUE VASE blared the tabloid headlines the next day, citing me as the culprit, the sods.

****

The *Big Breakfast* welcomed some of Hollywood's finest into the house. Nine times out of ten, these megastars were just amazing; they knew how to play the game, they knew how to give an interview and they conducted themselves brilliantly.

A shining example was the legendary comedian Chris Rock, who was promoting his latest film, *Down To Earth*. I was a huge fan of his - I loved his stand up – and I was so excited to meet him. However, when I turned up for the interview at the relatively early time of 10 a.m., I could see that he was still half asleep and suffering from severe jet lag. He was so apologetic though, and so pleasant, that I shelved my usual cheeky, piss-taking questions and played it pretty straight. He ended up being a dream to interview, despite his tiredness, and I came out liking him even more.

I liked Mariah Carey too, but she was one hell of an odd ball, albeit a very pleasant odd ball. I had been allocated twenty minutes with her, which is a ridiculous amount of time to get with a big celebrity. I walked in to the interview room to find Mariah lying on a long sofa. She got up to greet me, wearing the highest heels I'd ever seen and a top that left nothing to the imagination. I couldn't take my eyes off her chest, not just because her top shelf was almost hanging out, but because her boobs looked a bit wonky. I remember thinking *Jeez, with all her riches, and living in the land of plastic surgery, you'd have thought she'd have got them done properly*.

Much to my surprise, she started flirting with me.

'You're cute,' she said.

'Not so bad yourself, love,' I replied. 'D'you need a guide to show you around London?'

'Only if I can bring my security with me,' she said, gesturing towards a guy who could hardly fit through the door frame, he was that massive.

'Nah, I couldn't afford to feed both of you,' I said.

We wrapped the interview – we'd gone on to do the usual PR fluff about her latest album - and she came over to give me a little kiss.

'If you ever fancy a funny English guy, I'm free,' I said.

'Hey, why don't you come over to America next month and be in my new video?' she said.

'Seriously?'

'Most definitely,' she purred, before asking her PR people to arrange my flight to LA for the shoot. I couldn't believe it. *Mariah Carey's properly into me.*

Three weeks later she was hospitalised for some reason, which put paid to my starring role on MTV. It was nice while it lasted, though. Can you imagine me as her bit of rough? That's a huge laugh in itself!

On the other end of the showbiz scale, however, I'd sometimes find myself having to deal with arrogant arseholes who, fresh out of a three-week stint in the *Big Brother* house, thought they'd hit the heights of fame and were going to set the world alight. One of these non-entities was a guy called Darren, who swept into the *Big Breakfast* house like he was some kind of Hollywood movie star.

Since being booted off the reality show he'd done some sponsorship deal with a soup manufacturer, and he told the producers in no uncertain terms that he was only coming onto the show to promote his chicken soup, and was loath to talk about *Big Brother* during my interview with him. If that wasn't going to happen, he told them, then he'd walk. While the producers seemed to cave in, Ben the editor wasn't having any of it, and told me to ignore his diva demands.

'...and here's Darren from *Big Brother*,' I announced, before talking about anything but his bloody soup. He was fuming, as were his representatives.

'Sorry,' said Ben as the end credits rolled. 'We just ran out of time.'

Of all the big-name guests that we welcomed onto the *Big Breakfast,* only three, in my opinion, were absolute dickheads. One – much to my disappointment – was the late Paul Daniels. He'd been a hero of mine when I was a budding magician and, to be fair, had always answered the letters I'd sent him asking for advice, and had gladly posed for pictures following the theatre shows I attended. So I was massively surprised that this kind-heartedness wasn't in evidence when Paul appeared on the *Big Breakfast*. He had been invited onto the show to be interviewed by me, as well as our resident puppets, Zig and Zag, who Ben had reinstated after a long, lamented absence (the puppeteers were two great lads from Ireland - Mick O'Hara and Ciaran Morrison – who were just brilliant at bringing them to life).

The plan was for Paul to talk about David Blaine and all things magic, as per usual, we'd arranged for a car to pick him up and bring him to the studio. Paul, however, decided to turn up in his own van, and when he walked onto the set he looked like he'd just been kidnapped. He was a total mess, and for some reason he was wearing a Russian-style Cossack hat teamed with a paint-spattered coat.

The director got one of the floor assistants to ask our guest if he'd kindly remove his coat and hat. He refused, point-blank.

'No,' he said, 'I am fine as I am, thank you.'

The assistant then tried to go through the item and script with him, only for Daniels to cut her dead, in a really patronising manner.

'I've been doing this for years, dear,' he said, 'and I know how it works.'

All the while, I could hear my director in my earpiece, calling Daniels all the names under the sun and demanding to know why the 'arsehole' wouldn't remove his coat.

I tried to make polite conversation with my guest, asking him if he'd ever thought about trying to make Big Ben disappear.

'Don't be so bloody stupid,' he said, humourlessly. 'If people know it can't move, then it's not going to move, is it?'

'Well, David Copperfield made the Statue of Liberty disappear,' I answered, in wind-up mode, 'but maybe he's just a better magician than you.'

He gave me a filthy look, and the interview went downhill from there. He quite clearly had no interest in the show, and had just come on to plug his latest tour. His attitude was simply appalling and, as someone who'd once worshipped him, it was a bitter pill to swallow.

I made a point of going to see one of his shows at a venue in Essex, part of me hoping that he'd blow me away and alter my opinion of him. I actually came out feeling quite sorry for my one time hero. The hall was half-full – there can't have been more than 200 people there – and it was a far cry from his mid-1980s heyday which had seen him win the prestigious

Golden Rose of Montreux award, and saw him regularly attracting 16 million viewers on the BBC. *Maybe it was the magician
in him that had made those of millions of viewers disappear* I thought
to myself as I made my way home.

'Never meet your heroes,' goes the old adage, and that was
certainly the case with my other nightmare guest, none other
than the comedian Steve Coogan. I adored my fellow Mancunian's body of work – I was a huge fan of *The Day Today* and
Knowing Me, Knowing You – and, in the days when I had hair,
people would often tell me that we looked alike. Once, when
I was in sunny Cannes, covering the film festival for the *Big
Breakfast*, I was informed that we'd secured an interview with
my comedy hero. The crew and I were elated at the prospect
of meeting the genius behind Paul Calf and Alan Partridge,
but – sadly – our excitement proved to be short-lived once we
started to chat. What a miserable fucker. Sorry, Coogan fans,
but that's how I found him. He couldn't have been more rude
and arrogant if he tried, and I came away from the interview
feeling so disappointed.

If I thought I couldn't meet a more obnoxious celebrity,
I was very much mistaken, because Dennis Waterman took
the biscuit in that regard. I'd loved watching him in *Minder* –
he and George 'Arthur Daley' Cole were a brilliant double act
– and, in 2001 I was delighted to get the opportunity to meet
him. Waterman was starring with ex-*Eastenders*' actress Martine McCutcheon in *My Fair Lady* in London's west end, and I
was dispatched to interview them both on the opening night,
during the after-show party.

Martine was nice enough. Her soap alter-ego, Tiffany, had
just been killed off, but that didn't stop me asking a daft question about whether or not she'd be returning to *Eastenders*. She

didn't get the joke, bless her, and patiently explained how she'd been run over by Grant Mitchell. I promptly pretended to burst into tears before hugging her and, judging by her startled expression, she clearly thought I was some kind of northern nutter.

I then filmed quick pieces to camera with VIP guests like Dale Winton and Barbara Windsor - who were both lovely – before the *My Fair Lady* publicity team introduced me to Dennis, who was swigging from a huge glass of whisky. Before I could say anything, and before the cameras had started to roll, he looked me up and down and glared at me. 'Who's this cunt?' he snarled.

I couldn't believe what I'd heard. What a nasty bastard. As if I was going to take that one lying down.

'Who are *you*, you fucking has-been?' I shouted back, or words to that effect. 'You're a fucking joke, you washed-up alcoholic...'

The next thing I knew Waterman had swung for me, and we were being pulled apart. His red-faced PR team dragged him away, as he clung onto his tumbler of whisky, and the interview was swiftly abandoned.

Later that evening, back at home, I remember feeling really annoyed that I'd lowered myself to this idiot's level. I should have just ignored him, or perhaps even laughed it off. Our altercation was the talk of the *Big Breakfast* set the next morning, although Ben Rigden was gutted that it hadn't been captured on camera, and our publicity team came over to advise me not to say anything to the press. Dennis Waterman was, without doubt, the biggest celebrity arsehole I have ever had the displeasure of meeting. I know that at times I've pushed buttons or been arsey but never without provocation and there's just no need for that kind of attitude.

Morons like Waterman were in the minority, fortunately, and I counted myself so lucky to be jetting around Europe and the USA to interview big-name stars. That said, it wasn't as glamorous as it sounds, since our schedules were unrelenting. Occasionally you might get the odd afternoon to look around a city or do some shopping, but most of the time it was a case of landing at the airport, filming a couple of links, going back to the hotel, having a quick snack, getting some kip, doing the interview the next day, and flying back home soon afterwards. (Wow I just read that back and it sounded whiny even to a Manc like me!) Television awards were probably my favourite gigs, because they gave me the opportunity to ask really cheeky questions (although I was careful not to be too insulting, like Dennis Pennis). I'd always see the same old faces – guys and gals from *The Bill*, *Emmerdale* or *Coronation Street* who'd attend the opening of a can of Coke - but they were good fun nevertheless.

Eastenders' actor Michael Greco, who I'd got to know through celeb football circles, was always up for a laugh and never took himself seriously. Sometimes, however, he'd turn up with his colleague Dean Gaffney (who played Robbie Jackson) in tow, who could be a bit temperamental. I remember asking them both if they had a speech lined, up, and telling them I a had a couple of pre-written speeches if they wanted to buy one off me. Michael played along – he even read them out – but Dean just stared at me, blankly. A few months later I saw Dean at a football event and he accused me of taking the piss out of him, and I told him to get a grip and stop being a knob (we would eventually kiss and make up, you'll all be delighted to learn).

CHAPTER 18

Cannes Film Festival

As 2001 approached, the *Big Breakfast* began to get a complete hammering from the press, with claims that it was past its best and ripe for change. We were still attracting better viewing figures than *GMTV* and *BBC Breakfast*, though, and our production team remained convinced that there was still an appetite for a funny, entertaining morning show.

'Ignore what you read,' announced Ben Rigden who, as well as being a top editor, was a brilliant motivator. 'Just carry on what you're doing.'

While I continued to enjoy my Friday morning presenting stints, my co-presenter, Amanda Byram, was starting to get right up my nose. She had a habit of ruining my newspaper reviews, chipping in at the wrong point and trying (and often failing) to be funny. All she had to do was just sit and listen, and laugh if she found something funny, or pretend to laugh if she didn't; quite simple really. There were occasions I had to put her straight on air, and when I watched it back later I'd realise that she'd made me look like a total cock. Richard Bacon and Paul Tonkinson had experienced similar issues, and I shared their pain.

One morning, during a show, my friend and former agent David Hahn had come to visit me on set – I was doing an interview for a reporter friend of his – and during a break in transmission I introduced him to Amanda. David was brilliant at sussing people out – he could sniff out the truth from the bullshit – and I could tell by his body language that he wasn't particularly taken with my co-presenter. As soon as she left, he took to me to one side.

'Mike, I'm telling you this because I have your best interests at heart,' he said, 'but it's so obvious that Amanda doesn't like you. She's threatened by you, I reckon. It's written all over her face.'

I was taken aback, but Dave was adamant, even more so after he'd watched the whole programme. His judgement turned out to be spot on, because shortly afterwards I discovered that Amanda was trying to edge me out of the Friday show. When I was presenting an item she'd apparently stand at the back of the studio with the MD, Mary Durkin, and continuously slag me off.

It came as no surprise when, after a couple of months in the presenter's chair, Ben broke the news that Richard was returning to the Friday show, but that I'd still be able to sit in him for him occasionally. I never questioned Ben as to why - I respected him too much to make him feel awkward - so I just said no problem, and left it at that. From then on, I kept Amanda at arms' length – to me, she couldn't be trusted – but I kept on polite terms with her. She'd occasionally moan about Richard to me - behind his back, of course – but I was always firmly Team Richard.

I was gutted to be taken off the Friday show but my mate Paul Connolly told me not to let it get me down, and to continue doing what I did best, namely the outside broadcasts. Paul, Gaz and I were still churning out decent OBs, including a trip to Scotland to meet a farmer who'd trained his sheepdog to round up his ducks and herd them into a pen. We decided to challenge Paul to do the same, dressing him up as a Border Collie as I played the role of the farmer.

The drive up north was probably one of the funniest journeys I have ever had. We travelled in two different vehicles - the crew were in one, and I was in the other – and each time we passed each other I decided to take off an item of clothing. Eventually I was sat driving in my pants and to make Paul laugh even more, I put on the huge dog's head that we'd bought for the OB. My mate was pissing himself so much when I drove past that he nearly crashed. Before long he was almost starkers, too, much to the bemusement of passing motorists.

The laughing stopped abruptly, however, when the Old Bill pulled us over on the M6. The officer did the biggest double take when he was confronted with a driver wearing just his undies and sporting a dog's head. Luckily he let me off – being on the telly has its perks sometimes - and I remember him walking back to his cop car, chuckling. I can only imagine how his report read: *'Half-naked television presenter apprehended after motorist complaints, clad only in underpants and a dog's head...'*

We eventually arrived at the farm, and Paul got dressed into the complete dog outfit. The poor farmer was totally bewildered when I whistled for 'my dog, Ben', only for Paul to crawl on. All I could hear in my earpiece was guffaws coming from the *Big Breakfast* studio.

'There's no way he'll get those ducks in the pen,' said the farmer, shaking his head. But Paul did, and within the time limit, too. When the last duck waddled in, I jumped on the 'dog' as if he'd just scored the winning goal in the FA Cup final. It was brilliant television.

Another memorable days' filming came from the York-shire town of Barnsley, on the same night that England beat Germany 5-1. The show was coming live from someone's house the following morning, and we decided to do some filming in the town centre the night before, on a street lined with bars and pubs. The initial idea was for me to get dressed up as a jockey while having a drink in every bar – like a pub 'Grand National' – the challenge being to compete the 'course' while still standing. I'd never been a big drinker, but I was prepared to give it a go.

Our legal department had different ideas, though, inform-ing me that I wasn't allowed to be seen presenting while drink-ing alcohol. Time for Plan B, then, which involved getting Paul the producer to do the 'Grand National' instead, while I re-ported on it. We began filming, and after visiting six bars Paul was absolutely rat-arsed. By the end of the pub crawl he was paralytic, and collapsed in a heap on the floor. Just as I was about to deliver my closing piece to camera, with my sozzled mate in the background, a local girl came over, pulled down her knickers and sat on his face. I was laughing so hard I could hardly get my lines out.

'On a night when England defeated Germany,' I said, 'Barnsley defeated our producer Paul...'

This kind of TV wouldn't go out now, but at the time it was so much fun.

****

In March 2001 the Oscars were due to take place, and the *Big Breakfast* had dispatched Melanie Sykes to cover them. I was gutted when I found out, since Mel only did the odd re-port for us and I thought I'd worked hard enough to have earned a chance at it. I was instead given the job of doing a live OB from the forest where the opening fight scene from *Gladiator* was shot, featuring Russell Crowe.

We'd made a big deal of the fact that I was going to have 'two *Gladiator* stars' appearing with me, when in reality it was just two extras, who we helpfully identified by pausing a clip from the movie's fight scene and using two big arrows to point them out. It was funny, though; typical *Big Breakfast* cheekiness.

I then handed over to Melanie in Los Angeles, who was reporting from the legendary *Vanity Fair* after-show party, interviewing some of the Oscar winners. I'll be totally honest, I felt grumpy and jealous as I watched from the truck, particularly when Mel reeled out a load of bland questions about what it was like to win and what the actress was wearing, the usual boring stuff.

Once we'd wrapped the OB, Paul and I discussed how different the Oscars coverage might have been had I presented it. I know we wouldn't have been talking about dresses, unless of course I'd been wearing one!

'Chin up,' said Paul. 'You might get the chance next year.'

As it happened, Melanie allegedly got herself embroiled in a contractual wrangle about working beyond 9 a.m. The production team were furious, and I don't think it was any coincidence that she never worked for the *Big Breakfast* again. Although it could also have been the bland interview…

That August, Paul, Gaz and I flew up to the Edinburgh Fringe Festival for a week of live OBs. Since we couldn't be bothered going to see every comedy show, we asked the various acts to put their flyers into a massive tombola for us to pick one out and give it our own special 'Squeaky Five-Star' recommendation. We were absolutely deluged, since everybody wanted some valuable publicity on the *Big Breakfast*. Some of the lucky recipients expected us to actually sit through their shows, but that was never going to happen. The fact of the matter, I'm sorry to say, was that the Fringe Festival was filled with a load of old rubbish.

One morning we were scheduled to have 'Swing Your Pants' comedians Trevor and Simon on the sofa so, the previous night, we'd felt obliged to go to their show. I found it painfully unfunny, so much so that I almost dropped off halfway through (like Chris Rock, I blamed the jet lag; that London to Edinburgh flight was a killer). Meeting the former *Live and Kicking* duo the following morning, therefore, was a bit uncomfortable, especially when they asked me if I'd enjoyed the show. It was Bonnie Langford who taught me what to say in these awkward situations.

'It was, er, different,' I smiled.

'Yeah, we wanted it to be,' they said, without any sense of irony.

One morning we interviewed Emo Phillips – the Canadian comic with the weird, high-pitched voice - having watched his excellent show the night before. I remember chatting to him during the break, expecting him to revert to his 'normal' voice, but then realising when he opened his mouth that it *was* his normal voice. Thankfully no faux pas from me on this one as I didn't ask him to speak normally!

We did a lot of roving reporting in the city centre, too. One day we were filming in front of Edinburgh Castle and, as I waited to do a link, a couple of middle-aged Americans came over to ask me where the castle was. The bloody thing was right behind me; how the hell could they miss it?

'Ah, they've moved it to Glasgow,' I said.

'Oh really? Gee, what a shame,' commented the guy. 'What on earth did they do that for?' 'Tax reasons' I said .

This daft response prompted us to do some secret filming with overseas visitors, with me trying to convince them that the famous castle was shut 'because it was full of soldiers', or 'because they'd lost the big front door key'. I even persuaded one American that this was in fact a replica castle, and that the real one had been bought by the Chinese government and was now somewhere in Beijing.

It was always in the spirit of fun and whilst we might have made fun, we were never malicious and I think that's what kept us going for so long.

****

Another showbiz institution that we were lucky enough to attend was the Cannes Film Festival. I remember the *Big Breakfast* producers ringing me one Friday morning, telling me to drop everything and head over to France that night. It seemed there was a new 'must see' animation film coming out, and my bosses wanted me to interview one of its main voice-over artists. The film was *Shrek*, and the star actor was Mike Myers.

Until then, I'd never really been a fan of CGI films, but *Shrek* was something else. It was so clever, funny and original; the whole cinema in Cannes gave it a standing ovation, and rightfully so.

'We'd be grateful if you could just stick to questions about *Shrek*,' said Myers' publicist before our scheduled interview, 'so no mentions of Austin Powers, if you don't mind...' *Yeah, right luv...* I remember thinking to myself.

I opened up the interview by mentioning the things we had in common: other than our names, we were both born in the north of England (him in Liverpool) and we both started our careers in kids' TV (him with ITV's *Wide Awake Club*. We had a nice chat about *Shrek* and then, risking the wrath of the PR girl, I brought up the subject of Austin Powers.

'When's the sequel out, then?' I asked. He looked at me, lowered his voice and leaned forward.

'Between you and me, we start filming the new one next month,' he winked as his colleague nearly blew a gasket. He'd given me a massive showbiz exclusive, and the team at the *Big Breakfast* were made up. As I always said, if you don't ask, you don't get.

The crew and I stayed in a lavish five-star hotel on the outskirts of Cannes, a far cry from the street I grew up on and we spent much of our time hatching plans and ideas. Similar to what we did in Edinburgh, we launched our own special endorsements for the various films that were being promoted and touted around the town (the place was teeming with people trying to flog a movie, produce a movie and direct a movie). We decided that we would offer our own award – the Squeaky Palm Door - to deserving films.

The lads and I had a blast in Cannes. We'd do a live report in the morning, then would spend the rest of the day filming another piece that would be edited that night and sent over to London, to be aired the following day. I remember having a chat with the martial arts actor Jean-Claude Van Damme, on his private yacht. We'd planned my opening line to be 'Hi Jean-Claude, all your films are really crap, aren't they?', the hope being that he wouldn't understand what the word 'crap' meant and that he'd just sit there and nod his head.

'Hi Jean-Claude, do you agree that all your films are -' I said, before he interrupted me.

'I am back,' he said. 'Look at me. Go on, hit me.'

He then lifted up his shirt and beckoned me to punch him in the stomach.

'Go on, PUNCH ME!' he yelled, so I did, and gave it my best shot.

'Anyway, Jean-Claude, as I was saying, all your films are really crap, aren't they?'

'What does 'crap' mean?' he replied.

'It means 'cool' in English, Jean-Claude...'

'Well, yes, then. I agree. All my films are crap.'

We finished the rest of the interview, and as we prepared to leave we saw a PR woman explaining to him the true meaning of 'crap'. We scarpered before he got the chance to kung-fu kick me to within an inch of my life. Mad as a box of frogs but brilliant TV.

The *Big Breakfast* crew were invited to so many Cannes parties, but as we were up early a lot of them were just too late or to be fair full of people kissing ass. One we did accept, however, was a bash hosted by multi-millionaire fashion designer Pierre Cardin, which was the hottest ticket around. I'd never seen anything like it. His luxury mansion was amazing, with an infinity pool outside, and paintings on the wall that were so valuable that the Mancunian in me wanted to stuff one under my top. I remember looking at Gaz and Paul and thinking *what the actual FUCK are we doing here?*

I'd never seen so many pretentious people in one place, though. Actors, directors, producers, models... all the superficial luvvies were out in force. The food was plentiful and the drinks were flowing; in one room people were inhaling oxygen, for crying out loud. The lads and I didn't fancy that so we grabbed a glass of Cristal champagne and had a mooch around Pierre's gaff.

At one point I found myself in conversation with a model. She must have been about six foot four and possessed the longest legs I'd ever seen.

'What d'you do for a living then, love?' I asked, and she just gaped at me as if I'd lost my mind.

'What do you *think* I do?' she asked. I looked her up and down.

'Hmmm,' I mused. 'D'you drive a van?' I said.

She wasn't impressed, and before I knew it had flounced off to join her model mates. No sense of humour these ladies, maybe their shoes are so uncomfortable that life isn't funny…

I also met a couple who were trying to finance their film which, to be fair, didn't sound like it was going to trouble any box offices. I took an instant dislike to the guy – I didn't like the way he ordered his wife around – and thought I'd amuse myself by leading him up the garden path.

'Sounds like a great movie,' I said. 'Funnily enough, I'm looking to invest in something while I'm in Cannes, so tell me more...'

When he heard me talking money, he began to treat me like royalty, trying to convince me to throw my millions in his direction. Eventually the guy got around to asking me what I did.

'I work at McDonalds in Cannes,' I said.

'What?' he replied. 'You're shitting me, right? How the hell you going to get the money to finance my film?'

'I'll do extra shifts,' I laughed, and to my surprise found yet another party guest storming off in a huff.

Then I decided I wanted to meet Pierre Cardin himself, so I tried to muscle my way into the private room that he'd locked himself into.

'Can I meet Mr Cardin, please?' I asked the security guys on the door. 'I've bought one of his jumpers and it's shrunk in the wash, so I'm wondering if I can exchange it?' Needless to say they wouldn't let me past.

We left the house at 3 a.m., knowing that we had to be up in two hours. Instead of heading back to the hotel, we went straight into town and grabbed a coffee, chatting in a café until we were due to start the show. That morning was going to be a big day, we reckoned. Hollywood's finest were due to be arriving in Cannes and, as tradition dictated, would be walking up the famous red-carpeted steps, past the world's press, and into the theatre.

A few hours' later, during our live OB from the foot of the steps, a mischievous Richard Bacon dared me to run the stairs. As I surveyed the security guards lining the area, all I could hear in my earpiece was everybody in the house chanting *DO IT…DO IT…DO IT…*

'For you, Richard, I'd do anything,' I said, before jumping the barrier and running up the red steps. The next thing I knew I was being pinned to the ground but, ever the professional, didn't take my eye off our camera.

'Richard,' I squeaked, as a security guard sat on my head, 'it's back to you in the house…'

I was dragged away like I was some crazy criminal, and Paul's explanation that we were a television company and that it was 'just a bit of fun' went down like a lead balloon with the organisers.

CHAPTER 19

MTV Music Awards & Meeting Prince Charles

I returned to England to find that Richard had decided to have a week off, and that I was going to be in the house with Amanda while my colleague Ed Hall did the OBs. I couldn't wait to get cracking, but was determined that Amanda wouldn't get all the plum jobs on the show, as had previously been the case. Fighting my corner would be our new director (and my old mate) Dino, who I'd worked with at Nickelodeon. It was great to have Dino around, and he was such a calming influence during the madness of a broadcast. He'd chat to me through my earpiece, he'd help me with pronunciations, and he'd even prompt me with the odd funny line.

That week didn't prove to be plain sailing for me, though. It wasn't always easy being funny for five days a week, and by Wednesday my form had dipped; I was the first to admit that I wasn't at my best. By Thursday and Friday, however, I was back to my best and, as per usual, we finished the week with The Friday Song, made funnier by the fact that Amanda and I couldn't sing for toffee.

I also did a weeks' presenting stint with Richard, when Amanda went off on a break. This new combination was the talk of the production team. *How was it going to work? Who was going to take the lead? Who was going to do the paper review?* There was no battle as far as I was concerned, though; I loved working with Richard and, mindful of his broadcasting experience, I was more than happy to play second fiddle.

We were often like two naughty schoolboys, to be fair. Richard loved to play 'show chicken' which entailed both of us getting out of our seats and, as the vision mixer counted down from ten to one, seeing who'd dare to be last to sit in his chair. We'd often get told off by the editor, who wasn't remotely amused. 'It's just not funny, lads,' he said, wagging his finger as we sniggered to each other.

Richard was a supremely talented and intelligent presenter and was a joy to work with. At no point did we find ourselves at each other's throats, or fighting over items. That week, I remember us both interviewing two-time world heavyweight champion George Foreman. I was really excited about him being on the show – I loved watching footage of the legendary 1974 'Rumble in the Jungle' fight with Muhammed Ali – but, according to his PR, George wasn't interested in talking about boxing. He'd since become a successful entrepreneur, selling millions of his Lean, Mean Grilling Machines, and that's all he wanted to plug.

As soon as he walked on the studio floor you could feel his presence. The man was huge, and when he shook my hand I thought he was going to wrench off my arm. He took his place on the sofa, and before Richard could ask his first questions he launched straight into a pitch about his best-selling gadget.

'My grills are healthy, they cut out the fat, they're great for cooking, everybody needs one...' and so on. Richard cut him short and, totally ignoring the PR's warnings, dared to bring up that great fight. As it turned out we couldn't shut the bugger up, and he gave us some great insight into his boxing days.

I rarely had my photo taken with any of the stars we interviewed, but I made an exception that day because George was a gem. When I returned to my dressing room there was a gift waiting for me: yep, my very own George Foreman grill.

One morning, following the opening titles, the show began with my co-presenter theatrically pretending to punch me in the face. My mum had tuned in that morning, though, and as soon as the show finished she was on the phone.

'Why did he punch you? Why are you two fighting? What happened?' she asked.

'It was just a gag, mum, Richard and I are fine,' I laughed, trying to calm her down. (it's on you tube, have a look)

My five-day double-act with Richard went far too quickly.

****

In November 2001 I was to have one of my biggest "Fail" moments, Paul, Gaz and I flew over to Germany for a week to cover the MTV Music Awards. I met them at Stansted Airport, only to find that I'd picked up my girlfriend's passport instead of my own. Despite my pleading, and despite the check-in operator recognising me off the telly, they refused to let me board. Fair enough, I suppose. Paul and Gaz flew out, and I arranged to fly out the next morning. The editor at the time, Mike Agnew, wasn't happy, but he became even more pissed off when I managed to miss the second flight, too, having spent hours waiting in the wrong queue. Mike even sent a colleague over to the airport to ensure I got it right third time. It badly messed up our filming schedule, though, and that week *Heat* magazine printed a picture of me wearing a dunce's hat.

WHICH TV PRESENTER MISSED TWO FLIGHTS TO GERMANY? Was the accompanying headline. Well you can't get it right every time can you?

The awards ceremony (presented by Ali G, Sacha Baron Cohen's Staines-based alter ego) was amazing, as was the after show party. I remember chatting to a gorgeous brunette at the bar – she had the most amazing eyes - who told me she was a singer from Canada. She'd just had a hit in the UK, she said, so I asked her to sing a verse to me.

'I'm like a bird, I'll only fly away...' she sang, in this beautiful voice. 'I don't know where my soul is, I don't know where my home is...'

'Oh yeah, think I might have heard that,' I lied.

It was only when Rob the cameraman came over that I realised who she was.

'You do know who you're talking to, don't you?' he asked.

'Er, no mate...'

'Nelly Furtado, you dickhead. She's only sold twenty million albums worldwide.'

The next day I was with the crew at the press tent, as was Nelly. When she spotted me she came over.

'Hi Mike, how are you?' she smiled, before giving me a kiss on the cheek.

'Yeah, all good thanks, Nelly,' I replied, as Paul and Gaz stood there, open-mouthed. 'Take care, and nice meeting you.'

To be fair, I hardly ever got star-struck. One morning there was a real buzz around the *Big Breakfast* house because someone called Usher was the star guest.

'Who the hell is Usher?' I asked. Everyone walked away laughing, thinking I was taking the mickey, but I honestly wasn't. Then I was told that this fella – a singer, apparently - was coming in with his mum.

'Has he won a talent show or something?' I remember asking the editor. 'I mean, who brings your mum with you?'

We started the show, and the studio was packed with people you didn't normally see - staff from the offices, and the maintenance guys – who'd all come to have a nosey at Usher the megastar. Even our sixty-something cleaner was there, and I remember thinking *how the hell did she know who he was and I didn't?*

Usher came in – with his mum, who actually turned out to be his manager - and sat on the sofa and shook my hand.

'I've been watching you, you're a funny guy,' he smiled. I didn't know whether to say 'Hi, thank you, I haven't got a clue who you are,' or 'Hi, thank you, I love your music.'

We came out of a break and I linked into the interview by saying, 'Viewers, will you please welcome one of the biggest pop stars of this century... it's only Usher!'

He sat on the sofa, and Amanda and I struck up a conversation. I pointed out that he'd brought his mum with him, and was soon inviting Mrs Usher onto the set and taking the mickey out of her son for being a Mommy's boy, which they loved. He then revealed that she used to be a choir mistress.

'Right, that's it then,' I said, thinking on my feet. 'Mommy Usher can teach our crew a song during the show and we'll come back later to see how they get on.'

Usher's music video at the time featured him sliding sideways into a car, so we rigged up a mock car in the garden so that he could teach me how to do the same. I played the fool by getting stuck, of course.

Mommy Usher was brilliant, and by the end of the show had taught the crew to sing a fantastic song. The whole 'Usher' thing worked so well – it was fabulous television – and I'm convinced this stemmed from the fact that I treated him and his mum like normal human beings. After the show Mommy Usher gave me a big kiss ('that's the most fun I've ever had on a television show,' she said) and Usher thanked me and shook my hand. I've never seen him since; but he remains one of the "stars" that stands out as genuine and lovely to be around.

You'd think that being on TV I'd be clued into to what was happening in celeb world, but I was forever chatting to big stars without realising who they were. Once I flirted with the actress Jennifer Love Hewitt, not having a clue that she was a Hollywood movie star. Another time, I'd taken my dog Ben into work with me (our wardrobe lady, Babette, used to bring her dog in, too, so I thought they could keep each other company). That particular morning, a glamorous blonde woman came out of her dressing room and made a huge fuss of Ben, and we struck up a ten-minute conversation about our love of dogs. She told me that she was on the show – I presumed she was chaperoning one of the guests – and she went on her way.

'Squeaky, what were you chatting to Kim Cattrall about?' said Babette when she came into my dressing room bearing my clean clothes. I didn't watch *Sex In the City* so hadn't realised that I was talking to one of America's most famous actresses. Something similar happened with *Neighbours* actor Ian Smith, who played Harold Bishop. Like with Usher, the studio had been packed with people wanting their photos taken with him. *Why is everyone making a fuss of that balding guy with glasses who I was sat next to in make-up?* I asked myself, none the wiser.

One big star I *did* recognise – who wouldn't? - was Britney Spears, who I interviewed in Chicago, just before Christmas. Paul Moore was our producer, and Paul Connolly had written a very funny interview, so I reckoned it would be a piece of cake (I was also really looking forward to visiting the 'Windy City'; another place to tick off the bucket list). We were told to meet Britney in the penthouse apartment of a five-star hotel. Going in before us were the crew from Channel 5's *Pepsi Chart Show*, who presented her with a special award, basically a block of wood with her name on it.

We were able to watch as the they handed over the award, before Britney expressed a sincere thank you to all her fans. As the Channel 5 guys left, and we took their place, we saw Britney fling the block of wood to one of her 'people', who just casually threw it in a bag.

'Okay, you've got twenty minutes,' said one of her flunkies, talking to us like we were something he'd just trodden in.

'Twenty minutes from when we start filming, right?' I asked.

'No,' he scowled. 'Twenty minutes from now,' he said, at which I lost the plot, and in my best Mancuunian Diva way -

threatened to walk out, telling him that I hadn't flown all this way to get fobbed off by some ignorant PR person.

Paul looked at me as if to say *Mike, what the hell are you doing?* but we'd travelled a long way, and were expecting a decent interview, her PR lacky wasn't getting the better of us. They backed down, and we began filming the interview. At one point, I produced a big poster of Justin Timberlake, who Britney was dating at the time, and started to draw on it with a marker pen.

'Would you still fancy Justin if he had a moustache?' I asked, and – credit to her - she played along.

'I guess the bit with the picture of Justin will be edited out, yes?' asked the PR guy afterwards. 'It was just joke, right?'

'Yeah, of course,' I said, winking at Paul. As if.

I then asked Britney if she could sign a CD cover for my niece Nicole (she was a massive fan and I'd bought her the record for Christmas). She refused point blank, though.

'I'm sorry, Britney doesn't sign anything,' said her irritant of a PR guy.

'Oh, right,' I said. 'That's OK I'll just go back to the UK and tell my seven-year-old niece that you refused to sign a CD. I'm sure it'll make a great story for our tabloids.' She couldn't have signed that CD quick enough.

Moments later her entourage had swept out of the apartment, telling us that we could stay and 'enjoy it' if we liked, as if we were some British bumpkins who hadn't seen such luxury before. Mind you we promptly checked out of our three-star Best Western and moved into the apartment for the night.

We ordered a shit load of room service – steak, lobster, brandy, wine – as well as every film on the movie channel. Naturally we billed everything in the PR guy's name. Again these things may seem petty but you had to experience the attitude of these folk to realise that it was sometimes the only way to let off steam. Besides, no doubt it would have been small change to them.

As Christmas approached, we spent many afternoons pre-recording lots of seasonal items, which always took much longer than our live shows. We'd always film a 'potted Panto', inviting a whole host of guests to play various parts, including S Club 7, Westlife, Boycie and Marlene from *Only Fools and Horses*, Neil and Christine Hamilton (a very odd couple indeed) and actors from *Brookside* and *The Bill*. Amanda, Richard and I would play various roles, too, but it often went pear-shaped. One day Richard and I got the giggles and, no matter how hard we tried, we couldn't stop laughing, both of us blaming each other and incurring the wrath of the production team. The out-takes that we showed on the Big Breakfast were often funnier than the potted Panto (I've still got the footage on old-fashioned video somewhere).

In January 2002 I found myself in New York again, this time to interview Mel Gibson who'd brought out a new film, *We Were Soldiers*. Due to its serious content – it was about a French unit on patrol in 1954, during the first Indochina War - we decided against doing our usual piss-take and instead planned to play it straight. When the PR company introduced me to Mel, he seemed really on edge, sparking up his cigarette with shaky hands.

'Ah, you're the guy they told me to watch out for,' he said. I felt like putting my arm around him and saying 'Don't worry, Mel, we're going to treat you gently...' And we did, chatting about his latest project as well as his *Lethal Weapon* days. I lightened things up towards the end, though.

'So your company made the film, Mel,' I said.

'Correct,'

'And your company paid for me to fly over to New York.'

'That's right.'

'Well I'm a bit disappointed you flew me economy...' I said, which made him laugh. We then wrapped up the interview and posed for photos before shaking hands and wishing each other all the best.

Later that day we headed back to JFK airport.

'Ah, Mr McClean,' said the girl at the Virgin Airlines check-in desk. 'You've been upgraded to First Class courtesy of Icon Entertainment...'

Mel Gibson's production company, had come through. Thanks Mel...

He wasn't the first Aussie movie star I'd met; the previous year I'd come face-to-face with Russell Crowe, who'd been in Germany to promote his acclaimed new film, *A Beautiful Mind*. I'd not long learned that I'd been chosen to cover the Oscars that year, so I was floating on air. My first task was to interview the director of the film, Ron Howard, who many (including me) still remembered as Richie Cunningham in *Happy Days*. For some reason there was only one camera, so Ron shifted to one side of his seat so I could squeeze in next to him. After chatting about *A Beautiful Mind* I asked him if there was any truth in the rumour that he was going to be directing *Fonz: The Movie* and he nearly fell off his seat laughing, especially when I told him I was willing to dye my hair ginger to play the part of Richie.

Our interview with Russell Crowe was a few hours away, so we killed some time by going through the questions (as always I had my two sets; one for me, and one for the benefit of the PR team). I admit to feeling a bit nervous; over the years, the actor had a gained a reputation as being difficult with the media, and, the previous day, he'd not exactly endeared himself to the press pack by cancelling a whole raft of interviews. Some reporters were forced to fly home without any footage, and others had to shell out for an extra night's stay in a hotel.

As we awaited our turn, alongside representatives from the world's leading newspapers and TV channels, Crowe's PR woman came out to announce that she had some bad news. Everybody groaned, expecting the inevitable.

'I'm so sorry, but Russell is cancelling all interviews this afternoon...' she said, scanning the room, 'with one exception.'

Every single reporter held their breath and crossed their fingers, hoping that they'd be The Chosen One.

'Is there a 'Squeaky McClean' in the room? she asked, and I slowly put up my hand. 'Mr Crowe will see you in five minutes,' she smiled.

Everyone looked daggers at me and I was back to being an extra in the Green Room for a moment! *Why him?* they were probably asking, as I waited for a hole in the ground to swallow me up.

'I hear you're a funny fucker,' was Russell's opening gambit when I entered the interview room.

'I hear you're a miserable bastard,' I replied, and from then on it was plain sailing. After we wrapped up, I asked him why he'd cancelled the other interviews.

'I just had had enough of the same boring questions,' he admitted.

'Oh, and by the way,' I added, 'I'm covering the Oscars for the *Big Breakfast* this year, so if you win one, could you do me a massive favour and give me a live interview?' He agreed, shaking my hand.

'And was I funny enough for you today, Mr Crowe?'

'Yeah, very. Now fuck off,' he replied.

One day, Paul announced that him and Gaz were no longer going to produce the *Big Breakfast* OBs. Paul had got another gig, Gaz was moving onto pastures new and they'd be handing over the reins to a new team. I was gutted. No-one wanted a winning team to split up, and no-one in broadcasting knew me better than they did. They'd always called me 'Magic Michael', but I could only produce that magic with them, and I knew that it wasn't going to be the same again.

Softening the blow was the arrival of another producer who 'got' comedy and who was brilliantly creative. Sarah Clarke was lovely – we clicked immediately – and, much to my relief, she knew instinctively what worked when it came to OBs.

One morning, following a show, I got a call asking me to report to the office with my passport. *Brilliant*, I remember thinking. *I must be off to some exotic overseas location.* That wasn't the case, as it happened. Sarah informed me that we were going to a posh charity function that was being attended by His Royal Highness the Prince of Wales, and that I needed my passport for a security and criminal record check (luckily my tyre-stealing incident in 1989 had been overlooked). The event was to be held at a stately home in the middle of Buckinghamshire, and some of the world's biggest 'A'-listers had been invited, like Sir Elton John, Kate Moss, Sting, Rowan Atkinson and Sir David Frost.

As we drove into the grounds, we passed a line of helicopters, with hundreds of Mercedes, Bentleys and Ferraris parked up nearby.

Wow, I thought, *if the lads from Manchester were here now they'd have a field day. Half of these cars would be on the back of a lorry by now...*

As was usually the case at these VIP gatherings, the camera crew and I waylaid a few guests as they walked down the red carpet. Suddenly there was a massive commotion, and Prince Charles himself approached, alongside his wife Camilla. We'd been told beforehand not to speak to the royal couple or ask them any questions, but I didn't do protocol.

'Have a great night, your royal highness,' I yelled as he ambled past.

'You too,' he said, stopping and looking back at me.

Technically the future King of England had spoken to me – the only interviewer to get a sound bite – and we milked it for all it was worth on the following day's *Big Breakfast*.

Following Prince Charles on the red carpet was Sir Elton John.

'*Elton...Elton...Elton...*' shouted the assembled press.

'Fuck off,' came his short-and-sweet reply, which I found highly amusing.

CHAPTER 20

Hollywood Here I come

Reports continued to circulate that Channel 4 were about to kill off the *Big Breakfast*, and were effectively strangling it slowly. There were a few ominous signs; many big-name guests were being invited onto other shows rather than ours, leaving us with *Big Brother* contestants, crappy boy bands and various crackpots who could read the mind of dogs or balance cups on their heads. The powers-that-be also began to censor us; for instance, we'd devised a funny little game whereby a guest would get a short electric shock, yet the next thing we knew we'd received orders from 'on high' to put stop to it.

Every time I went out, I'd be collared by people telling me how shit the show had become, and how they didn't watch it any more. Typically, they'd often lay the blame on me and the other presenters, not realising that it was the Channel 4 head honchos that had the final say on guests and content, not us.

That same spring, my agent Nick rang to ask if I was free to do another panto, namely *Peter Pan* in Richmond with Bonnie Langford and Robert Powell, with a weekly purse of £5,000.

'Get the deal done, Nick,' I said, mindful that I might not even have a job by Christmas.

In December 2001 I was dispatched to cover the British Comedy Awards, something that I'd always hoped I'd attend as a nominee. Ricky Gervais was hot property at that time, having enjoyed massive success with *The Office*, and I was delighted to be granted an interview with him. He took the piss out of me, trying to make out that I was being rude to his wheelchair-bound producer, Ash Atalla, but I gave as good as I got.

'Shut it, Gervais,' I said, 'I'm done with you,' which made him laugh.

I got to meet a whole host of my comedy heroes that night, including Graham Norton (without doubt the best television talk show host around), Ronnie Corbett and Ronnie Barker (both comedy heroes of mine) as well as Harry Enfield with his mucker Paul Whitehouse. A truly memorable evening and as an extra bonus no hero bubbles burst!

A few days' later, Elsa the producer dispatched me to Soho for a preview screening of a film *Ocean's Eleven,* starring Brad Pitt, George Clooney, Andy Garcia, Matt Damon and my favourite American comedian, Bernie Mac. I loved the film, and the following weekend Elsa and I were invited to interview some of the cast. First up was Andy Garcia, who didn't exude much warmth and mumbled so quietly I thought he was on mute. In contrast, Matt Damon was friendly, funny and played along with all my gags. The director, Steven Soderbergh was another cool guy, relating some great anecdotes about the cast and the film-making process.

After a lunch break, it was time to meet the main men, Pitt and Clooney. For a laugh I'd attached each of Pitt's questions to a different pair of knickers – a thong from my mate, some belly-warmers from my Nan - but the movie's PR people weren't having any of it.

'We're not letting you in if that's the road you're going down,' they said, which really pissed me off, but I still managed to smuggle in the big baggy pants, with Paul Connolly's 'Ask for forgiveness, never permission,' mantra in my head. I began the interview by pulling his leg about his girlfriend Jennifer Aniston, trying to make out that I once dated her ('Yeah sure, that's all water under the bridge,' he grinned, playing along brilliantly). We then chatted about *Ocean's Eleven* before I finished in style by pulling out Nan's big knickers.

'My nana asked me to say hello, and says she'll never forget that night you had together,' I grinned, handing over the belly-warmers.

'Tell your nan I will never forget that night either,' he replied, 'and I'll always keep these close at hand.' He honestly couldn't have been nicer. What a top guy.

George Clooney was just as amiable. While I didn't have any knickers for him I still managed to make him laugh with a few cheeky asides, which chuffed me to bits. Needless to say the PR woman wasn't happy with my knickers ruse; not one little bit.

'I'll be making a complaint to your boss,' she hissed.

'Sure, no worries,' I replied. 'The show's on its last legs so I'm pretty sure he won't give a shit.'

Why do PR folk insist on treating their 'stars' like precious snowflakes? In my experience, they're so bored with the standard questions that they'll cheerfully do anything to relieve the boredom.

****

In March 2002, I flew out to Los Angeles for the Oscars. I remember sitting on the plane and having to pinch myself. Here I was, Mike McClean from Manchester, jetting off to cover the biggest showbiz event in the world.

Eleven hours later I landed in Los Angeles and checked into The Standard hotel. It's probably the most recognisable hotel in LA – it's used as a location in many movies – and even as I walked in there was some filming going on. A guy was standing in the lobby holding a gun, and when he fired it I nearly cacked myself, dropping my bags and running for cover until the shout of '...and *CUT*!' made me realise that I'd unwittingly wandered onto the set of some cop show. I got to my room and had a quick nap, before meeting up with Sarah over dinner, where we discussed the plans for filming. Drew Barrymore was in the hotel bar and, like with my mate Madonna, we had a really animated conversation.

'Is that seat free?' she'd drawled.

'Yeah, go for it,' I'd replied.

The first item that Sarah, Sean and I filmed in LA was called *Botox and Bagels*, which followed some individuals as they had various surgical procedures at a clinic in Beverly Hills A female prison officer came all the way from San Francisco to have some Botox during her lunch hour, before going straight back to work. Another woman arrived to have a boob job in the morning, and was picked up by her son in the afternoon, which I found a bit weird.

We also chatted to one guy, who worked as a personal assistant to a major movie star. Part of his job was testing out surgical procedures on his boss' behalf, to check that that they were safe and successful. He'd already undergone Botox, and had reported back to the A-lister as requested.

'He's told me he wants a penis enlargement next,' shrugged this guy, 'but I don't fancy being a guinea pig for that...'

Sarah and I tried to get him to reveal the identity of the famous actor, but to no avail.

The day after, we went to meet a man who'd written a book about things you could do with everyday objects. Peanut butter, according to him, could be used as a substitute for shaving foam, furniture polish and chewing gum remover (they all work, by the way; I tried). He told us how he cleaned his toilet with Coca-Cola, and how he used Pepto-Bismol as a face mask.

Sarah suggested that I go and try the latter, so I smeared a load of the stomach-ache reliever onto my face, waited for five minutes and tried to rinse it off. But would it shift? Would it hell. This pink gunk remained attached to my face for ages, much to the crew's amusement. It was one of those awful moments when you think the worst is going to happen and for me it would have been filming the Oscars covered in Pepto-Bismol.

The *Big Breakfast* happened to have an office in Hollywood which was used by a producer, Debbie, as a base to edit and send various interviews back to our London HQ. Since the show was finishing, this very well-connected producer decided to throw a party for all her celeb mates, and asked us to come along too. Located nearby were the New Line Cinema studios; at the time they were filming the third *Austin Powers* movie and, before the party started, I couldn't help but sneak in and have a nosy at the set. I was about to take some photos when a security guy came over to ask what I was doing.

'I'm a friend of Mike Myers,' I said, but he never believed me for one minute and quickly escorted me off the set.

I headed over to the party and, as I did so, I saw a guy whose face I recognised but whose name I couldn't remember. Suddenly I realised who it was; none other than Alan Dale, a.k.a. Jim Robinson from *Neighbours* and, latterly, John Ellis in *Entourage*. I got chatting to him – what a lovely guy he was – and asked him why he'd decided to leave a popular show like *Neighbours* and head to a country where it was notoriously hard to find work. He told me he'd simply had enough of the Aussie soap, and felt it was a case of 'it's now or never'.

'You should do the same yourself,' he said, when I told him about the *Big Breakfast* scenario. 'It wouldn't take you long before you cracked it.'

I had to laugh, telling him that it had been hard enough to make it in the UK, let alone the States.

Now I do have the odd "What if?" moments but I'm pretty sure I made the right decision.

****

We spent an afternoon filming with Chris Evans, since we were keen to interview all the past *Big Breakfast* presenters for the last ever show. Chris, along with his wife Billie Piper, had bought a mansion in the Hollywood hills. Theirs wasn't any old house, though; it turned out that it had once been owned by Lionel Richie, and that Chris had apparently outbid Courtney Cox and her husband when it came on the market. He had illustrious neighbours, too, with Leonardo DiCaprio on one side and *Friends* creator Dave Crane on the other.

Chris showed me around the house, which was absolutely unbelievable. The view across Hollywood was amazing, and it was totally surreal to sit in the same living room where a music legend had written one his most famous hits, *Dancing on the Ceiling*.

As the crew were setting up, Chris and I had a really good chat. I was gobsmacked to discover that he knew all about my career – he reminded me that his wife Billie had appeared with me on Nickelodeon and *Mad For It* - and said he'd loved what I'd done with the *Big Breakfast*. Can you imagine what it was like to be told this by a broadcasting legend? It honestly made me feel ten feet tall.

He continued to regale me with stories about his own days on the programme – I honestly could have listened to him for hours – but he did recognise that the time was right for it the *Big Breakfast* to end. He was sorry that was the case, though, and reckoned Channel 4 would come to regret it.

We'd worked really hard in LA – we'd condensed so much into a few days – but on the plus side, this meant that we had three days to ourselves to do what we wanted. Sarah and I had a day at Universal Studios, which was just unbelievable. I think my favourite part of the day was seeing a car lot filled with famous vehicles like the *The 'A' Team* van, the *Back To the Future* DeLorean car and KITT, David Hasselhoff's motor in *Knight Rider*.

That night we attended the premiere of Wesley Snipes' new film, *Blade II*, at the Kodak Cinema on Hollywood Boulevard, the same venue as the Oscars. When I arrived, Sean was deep in conversation with one of the movie's stars, former Bros drummer Luke Goss, who had seemingly given up on the music industry and was trying his hand at acting. My first impressions of him weren't great; he clearly didn't want to chat to me and gave out one of those limp handshakes, which is always a bad sign in my book. When I mentioned I was a presenter on the *Big Breakfast* his attitude suddenly changed, though, but by then it was too late, and I made my excuses and left.

I got myself a drink and just stood at the window, staring out towards Hollywood, recalling how jealous I'd felt the previous year when Melanie Sykes had got this gig. As I was admiring the view, a guy came over.

'Isn't it amazing?' he said, and we got chatting. It turned out that he was an up-and-coming actor who'd just bagged himself a role on a TV show.

'I'm not sure if it's going to take off, though,' I remember him saying, adding that the show was called *CSI Las Vegas* and that it was going to be broadcast on Channel 5 in the UK.

'Best of luck,' I said, not realising that the person I was chatting to was the brilliant Gary Dourdan, who would go on to achieve great success in his role as Warrick Brown.

Since Wesley Snipes was due to fly over to London for the UK premiere (and be interviewed on the *Big Breakfast*) I was taken over to be introduced to him. He seemed nice enough, and I had my photo taken with him and said I'd look forward to seeing him on the show. As I was chatting with him, he beckoned over one of his minders, handed him a ticket for his private after-show party and sent him in the direction of a gorgeous-looking dark-haired woman.

'Can I have one of those, Wesley?' I asked (I wasn't one to miss a chance).

'You can if you look like her,' was his response.

Then Sarah and I found a quiet corner where we could do our live phone call to the *Big Breakfast* (the time difference meant that the show was on at the same time as the party).

'Hey, Mike, how's it going?' asked Richard from the house.

'Well Richard, you won't believe this, but I'm at the premiere party for *Blade II* and I've just tried to blag a ticket to Wesley Snipes' private party,' I said, hearing the whoops coming from the studio.

'But I wasn't as hot as the woman he's just invited so I don't think I had a chance,' I added.

'Keep up the good work, Mike,' said Richard.

The next day we went to Venice Beach, which was full of oddballs. I remember taking a photo of a dog wearing sunglasses, and as I did so its owner demanded that I pay her $20 for the picture.

'As if,' I said, thinking she was joking.

'If you don't delete it, I'll call the police,' she yelled.

I knew that everyone in LA was super-savvy about filming and image rights, but this was ridiculous.

It was probably a super famous dog but as I didn't reconise a lot of human celebs this dog didn't stand a chance.

****

The Oscars' day buzz was amazing, not just regarding the ceremony itself but the after-parties too, the most prestigious of which were hosted by Sir Elton John and *Vanity Fair* magazine. I was due to film from the latter. I felt as nervous as hell as I ate my breakfast; I knew that the production team were expecting good things from me and the LA team plus, since it was to be our final live Oscars report, I wanted it to be memorable. We headed to the Vanity Fair venue at about 6 p.m. and immediately noticed hundreds of outside broadcast trucks lining the whole street, for miles and miles. Ours, luckily, was right parked right near to the venue, next to the biggest Winnebago I'd ever seen in my life.

'Who the hell is that for?' I asked Sarah.

'It's for us, Mike,' she replied.

I couldn't believe it. This thing was as big as a family home, with eight bedrooms, two bathrooms, a kitchen, and a TV room. And not to mention the swimming pool with diving boards (okay, a lied about the last bit). Inside we were greeted by two assistants - my make-up artist and my dresser – who had worked on numerous films including *Rocky*, *Die Hard* and *Beverley Hills Cop* (as well as all their sequels). It turned out that the Winnebago belonged to them – hence all the photos of stars tacked to the walls – and they went on to dish out some scurrilous gossip about the actors they'd worked with, none of which I could repeat in public. I know, I know! But having told you so much already though I need to keep the lawyers at bay as it is!

Sarah, Sean and I went outside to film some links. During the Oscars it was the norm for presenters to wear a tuxedo but I wasn't the norm. Instead, I teamed my shirt, jacket and bow tie with a pair of Northern Ireland football shorts (given to me by my mate Kevin Horlock) and some trainers. People stopped and stared as we filmed the links, probably wondering who the hell this crazy English guy wearing a daft outfit was.

The hours passed, and soon it was time for the ceremony itself, which we watched from the Winnebago. Our assistants were texting various actors as they won or lost – I couldn't believe how well-connected they were – and Sarah, Sean and I kept tabs on which big names had bagged the Oscar statues.

At about 11 p.m. I headed to my tiny little reporting spot outside the *Vanity Fair* party, right next to our rival crew from *GMTV*.

'Are you okay, Mike?' asked our editor Ben as I inserted my earpiece.

'Yeah, I'm good,' I said, but deep down my nerves were kicking in. I didn't usually get jittery, but the importance of this occasion had got under my skin. I then heard the *Big Breakfast* opening title sequence, before Richard kicked off the show.

'...and live in LA, at the biggest party of the year, is our very own Mike Squeaky McClean,' he said, at which I waved and exchanged a few words. The plan was, if I grabbed a great star guest, we'd either pre-record it or Richard would throw live to me.

Our first interviewee was *The Hours* actress Julianne Moore, who I chatted with politely for a minute or two before handing back to the house.

'Mike, are you okay?' asked Ben. 'You don't seem your usual self. You're being too nice. It's not the Squeaky we know and love. Relax and play with them like you usually do.'

He was bang on the money. He'd sensed I was nervous and knew that I needed a little pep talk. That's the sign of a great producer; someone who doesn't scream or shout, but who instead puts a metaphorical arm around you and gives you that little boost.

Soon enough, I saw Samuel L Jackson approaching.

'Samuel! Samuel! Samuel' I shouted, and he came over.

'Squeaky McClean from the *Big Breakfast*,' I panted, shoving the microphone in his face.

'I know that show,' he said. 'It's not been the same since your man Johnny left,' he said, which was a bit mean of him, considering I'd not brought up some of the shit films he'd starred in.

'Never mind that,' I continued, 'what are you doing here, because you've not been nominated for anything...?'

'I came here because you kept shouting Samuel. I came here because I didn't want you in my ass anymore,' he grinned.

'Well, thank you firstly for letting me into your ass, and secondly, seriously what *are* you doing here?' I said, before yelling for security to deal with the intruder on the premises. I was up and running, and soon Ben was in my ear again.

'That's more like it, Mike. Go for it.'

I did just that. I ripped into everyone I met, while doing my utmost to remain as polite as I could. Paul McCartney and his then wife, Heather Mills, came over and I remember mentioning to Paul that Sharon Stone was looking forward to meeting him, before suggesting that he should get rid of his missus for five minutes and get together with Sharon.

'Have you seen *Basic Instinct*? I quipped, winking at him.

Sharon Stone herself came over, too, and I asked her to confirm if the rumours were true that they were making a sequel and, if so, would she consider wearing knickers when she re-enacted that famous scene? The house roared with laughter but she just gave me an icy smile and moved on.

The legendary Sidney Poitier had won an award and, much to my delight, sidled over for a chat. I didn't have the heart to be cheeky with Hollywood royalty, however, so I just asked if I could hold his award.

'Come on Sidney, I'm not going to nick it,' I said, 'those days are over.'

He let me hold it, but he grabbed the base, firmly.

It had taken me a while, but I'd finally got into my stride and actually started to enjoy the filming, especially since all the big names were stopping to say hello. Up next was Puff Daddy, or should I say Sean Combes, since he'd put his old name to rest, apparently. Not as far as I was concerned, though.

'Mike, who's with you right now?' asked Richard from the House.

'Well, Richard it's none other than the master of pop, Puff Daddy,' I grinned, noting that he was sporting a pair of huge earrings.

'Puff, thanks so much for being live on the *Big Breakfast*,' I said, 'but could I ask if your earrings are from Argos or Ratners?

'No, man,' he said, name-checking some top jewellery designer as the joke whooshed over his head.

'And what about the name change?' I asked. 'Puff Daddy was way cooler than Sean Combes. Which idiot came up with *that* name?'

'No, man... that *is* my name,' he said, deadpan.

Then it was time to reacquaint myself with Russell Crowe, who played an absolute blinder for me, despite missing out on an Oscar for *A Beautiful Mind*. I'd quickly prepped him off-camera, asking him to come over and say 'Hi Mike,' at which I'd just blank him. An old gag, but a funny one.

'Hey Mike,' he smiled, as the cameras began to roll. 'How are you?'

'Russell, can't you see I'm working, mate?' I replied with mock exasperation, shooing him away with my hand and looking over his shoulder for other stars.

'But you said if I won that Oscar that I should come and see you,' he said, forlornly.

'Yeah but you never won the Oscar did you?' I said, gesturing for him to move along. He nodded sadly, before walking off with his tail between his legs.

Squeaky McClean telling Russell Crowe to sod off was the gag of the day and, as we went into a break, I ran after him to shake his hand and thank him.

'No worries, all the best,' he said, with his best *Okay, now piss off* look.

The two-hour show flew by and soon enough we were saying goodbye and handing back to the house. There were still loads of celebrities coming into the *Vanity Fair* party, so we hung around for another hour or so to do more interviews and film our closing links.

We returned to the truck, where the make-up girls told us we'd been on American TV. As we reflected on the ceremony, none other than Chris Tucker of *Rush Hour* fame popped by to say hello to the ladies, as he'd once worked with them. He sat and had a drink with us – he turned down our invitation for an interview, sadly – and we chatted about how he loved doing stand-up, and how he hated travelling (I couldn't disagree). He was incredibly down-to-earth, so much so that he hadn't bothered with the *Vanity Fair* after-show and was going to a friend's house party instead.

My crew and I headed back to our hotel for a celebratory drink. As we clinked our wine glasses, Sarah announced that the Channel 4 big cheeses had been delighted with our Oscars coverage, saying it was one of the best they'd ever watched.

'A job well done, Mike,' she said.

I felt a real sense of achievement coupled with sadness. I wish I'd been able to do more Oscars, but maybe knowing it was to be the last for *Big Breakfast* meant I'd really given it my all.

CHAPTER 21

R.I.P. Big Breakfast

Not long after my return to London, the news broke that the *Big Breakfast* would be officially taken off air on March 23rd, only a matter of weeks away. While it wasn't a huge shock, it caused much sadness among all the people who'd worked on the show over the years. My two-year stint had been a wonderful, once-in-a-lifetime experience, and I can safely say that – although some days had been better than others - I'd never been bored once. I'd also I made some great friends along the way, and I had learned so much about broadcasting. We were like one big family in the *Big Breakfast* house, and I knew I'd miss it terribly.

One positive development over the past few months was the arrival of Lisa Rogers, though, who'd been brought in as an additional presenter. We got on so well that many people speculated that we were romantically involved, although that wasn't the case (she was actually dating *Royle Family* actor Ralf Little). If I'm honest, I did fancy her a little bit, though. She was so funny and down to earth - like me, she had no massive desire to be famous and saw presenting as just a job – and there was never any clash of egos.

My last few weeks on the show were mainly spent presenting items from the house, although I did have to do an OB in Southampton about keeping fit. As per normal we descended on a rough estate the night before to have a look at the street we were due to film on. Our task was to get the people of Britain back in shape, with the help of some guys from a nearby army boot camp.

The next morning, I did my normal knocking on doors, but on this occasion I wasn't accepting no for an answer; I wanted everyone out. One door was answered by a youngish woman.

'Hi, it's Mike McClean from the *Big Breakfast*, you're live on Channel 4, so please don't swear,' I said, barging into her house.

'Do you like to keep fit?' I demanded as the film crew followed me in.

'Er yeah, sort of,' she said, looking a bit flustered.

'Well, it's all about what you eat, so let's have a look in your fridge,' I said, as she hesitantly allowed me to tramp through her lounge and into her kitchen. It wasn't the nicest gaff in the world – it stank of allsorts – and we passed two kids eating chocolate biscuits in front of a huge telly and another taking a dump on his potty.

As I neared her fridge this woman started to give me daggers, while frantically gesturing me away from it. *She's probably worried because she's got loads of junk food in there,* I thought, but I nonetheless grabbed the handle and flung open the fridge door, only to be confronted with the biggest block of cannabis I'd ever seen. *Shit.* I quickly shut the fridge before the cameraman got near it, and linked immediately to a commercial break.

'Mike, we need to see what's in the fridge,' said the director down my earpiece.

'Mate, we'd be raided by the drugs' squad if we did,' came my reply.

A few weeks before the last show, I met with Ben Rigden to discuss the very final live OB. His idea was to winch the huge, iconic *Big Breakfast* gnome from the house, lower it onto a truck and personally deliver it to Channel 4 headquarters. The twist in the tail was that the gnome would be fitted with a new hand, which would be doing the V-sign.

'I totally understand if you don't want to do it, though, Mike,' he said, 'but have a think about it...'

At first I wasn't sure that it was a good idea, especially if I wanted to carry on working for the channel. However, the more thought I gave it, the more I thought *Sod it, I'm going for it.*

The last show was to be a three-hour special, featuring a plethora of celebrity guests and former presenters. The script meeting that morning was really subdued; everyone just sat around the table with glum expressions, hardly saying a word as Ben ran through the show. Usually, any spare scripts would just be binned by the cleaners, but that day they were all snapped up as treasured mementoes. People had even applied for tickets to be in the audience that morning, which meant that almost five hundred people were in the garden.

Hearing the continuity announcer saying '...and now, on Channel 4, the very last ever *Big Breakfast*...' was so weird, followed by the final airing of those famous opening titles. Richard kicked off proceedings, with Amanda as his co-presenter, and a few minutes' later they linked to me as I sat with Zig and Zag. I then left the studio, clambering into a car and heading to the Channel 4 offices to prepare for our crazy gnome stunt.

I was a little nervous, I admit, because I'd been told by Chris Heath, who was producing this OB, that all channel's head honchos were at the HQ that morning, including Sharon Power, who'd been responsible for axing the show. It was definitely going to ruffle a few feathers.

'Mike can you tell us where you are?' asked Richard when I finally reached my destination.

'No, not yet... all I can tell you is that I'm at a secret central London location. All will be revealed later in the show...'

The programme continued, featuring lots of nostalgic footage and blasts from the past, and soon it was time for the unveiling of the big gnome. Chris got us into position for the last ever link, and Richard asked me to reveal all.

'Well, Richard, I'm at the head offices of Channel 4 to drop off a very special present to the powers-that-be,' I said, at which the *Big Breakfast* gnome, with his brazen two-fingered salute, was wheeled in front of the cameras. Through my earpiece, I heard a huge cheer rising up from the house. I then jumped back into the car, and raced back to the house for the show's finale. It was heartbreaking - Lisa Rogers was in tears, bless her – and I felt genuinely gutted that it had all come to a premature end. (google it, it's very funny)

Following the closing titles, all the crew had breakfast together, before having group photos and meeting and greeting the hundreds of fans who'd come over to watch the show. Once all the punters had left, we held a staff auction where we could bid for all manner of *Big Breakfast* memorabilia including props, cue cards, furniture and costumes. Richard bid for the cue card with the address on it, and I bid for the cue card with the phone number on it.

However, the two things that everyone coveted – the iconic *Big Breakfast* chairs - were nowhere to be seen. Ex-presenter Johnny Vaughan wanted them, Amanda Byram wanted them, our editor Ed Forsdick wanted them, even our cleaner wanted them. But they'd vanished, apparently, and Ed was going crazy.

'Where are those fucking chairs?' he shouted at various runners, asking them to find them, and find them quick.

What Ed didn't know was that there was only ever going to be one person who got those chairs. I'd arranged with our chef, Abdul, to shove them into his van straight after the show ('Not a word, Abdul, not a word,' I'd said) before getting him to deliver them to my house. As the frantic search continued I just looked on and smiled, knowing that I'd be cosying up on them that very same evening.

Sorry guys, but at least now you know where they went!

****

The new incarnation of the breakfast show was to be called *RI:SE*. Many people asked me if I'd be working on it, but the answer was no. Even if they'd offered me a position I'd have declined; it would have been like playing for Manchester City and then defecting to Manchester United. Not a chance.

Like a lot of people, I was keen to see what this new-look programme was going to be like. It pained me to admit it, and I tried to keep a professional perspective on things, but it was a pile of shit. In reality, the production team was on a hiding to nothing, because the *Big Breakfast* was incomparable, for three reasons. Firstly, it had the best opening titles ever. Secondly, it had the best production team ever. And finally, it had the best set and location ever.

RI:SE was a diluted version of our show, and was rightly slated by most of the newspapers, including the *Guardian* which generally had its finger on the broadcasting pulse. By its second week, viewers had switched over to *GMTV* in their droves. By its third week, there were more people living on my street than *RI:SE* viewers. Unsurprisingly, it only lasted a year.

Even now, I can't explain why Channel 4 got rid of the *Big Breakfast*. Yes, it probably needed a bit of a re-haul – like many long-running shows - but if I'd have been in charge I'd have given it a summer break, and in the meantime freshened it up with some fresh new ideas. When it came down to it, though, it was a show that cheered up millions of people in the morning, sending them off to work feeling happy and up beat, and giving them something to chat about with their colleagues in the office.

In an increasingly troubled world, and during these times of austerity – I believe we need entertaining, light-hearted shows like the *Big Breakfast* more than ever before. I'd personally love to see it return to our screens, and I remain convinced there's still an audience for it. Would I jump at the chance to present it again? Damn right I would.

****

I was in desperate need of a holiday after all the *Big Breakfast* shenanigans, so Les and I jetted off to Ibiza for a chill-out
week of fun and laughter. While I was abroad I had people
constantly coming up to me to ask why the show had ended,
and what my next job would be. As for my immediate future,
I honestly I had no idea what was around the corner. In the
first instance, I just wanted to get some sunshine and let my
(thinning) hair down. I certainly did that with Les.

When I returned to the UK, and having looked after my
earnings over the years, I decided to pay off my parents' mortgage. It was the least I could do. I'd always been a saver, knowing full well that this ride in TV-land wasn't going to last for
ever, so I had squirrelled away enough money to pay for my
house and my car, as well as a little place in Spain. Being careful with my cash, and being resolutely debt-free, was something I inherited from my mum, I suppose. When I was a kid,
I distinctly remember her trying on a lovely pair of shoes, before deciding against buying them because she didn't have the
money, also because she didn't pay for things on the 'never-
never.'

Being newly unemployed, it was time for me to touch base
with my agent. I remember ringing Nick to ask him if there
was any work lined up for me, and being disappointed to hear
that there wasn't. I did get a phone call from a previous agent,
though - Jackie from my Nickelodeon days – who was now
working at ITV.

'We're doing this new show, Mike,' she said. 'Ant and Dec
are presenting it. We're sending a load of celebrities out to
Australia to live in the jungle for a few weeks. You'd get a
£11,000 fee if you were up for it.'

I was seriously considering doing *I'm A Celebrity, Get Me Out Of Here* until my old producer from the *Big Breakfast*, Elsa Sharp rang me up. She informed me that a new channel was being launched - BBC Three - that was planning to promote up-and-coming comedy talent, and that was right up my street. She was producing a new eleven-week series called *CCTV*, a hidden-camera game show, and she thought I'd be perfect as the lead presenter. I weighed it all up and thought I'd give it a go.

The premise was to rock up at various towns around the country and encourage punters to take part in various challenges, with the opportunity to win a holiday. I'd be in a van instructing them what to do - I could see them, but they couldn't see me — and I was given a free rein to be funny.

Guy Templeton was our director; he had a great knack of ensuring that everyone worked hard and played hard, and we certainly did. I really hit it off with one of the producers, Sarah Church; our great friendship remained intact even when I got pissed one night and puked all over her, something that she never let me forget. Sorry, Churchie.

CCTV attracted good viewing figures for BBC Three, but not enough to warrant another series (the fact it went way over budget probably didn't help matters, either). I found myself out of work again but, now that I was classed as a 'celebrity' I started to be offered reality shows about cars, cooking, DIY, you name it. I accepted most of them. Work was work, and I had bills to pay.

It was fast approaching panto time, yet I wasn't really looking forward to doing *Peter Pan* in Richmond. I'd heard that

Bonnie Langford wasn't the easiest person to work with, although I was very much looking forward to meeting Robert Powell, as I was a big fan of *The Detectives*, the BBC2 comedy series starring him and Jasper Carrott.

As it happened, I learned a lot from Bonnie; she was such a great pro and had an incredible work ethic. Robert, on the other hand, was a bit aloof and, no matter how hard I tried to make conversation, he wasn't having any of it. *Fine, be like that*, I remember thinking.

One night I was doing a little on-stage routine with some kids when I asked one of them what his dad did.

'My daddy died,' said this little lad, and the whole theatre suddenly went quiet. I felt hundreds of eyes on me, with both audience and cast alike probably thinking *how the hell is he going to get out of this one?* Luckily I was on my toes that night.

'My daddy's not with me, either,' I said, 'and I reckon yours is now in an amazing place.'

'D'you mean heaven?' he replied, all wide-eyed.

'That's right,' I continued. 'And when you go to heaven you get wings and every time you're good for your mummy, your daddy gets another feather and he becomes the biggest and best angel.'

'Okay...' smiled the little boy.

'I know our daddies aren't here right now,' I continued, 'but they're always around us, and every day we can speak to them so they can hear us. And I know that your daddy will want you to be good for Mummy and, when you get older, to look after Mummy'.

I looked out into the audience and could see the adults wiping their tears away. I ensured that the little kid got the biggest goody bag ever and, as he left the stage, he received a huge round of applause.

After the show, as the crew wound down, we chatted about what a potentially distressing situation that could have been, the company manager came over and told me that the boy's mother was waiting to see me at the stage door. I told him to send her up to my dressing room. She gave me the biggest hug ever and explained that the panto had come as a welcome treat for her son, his dad had died only a few months previously, she said it was the first time she'd seen him laugh for ages. I gave them a tour of the theatre, got their programme signed and wished them all the best.

'Thank you so much,' said the woman as she bid farewell, 'and can I just say how sorry I am to hear about your dad, too.'

'That's heartbreaking, Mike,' said Bonnie Langford after the woman had left the theatre. 'When did your dad pass away?'

'He's not dead,' I said, explaining how I'd thought it wise to tell a little white lie in such difficult circumstances.

'My Dad's not with me - he's at home with my mum – but I just thought it was the right thing to say to make that little boy feel better.'

Bonnie agreed. That night I rang my dad in Manchester, just so I could hear his voice. We often take for granted that our parents will always be with us and this night was a reminder to me that all too soon they can be gone.

CHAPTER 22

Richard & Judy

Towards the end of April, my old *Big Breakfast* colleague Gaz got in touch. He was now working on the live outside broadcasts on the *Richard & Judy* show – he was doing really well, by all accounts - and wondered if I was free to cover a massive sci-fi convention in Blackpool. The usual OB presenter, Richard Blackwood, wasn't available and they needed a temporary replacement. I was made up that Gaz had thought of me because, if I'm honest, I'd missed the banter that we'd shared on the *Big Breakfast*. So I headed over to Blackpool straight away.

The commissioning editor of Channel 4 was going to be watching from the studio – as were Richard Madeley and Judy Finnigan - so Gaz wanted this film to be a good one.

'Hi, Mike. I remember when you presented us with a cake when we did our last *This Morning* show,' said Richard through the earpiece as I got prepared in Blackpool.

The OB was a great success; the big boss from Channel 4 liked me, as did Richard and Judy, who at that time were regarded as the King and Queen of British television. The only person who didn't rave about me was Simon Ross, the boss of the production company Cactus (and the brother of Jonathan and Paul). He didn't give me a thumbs up, but there again he didn't give me a thumbs down, either.

Gaz told me that he was going to try and get me a regular presenting gig, and asked me to come over to the studio to plan a forthcoming OB and meet the Cactus team. Simon

Ross and his lovely wife Amanda were the big bosses, Gillian DeBuitleir was the editor, and the rest of the Cactus team seemed to comprise of many of the ex-*Big Breakfast* staffers. I chatted with Richard and Judy, too; Richard asked me if I was going to do any more on the show, and I told him that I was discussing a feature idea with Gaz and Simon.

'I'm sure you'll be fine,' he said with a wink.

We filmed the OB, a light-hearted piece that focused on various towns and the famous people that had been born there. We went to Stoke, which was the birthplace of TV legend Frank Bough and presenter Anthea Turner. It got a good response when it was broadcast; Richard and Judy told me that they'd loved the way I interacted with the great British public (Judy even gave me a kiss and said 'keep up the good work') and Ben Adler, the commissioning editor of the show, was also a fan. Simon's response was yet again on the lukewarm side – he didn't think we should do any more – but in the end we filmed five more, which were even funnier.

Eventually I got the nod of approval from Simon, which meant that all the other *Richard & Judy* producers could now use me to film various reports for them. Some weeks I'd film up to five features, and my TV profile began to rise again. I got invited onto *Big Brother's Big Mouth*, hosted by Russell Brand, who welcomed me to the show as 'Richard and Judy's bitch'.

The OB team was a nucleus of really decent, funny guys, including Uncle Rod the cameraman, Sauce the sound man, another sound man called Serial Killer and cameraman John Ryan. Every runner that joined our crew was put through a test to ensure they could handle us. Gaz would tell them that

I was very religious, and that, each day at 11.30 a.m., I'd always like to stop work and say my prayers in the OB car. It was one of our favourite wind-ups.

'It's time to pray, Mike,' Gaz would say, handing me a bible. I'd then start to recite a prayer, instructing the crew - including the bemused runner - to kneel with me. We'd keep up the pretence for about two minutes until one of us inevitably burst out laughing, and the runner realised we were pulling their leg.

We played hard, but we worked hard too. Most days we'd meet at the office at 5.30 a.m. before filming on location until 7 p.m. My reports began to flow thick and fast and I was soon regarded as an integral member of the *Richard & Judy* family. I loved spending time in the office, and would sit with Richard and his PA, Naomi, just having a chat and a laugh. I got to know Richard pretty well, to the point that I could wind him up a little. I'd often pop in to Judy's dressing room just to say hello, and she'd always welcome me with a kiss. The Cactus environment had a great vibe about it, not dissimilar to the *Big Breakfast*; everyone got on well and we'd socialise out of work too, especially on a Friday. Amanda Ross would always invite me for a drink in the green room, where I'd meet our VIP guests and various movers and shakers from Channel 4.

Gaz and I would constantly bounce ideas off each other; we'd often have arguments in the process, but it was all constructive debate and all for the good of the show.

'You're like an old married couple,' crew members would tell us, which wasn't far from the truth.

The series ended in July 2002, and we had a big wrap party.

'Hope you'll be back with us in September,' said Richard. 'That's if you want to come back...'

'If you'll have me, yes,' I said,

I had saved a lot of money whilst working on the show and decided I wanted to buy a flat in Spain. I bought one in Torrevieja as it was on the Costa Blanca and the weather as always hot. In hindsight I wish I'd bought one near La Coruna so that I could have seen more of my extended family but unfortunately it's not the best for weather. One of the other reasns to buy it was so that mum and dad could pack up in Manchester and go spend 4 months there which they always did.

That August I had a complete break there and spent the whole month. Gaz came over for a week, too, which was great.

****

I was getting more and more pissed off with my agent, Nick. He wasn't finding much work for me, yet I was having to pay him monthly commission from my *Richard & Judy* gig. I had a meeting with ITV about doing *Dancing On Ice*, but that was scuppered when they found out I'd had an operation on my cruciate ligament, and thus wouldn't get insurance. It was a real shame; I'd have loved to learn how to skate and I think I'd have looked fabulous in Lycra.

That autumn I told Gaz that I wouldn't be able to do any reports over Christmas as I was doing panto in Shrewsbury. He then came up with the idea of making a fly-on-the-wall documentary out of it - the making of a panto – which Simon loved. The panto producer John Spillers was delighted, too, since it meant free publicity for him and the theatre.

As soon as rehearsals started, we began filming. The reports went out on Channel 4 every night, with Richard and Judy promising that they'd attend the opening night. This prompted a massive rush for tickets, and the entire 450-seater theatre was booked by people wanting to see the panto and catch a glimpse of the famous couple.

In the end, however, they couldn't make it, and the theatre manager wasn't at all impressed.

'Good luck when you mention it to the audience,' she said. 'You probably won't get out alive...'

Before the curtain went down I apologised on Richard and Judy's behalf, and the audience went mad, booing and hissing. In fact, they were so cross that I had to ask Richard to issue a personal apology the following Monday, which he did.

Once panto had finished, I found myself starring in one of the most successful television shows on BBC; *The Office Christmas Special*. I'd had a call from Nick, telling me that Ricky Gervais' people had been on the phone, and that they wanted me to play the part of a nightclub host, presenting a *Blind Date*-style segment. I'd never got around to watching *The Office* (I tended to prefer news and football on telly) but I'd heard it was brilliant. I met with the director, Stephen Merchant at the BBC in Shepherd's Bush, and read for the part. I then met with both Stephen and Ricky; I'd met the latter before at the British Comedy Awards – and he often appeared on *Richard & Judy* – and I was looking forward to seeing him again.

I can safely say that Ricky Gervais is one of the nicest guys I have ever worked with. Being such a massive star you'd think he'd possess a huge ego, but he struck me as so honest and down-to-earth.

'Feel free to ad-lib,' he smiled as I read through the part again. Whenever I said something funny he'd shriek with laughter, in that inimitable way of his. In fact, his laugh was so funny it made me dissolve into fits, too.

At one point, he asked me if I'd seen *The Office*. I was going to say yes, but then I thought I might make a dick of myself if he asked me something that I didn't know the answer to.

'No, I've never seen it, Ricky.'

That was it. He totally ripped into me.

'Oh, right, well fuck off out of the room then,' he said, laughing, before telling his assistant to send me some DVDs.

'You can stick your show up your arse, anyway,' I replied, which made him guffaw even more.

As I was leaving I passed a bowl of jelly sweets in a bowl on the table in front of him.

'Can I have one, Ricky? I asked.

'Course, help yourself,' he replied, at which I opened my bag and poured the lot in.

'The kids'll love these, thanks...'

I could still hear him laughing as I walked out of the building.

I don't think I realised how big *The Office* was. When I told everyone I was filming the Christmas special they generally couldn't believe it. Around that time, I remember hooking up with my good friend Oliver Skeete – the dreadlocked Olympic show jumper-cum-TV star we sat chatting about my role in *The Office*, and his forthcoming role in a James Bond film, with Pierce Brosnan. We were both in awe of each other; I was a huge James Bond fan and Oliver was obsessed with *The Office*. Isn't it funny how you often don't appreciate the things you're getting the opportunity to do?

Filming started a few weeks later. David Brent, Rickys' famous creation was dressed as Austin Powers and was one of the three *Blind Date* contestants, the other two being Howard from the Halifax building society advert and Bubble from *Big Brother*.

I was a bag of nerves, to be honest, not helped by the fact that the studio was filled with two-hundred extras acting as the audience. We rehearsed the scene in the morning, before breaking for lunch. Ricky and Stephen sat with us, the latter warning me not to be distracted by Ricky's efforts to make me laugh.

He wasn't wrong. We did the first take, which went perfectly, but for some reason we had to go again. I fluffed a line in the second take, at which Ricky tried desperately to make me laugh, although I managed to remain straight-faced. We then shot our close-ups, which is when he got me good and proper. I was just about to say my line, but immediately before he'd changed his dialogue, which made me piss myself laughing. From then on he kept throwing in a curve-ball, and I just couldn't get my lines out for giggling.

'Ricky, stop it, please,' I said, as Stephen told me to take a break and compose myself. I finally finished my scene, although my stomach was aching because I'd laughed so much. I went over to Stephen to apologise for all the stops and starts.

'Don't worry about it, Mike,' he said. 'He does it all the time.'

I loved every minute of working with Gervais and Merchant. They had such a great working relationship, which was obviously so key to *The Office's* success.

Back at *Richard & Judy*, we travelled to see a guy in the depths of Cornwall who'd never bought meat in his life, instead feasting on road kill that he found near his home. Fox, rabbit, badger, pigeon; you name, it he'd eaten it. He took us out for a drive to see if he could find anything, and came across a dead pheasant which he promptly bagged up and bunged into his freezer.

What an oddball, I remember thinking as he cooked me some fresh badger to try, while telling me that he drank his own urine every day. To prove it, he went to the toilet and peed into a glass, before re-emerging and drinking it right in front of us.

'That's brilliant,' said Gaz, 'but it would be even funnier if you could do the same, Mike...'

'I'll only do it if you drink yours first,' I said, at which Gaz got up and went to the loo, returned with a glass, and downed it in one.

'Your turn, McClean,' he said.

'Not a fucking chance,' I replied.

I'm actually surprised that knowing me as he did Gaz expected me to go through with it!

One report that I'll never forget involved a woman in her early nineties. I wasn't told much about it until I got to the location, despite asking Gaz where the hell we were heading. I probably deserved this after the pee incident to be fair..

'You'll see,' is all that he'd say.

We arrived at an airfield, and I clapped my eyes on two light aircraft emblazoned with 'Utterly Butterly' logos. They were used by a stunt team, who'd stand atop them and, while in mid-air, would climb out and walk along the wing. This 'wing-walking' is what I'd been tasked to do, the twist being that I'd be in one plane and this ninety-something woman would be in the other. I hoped that this was a wind up show and someone was going to pop out and say 'Haha... surprise... we had you there...' but it sadly wasn't the case.

This woman, incidentally, was amazing. She looked more like she was in her seventies, probably because she'd led a very clean-living life which comprised of lots of yoga and healthy eating. Unlike me, she seemed to be taking everything in her stride. I interviewed her before we both got strapped in, all the while thinking *why the hell would an OAP want to do this?*

For the first two minutes I wanted the whole thing to stop, but as soon as we got into the air I felt fine, and actually began to enjoy it. We flew past the airbase a couple of times and then the pilots started to do tricks, performing loop-the-loops and flying within inches of each other. My underpants looked like a map of the world by the time I'd finished, and I remember cursing Gaz for coming up with the idea. Looking back, though, it was a great experience, and it wouldn't surprise me at all if the woman is still alive and kicking.

****

The time had come to part company with my agent, since I was sick of paying him commission for jobs I'd got off my own back (representing myself, I'd later get jobs on ITV's *Red Bull Race*, followed by *Celebrity Fear Factor* and *The Match*, both for Sky). I also went to see Simon Ross and asked him if he was happy with everything I was doing for them.

'Yes, of course,' he said.

'Good. Can I get a pay rise then, please?'

He laughed and agreed to increase my fee to £550 per day. We shook hands and did the deal, and I promised that I'd never ask for another rise again. He also suggested I consider signing a contract, but that would mean obtaining permission from them if I wanted to do other shows. I had a think, but decided against it as I thought our agreement suited both parties.

'If you change your mind, I could always speak to your agent,' he said.

'I'll warn you, she pushes a hard bargain...' I replied.

At that time, I continued to get requests to do some stand-up gigs, but I was still reluctant to take the plunge.

'You're daft,' said Gaz. 'You need to get back on the horse.'

My relationship with Gaz was just brilliant. We worked well together and we were great mates outside of work. He confided in me a lot about various things, and vice versa. We travelled a lot over the years on *Richard & Judy*, and covered nearly every inch of the country.

The one report that gave us both a massively hyped status was the famous Squirrel Report. A squirrel had bitten a policeman in a police station just outside of Newcastle, and we were tasked with getting to the bottom of this crime. We got a train to Newcastle and, as it approached the city, a group of female students got on. It seemed Thursday night was student night in Newcastle, and before you could say *why-aye, man*, they were inviting us all out for night out on the town. We all partied at a club called Fleur's, necking the sambucas like there was no tomorrow. Our plans 'not to have a late one' (we were due to be up at 7 a.m.) went well and truly out of the window as we returned to the hotel in the early hours.

Everyone piled into my room for more drinks, until there was a knock on the door. I thought it might be security, checking what all the commotion was, but when I opened the door I pissed myself laughing. There stood Adam Ross, (Jonathan Ross's brother) who was our runner, dressed head-to-toe in the squirrels outfit that we had brought up for the report.

I finally got up at about eight o'clock and, leaving a roomfull of comatose bodies, headed down to meet the rest of the crew. I didn't feel good at all – despite drinking water for the latter part of the evening – but Gaz and Adam looked and felt worse. The three of us spent all day puking up; we had to apologise to the police officer and the squirrel expert we'd drafted in, giving them some spiel about suffering food poisoning. How we managed to get through the day I'll never know, but we managed to film everything we needed and headed back to London.

The report went out the following night, and the response was just unbelievable. Richard and Judy loved it, the bigwigs at Channel 4 loved it, and everyone in the office loved it. Even my mum loved it. I remember the next day going shopping at my local Costco and people approaching me to ask if I'd found the squirrel yet. It was just one of those films that we got just right; if only viewers knew the state we were in when we'd filmed it.

Later that day, my mobile rang. It was Richard, calling from his car phone.

'Hi Mike,' he said. 'Judy's here with me.'

'Hiya Mike,' piped up Judy.

'Listen,' continued Richard. 'We just wanted to say how good your report was. It was one of the best we've ever had on the show, isn't that right, Judy?'

'Mike, we loved it,' she said.

He didn't have to ring me to say that, but he did! It was a conversation I'll never forget. I thanked them both, while emphasising that it had been a proper team effort. I can look back at the people who have inspired me and those who are in my opinion the very best to work with and Richard & Judy definitely fall into this category.

My status on the show was now cemented, I'd carved my niche as their roving reporter. But, although I loved my little job, I still hankered after a show of my own, or a big Saturday night TV gig. I was pleased to be asked to present Catherine Tate with the comedy award at the 2004 Variety Club Awards in London, though. I was sat on a table with Catherine herself, as well as *Countdown's* Carol Vorderman who I must say was looking particularly attractive that night.

It was always customary for the presenter of an award to say a few funny lines or gags, but I wasn't sure whether it was wise. The room was packed with well-known comedians, but – still bruised by my stand-up experiences all those years ago - I felt nervous and intimidated. Going on stage before me was Victoria Wood, who'd told a few gags which had gone down okay, but hadn't exactly brought the house down. *Sod it*, I thought. *I'm going for it*.

I bounced up on stage, telling everyone how nice it was to be in London, and how nice it was to be sat at a table with Carol Vorderman.

'I got aroused,' I said, with a cheeky grin, 'which isn't bad for seven letters.'

That got a great laugh, as did the couple of gags that followed it. I came off stage feeling really pleased that I'd taken the plunge. Later that evening, Victoria Wood came over.

'Very funny, that... you did better than me,' she said, which was really nice of her. That's the thing with comedians, we're a friendly lot and we do like to support each other, well for the most part!

With this under my belt my appetite for stand-up was returning.

CHAPTER 23

Playing Football For Rod Stewart

In 2003 I was invited to take part in the *Celebrity Soccer Six*, a massive football tournament that took place at Chelsea FC's ground. It was the brainchild of a guy called Mark Abery, who ran the event and invited many of the biggest names in showbusiness, from Westlife to Take That, and from Mick Hucknall to Rod Stewart.

'D'you fancy playing in the comedians' team, Mike?' Mark asked me, telling me that we'd be pitched against teams headed up by Ant and Dec, Westlife and So Solid Crew, among others.

'Course I will,' I replied, 'but only if I can wear my lucky number five shirt.'

There were 25,000 fans at Stamford Bridge that afternoon. All thirty-six teams comprised six players with three substitutes, which included some ex-professionals. We had former Norwich City FC defender Rob Newman on our side, Ant and Dec's team had Newcastle United and Liverpool legend Peter Beardsley, Westlife's side had ex-England captain Bryan Robson and So Solid Crew fielded former Manchester United player Lee Sharpe. Add to the mix the likes of Ian Rush, Pat Nevin, Neville Southall and John Aldridge, and it was a proper Who's Who's of the football world.

The comedians' team comprised Les Dennis, David Baddiel, Omid Djalili, Paul Hendy and our goalie Terry Alderton, as well as two other comics I'd never heard of. In the dressing room, Baddiel was going on and on about playing in a decent team because last year, according to him, he'd been given a crap one.

He must be a fabulous player, the way he's talking... I remember thinking to myself.

Our first match was against Ant and Dec's team, and it became clear that Baddiel was a shocking footballer. My sister would have played better.

I took on the centre-half role, as I always did, and got into my deluded head that I was going to mark ex-England international Peter Beardsley out of the game. *If I keep him quiet I can cut the supply to his team*, I thought. As if. We got battered 5-1.

'Squeaky, get tighter on Beardsley,' I remember Terry shouting from his goal mouth.

'I have to catch the fucker first,' came my reply.

I think I did myself proud – I put in a good few challenges – but Beardsley was just awesome. At the end of the match he came over, shook my hand and told me that I'd done brilliantly, and had given him a hard time out there. I was in heaven.

Needless to say, we only won one game, beating the boys from *Brookside* and *Hollyoaks*. This was quite a surprising outcome since they had a great team including Phil Oliver and Nick Pickard (as well as his brother John) who were all top players.

The next year, I was delighted to be picked for Rod Stewart's celebrity side. The guy was crazy about football and I couldn't wait to meet him. My other team-mates were Bradley

Walsh (a really decent player), Jim Alexander (a great goalie who was in Sky One's *Dream Team*), a DJ called Mark Fabian and ex-Manchester United player Terry Gibson. Rod also drafted in two of his friends, Glyn Evans (a police superintendent from Essex) and Billy May (one of his old school mates). When I arrived at Stamford Bridge, I discovered that Rod had sorted out some new Nike kits and tracksuits for us.

'You must be Mike,' he said.

'Sorry, who are you again?' I replied with a wink.

'You're going to be trouble...' he said, laughing and shaking his head.

Bradley selected the starting line-up for the first match. To be honest, I was a little pissed off to be a sub, at the expense of Rod's mates (it was meant to be a 'celebrity' Soccer Six not a 'bring-your-mates' Soccer Six but I never uttered a word). We kicked off, and within two minutes the opposition had scored, our team's problem being that we had no defence and kept getting caught on the break. Bradley brought me on with a few minutes to go but it was no use, and we were defeated. Our next game was against the comedians, only this time they had a much better team. I was sub again – it was really starting to annoy me – and I came on for the last five minutes, the game finishing in a draw.

We had to win our third match to progress further in the tournament, and I decided to make a stand.

'Right, I'm starting this game. We keep losing because we're not defending, and that's what I do best. Rod, one of your mates can be sub this time.'

No-one could quite believe my cheek.

'Well, that's me told,' said Rod. 'You'd better be good, Mike, that's all I can say...'

As I walked onto the pitch, Bradley shook my hand and wished me well. Not only did we win, I had one of the best games of my life and even managed to score.

'Well played, Mike, looks like you're starting the next game then,' said Rod.

'You're not wrong,' came my reply. Yeah so I was pushing my luck but I knew it had to be done.

We reached the quarter finals, only to get beaten by bloody Westlife. What made it worse was they were all sat on stools.

I was so pissed off in the dressing room afterwards; I'd really wanted to win. Then Rod came over.

'Do you fancy playing for my team at home?' he asked. 'We have matches at my house most Sundays, and I'm always looking for decent players.'

I didn't need to be asked twice, and a fortnight later I found myself keying the code to Rod Stewart's front gate. He lived in Essex, which wasn't far from my gaff. When I arrived, one of Rod's mates was waiting for me.

'Hi, Mike, the lads are already on the pitch. Rod's left your kit hung up in the dressing room.'

I couldn't believe my eyes. Not only did Rod have a full-size pitch outside his beautiful mansion, he also had a proper dressing room with showers.

'What d'you think?' asked Rod once I'd got changed and jogged out.

'Pretty amazing for an ex-council house,' I said.

The pitch was amazing, definitely on a par with anything from Division One. The grass was cut to perfection – Arsenal's groundsman tended it, apparently - and Rod had installed proper goals and a dugout. The only thing he didn't have were floodlights, but only because the local council had refused planning permission.

I went on to play as a right-back for Rod's team for two years, either during the week or on a Sunday, and I loved every minute. He didn't mind you bringing along spectators, either, as long as they didn't hassle any of his celeb mates for photos and autographs.

Once, he and I were warming up, just passing the ball to each other, and he mentioned that he'd seen me on *Richard & Judy*. I remember feeling totally overwhelmed that this world-famous legend had been watching me on telly.

I also remember having a slightly awkward conversation with him before a football session. I turned up that day to find Manchester United's latest red Nike kit hung on our dressing room pegs. My heart sank.

'Please don't be offended, Rod,' I said, 'but there's not a cat in hell's chance of me wearing that.'

I explained that I was a diehard Blue, and he fully understood, saying that he'd never be seen dead in a Glasgow Rangers strip. He even went to the lengths of asking the lads to wear Celtic shirts instead, bless him.

Another time, Rod joked that he'd invited over a couple of players who were on his 'transfer list'. They turned out to be ex-Leeds United and Scotland legends Gordon Strachan and Gary McAllister, and I can safely say that I never wanted that ninety minutes to end. Gordon and Gary were just brilliant, encouraging us throughout the game and getting stuck in like the rest of us.

One Sunday I remember it being so hot that, after the game Rod let us jump into his pool. I was dying for a wee and couldn't help but relieve myself in his pool. I don't think there are many people who can say they pissed in a pop star's pool. Sorry, Rod.

****

In July 2004 I was booked onto a Sky One show called *Celebrity Fear Factor*, which entailed sending famous faces over to Argentina to take part in various dangerous stunts. I'd watched the show before and had loved it. I flew first-class from Heathrow to Buenos Aires; I'd never sampled such luxury before (I did get upgraded once, on an Easyjet flight, when they gave me a seat). Joining me in the first-class lounge were Shane Lynch from Boyzone, former gymnast Suzanne Dando, a *Brookside* actor, an *FHM* model Tanya Bardsley (The real house wives of Cheshire) and a girl from *Big Brother* (as well as a few I didn't recognise).

When we arrived at Buenos Aires we were told to stay in our hotel, since the city was pretty dangerous and notorious for muggings. Sod that for a lark. I was from Manchester, for God's sake. I had no qualms walking into the centre of town to have a look around, and what a place it was. There were murals of Diego Maradona on every street corner, and on the pavements there were lads doing amazing football freestyling tricks. I must have mooched about for four hours, yet didn't come up against any trouble or danger whatsoever.

I headed back to the hotel, only to find a mass kerfuffle in the reception.

'What's going on?' I asked the staff.

'Apparently a Mike McClean has gone out into the city on his own, and we're trying to locate him.'

Then a Sky producer spotted me. He wasn't happy.

'Mike, where the hell have you been? You were told it was unsafe to go out alone.'

'Bollocks, it's totally safe!' I said, explaining to him that the city was great, and that he shouldn't be such a TV luvvie.

That night, over dinner, all the other celebs were laughing, telling me how the production team were shitting themselves, visualising me being found dead in a gutter.

The following night saw our first challenge which was to take place in a freezing cold swimming pool, with two teams - Reds versus Blues - competing against each other. Our hands were tied together, and we were attached to a big disc that rotated in and out of the water. Our challenge was to untie our hands and free ourselves. They couldn't have picked a worse task for me, since I hated going underwater. When the time came, I soon discovered how difficult it was to hold my breath while using my teeth to loosen the hand-ties. At one stage I misjudged the turn, found myself gulping for air, and I honestly thought I was going to drown. I eventually managed to untie myself, but promptly learned that I'd been disqualified. I was gutted - I felt I'd let my team down – and returned to the hotel with a face like thunder.

For our second task we were driven to a disused boat yard. Two of us were elected by the other team to be hoisted up and dropped, head first, into a box of crabs and cockroaches. Two pairs of girls were chosen by both teams – I was gutted to miss out – but they all did it brilliantly.

Following that day's filming I felt like going into Buenos Aires again, so I asked Shane Lynch if he fancied it.

'I bet I can find us an Irish bar,' I said, and I did, and one that served Guinness. Shane was a lovely bloke and we had a really good night. He talked about his Boyzone days, and told me how he'd become a born-again Christian. I was also intrigued by all his tattoos – he was covered in them, from head to toe - and he proceeded to outline all the stories behind them. As we chatted more and more about life, God and showbiz we got progressively more pissed.

'Believe it or not, I gave up alcohol years ago,' he slurred after his sixth pint. I couldn't help but laugh.

'Well not tonight, my friend, not tonight...'

I was really glad to take part in our final challenge. Two cars were suspended in the air, and three celebs per team were locked inside; Suzanne and I were put in the trunk, and the girl from *Big Brother* was sat in the driver's seat. Our task was to escape out of the trunk, clamber onto the bonnet and then jump from one car to the other. The fact that I hated confined spaces and heights made me feel double-nervous.

The Blue team went first, completing their challenge in three-and-a-half minutes. At this point the scores were neck-and-neck, so we had to win this challenge. Up in the air we went, and the klaxon sounded. I'll never forget how petrified I felt when I opened that car-boot and looked down, particularly when the car began to sway. There was I shaking in my shoes, it was horrific and just for a second I thought I was going to lose my breakfast, I mean, how would you feel having the doubt of the previous day's failure and then being faced with your next two biggest fears? I don't know what propelled me to move, probably some innate competitive streak or possibly the fear of my mates taking the piss, whatever it was, I pulled up my big boy pants and got on with it…

Eventually we all got out, leapt across to the next car and rang our bell. We'd done it in three minutes fifteen seconds, and our team had won *Celebrity Fear Factor*. We all got £5,000 each to donate to our favourite charities; mine went to the NSPCC, who sent me lovely letter of thanks. I guess my time seeing abused children in the summer camps makes it a charity that's close to my heart.

CHAPTER 24

The Match

I was back in London, doing the reports for *Richard & Judy*, when I got a call from Luther Blissett. Sky One were producing a reality TV show called *The Match*, based around a football game at Newcastle's St James' Park between celebrities and ex-pros. Luther was going to act as the coach, and he wondered if I was interested in taking part. The celeb team was to be managed by Graham Taylor, and the 'Legends' team by none other than Sir Bobby Robson. Ex-players that had already signed up included Paul Gascoigne, Bruce Grobbelaar, Matt Le Tissier, Peter Reid and Chris Waddle.

I'd actually met Gazza few months earlier while playing in a charity game in Marbella, along with Bryan Robson and Lee Sharpe. It had been a dream come true playing in a game with those guys. The pre-match in the dressing room was one of the funniest hours I have ever had, spent listening to hilarious stories from Gazza and Robbo about their playing days. Gazza was pure gold, and got up to all kinds of mischief. Just prior to kick-off, Bryan Robson was about to put on the captain's armband when I grabbed it from him and pulled it up my own sleeve.

'You've had your day, Bryan. How's about me being the captain today?'

'Well if you're the captain, you can at least put it on the right fucking arm, you tit,' he grinned.

It was a great game, and playing alongside Gazza was a privilege, albeit on ordeal. Lee Sharpe had warned me that he took every single game seriously – friendly or not – and he wasn't wrong. If you despatched a shit ball to him he'd let you know in no uncertain terms, and you'd not do it again. I remember taking on one guy and, as I did so, I saw Gazza making a run. I chipped the ball into him and he turned and scored.

'Squeaky, fucking brilliant man,' he said, as I gave him the thumbs up. I was chuffed to bits. We won the game 4-1, and when I held the trophy aloft you'd have thought I'd won the World Cup, although I guess for me it was the closest I'd ever-come.

The premise of *The Match* was that the celeb team would live and train at St James' Park for two weeks. Players who didn't perform well in training would be put on the bench, and the viewing public would vote one of them off. I really didn't want this to happen to me so, a fortnight before the show was due to start, I rang the Academy Manager at Manchester City FC, Jim Cassell, to ask if I could train at the club's Platt Lane complex.

'Why don't you come in and join the academy lads?' he asked, which I did. I was put through my paces with City's young starlets – I held my own in a ninety-minute practice match - and it helped me immensely. Following my stint, that particular youth team went on to win the FA Youth Cup that year; no coincidence, surely.

I also spent a couple of days training at Southend United, as Terry Alderton knew the manager, Steve Tilson, and I was friendly with their captain, Kevin Maher. The Southend lads thought I was a new signing, however, and made sure I was welcomed with a good old-fashioned kicking.

I was determined to enjoy *The Match*; two weeks living like a professional footballer was an amazing opportunity, also being paid to do it was a nice bonus. The other celebrities who'd been signed up included actor Ralf Little, Harvey from So Solid Crew, Tom Craig from *Coronation Street*, TV presenter Ben Shephard and band members from groups Steps and Blue. Alongside them were sprinter Darren Campbell, comedian Terry Alderton, actor Gary Lucy, George Best's son Calum, Phil Oliver from *Hollyoaks*, cricketer Alex Stewart, *Holby City's* Rocky Marshall, singer Dane Bowers and a lad called Jonathan Wilkes perhaps better known as being Robbie Williams' best friend.

The first batch of filming took place during a weekend at England's training ground, Bisham Abbey, where we underwent a gruelling fitness assessment. This included a bleep test - which I hated - along with a blood test and a breathing test - it's a good job they didn't do a spelling test as none of us would have passed! We also had our first training session, together with a practice match. Most of the lads played football to a very high standard, which was essential if we were going to have any chance of beating Sir Bobby's ex-pros. Graham Taylor also rang us up individually to say hello and to tell us what he expected from us.

A week later, I headed up to Newcastle for the start of our preparation. Our mobile phones were taken off us immediately – the Sky producers saw them as a distraction – and this predictably pissed off a few of the lads. Graham Taylor showed us around the stadium, and then it was time to choose our room-mates (I ended up with Rocky Marshall and Tom Craig).

We had to train twice a day, which proved to be really hard work, both physically and mentally. Never before had I been in an environment that was filled with so many egos (which might surprise you having read this far into the book!). Ralf Little was without doubt one of the biggest camera pests I had ever seen, forever trying to get his face in shot. He was clearly a very good player, but in his head, he wrongly thought he was professional-standard.

I liked Graham Taylor, though, who I called Gaffer, as that's what all pro footballers tended to call their managers. He was firm but fair; he'd have a laugh with us but would dish out a bollocking if need be. Our coach, Luther Blissett, was a hard taskmaster and made me realise that I had so much to learn about the game as a defender. He taught me how to press high up the field, how to make the pitch big when you have the ball (and small when they have it), and how to shadow play. All this made me realise how committed professional football-ers had to be, and made me admire my friends, ex-pros Kevin Horlock and Kevin Maher, even more.

Every night Graham would sit us all down and reveal who was on the bench, which was unbelievably nerve-wracking. I knew that I'd trained well and worked hard, and the Gaffer apparently said on camera that I was a good defender who could read the game well, and who was a decent passer of the ball.

As we were being filmed twenty-four hours a day, some-times it felt like being in the *Big Brother* house. While we knew that we had to be careful, we'd often forget about the cameras, let our guard slip, and give the show plenty of good TV. The production team could be sneaky, though. After training one day they'd arranged for us all to have a night out in Newcastle, which we were all really excited about. We all got changed, boarded the bus and headed to a city centre club called The Apartments. When we got there it was packed with beautiful women; it was like letting kids loose in Hamley's toy store.

Most of the lads had girlfriends and wives but, as soon as they walked in, a fair few started chatting the women up, not realising that every move they made was being filmed. It was a set-up, basically. Myself, Tom, Craig and Rocky found a quiet corner in the club and had a few drinks, watching the other lads try and work their magic on these Newcastle stunners.

Back on the coach, however, it all kicked off. The lads had discovered that the cameras had gone inside the club, and threatened to go on strike if any incriminating footage was broadcast. Calum Best and Dane Bowers didn't seem to be too bothered – probably because they were single - but some of the lads had partners back home, who'd be watching *The Match*. Eventually a clear-the-air meeting was held, and the team promised that nothing damaging would be shown.

Back at training, things began to get heated, and egos were clashing all over the place. I had a row with Ralf, Harvey had a row with Ralf, in fact most people had a row with Ralf. During one session I shoulder-charged Calum Best off the ball (not easy when I was 5 foot 7 and he was 6 foot 2) and as he got up he tried to grab hold of me. In order to defuse the situation, I just kissed him, and everyone on the pitch started laughing, including Calum.

As the week continued, more players were voted out, such as Calum, Dane Bowers and Antony Costa. One morning Graham made us watch a video of the players we were up against, and it was a true reminder of their skill and quality. One of these players was the great Viv Anderson, who'd been one of the first black players to receive an England call-up. Ralf passed a comment that implied Viv wasn't the best, failing to realise that the ex-pros would be watching the show.

The Legends, it seemed, were taking things very seriously. During their training sessions they'd be smashing balls in left, right and centre as Sir Bobby Robson barked orders at them. Their pride was quite clearly at stake and they were desperate not to get beaten by a load of television personalities.

As training got more intense among the celebs, more arguments occurred, especially when the time came for Graham to pick a captain. We all wanted Alex Stewart as he had skippered the England cricket team, but Jonathan Wilkes was chosen. Jonathan was a nice enough guy – and he'd once been on Everton's books - but he sucked up to Graham Taylor so much, which got on everyone's nerves. \in my opinion, Harvey or even Ralf would have been much better skippers, in my opinion.

The day before the big match, Graham announced the team and I was devastated to be named among the substitutes. I honestly thought I'd done enough to warrant a place in the starting side, and was ready to walk out.

'Don't do that, Mike,' said Ben Shephard. 'You should be proud you've made the final team. Keep your head up, mate.' He was right, of course.

We then got kitted out for our match day suits, and I got chatting to ex-Chelsea and Manchester United goalie Mark Bosnich, who was giving our celebrity team some additional goalie cover. He was a very funny guy, with lots of great anecdotes, but he'd had some dark times too. Drugs issues had marred his career, but luckily he'd invested his money well (in property around London) which had kept him afloat financially. He told us stories about his childhood in Australia, and how he'd run around his back garden, naked, shouting 'windy day, mate.' We all found this very amusing and 'windy day, mate' became the catchphrase we'd shout whenever we saw him.

On the morning of the match we had a light training session and in the afternoon we relaxed and got our bags packed. We were also given our phones back, which meant we could finally call our families. It turned out that my parents had been invited down to be guests on the show – they were put up in a nice hotel, with room service paid for – which they were absolutely delighted with.

On the team bus, Graham gave a great speech about how proud of us he felt, and how hard we'd all worked. Then he played a brilliant montage video of the past two weeks and, as I looked around at the lads, many of them were wiping away tears. It was an emotional moment.

We arrived at St James Park, and I remember feeling like a real footballer as I disembarked from the coach, coming off fifth as my superstition dictated. The first thing I did when I got to the dressing room was sort my complimentary tickets out (for my sister, my best mate Degs and his girlfriend Claire). I then sought out my kit - I was pleased with my number 15 shirt, as it had a number 5 on it – and then Graham told us to go out and assess the pitch. On the way out I bumped into Peter Beardsley, and told him that I was only a substitute.

'You're not starting?' he said. 'Well, your gaffer's made a big a mistake, that's all I can say...'

I saw Bryan Robson, too, and said hello.

'Fuck off,' he snarled, 'I'll do my talking to you on the pitch.'

I was shocked, giving Peter an *is he serious?* look. Bryan then smiled and winked. Phew.

The stadium was packed with 55,000 fans; not only had the organisers sold every ticket for this charity fundraiser, millions would also be watching at home. The atmosphere was amazing, and I remember standing in the centre circle with Ben Shephard and Tom Craig and gazing in awe at this magnificent sight.

Twenty minutes later we were back on the pitch in our training kits, doing our warm up, and I remember asking Peter how the Legends' preparation had gone. It turned out they'd done most of it in the pub the night before, with half of them drinking in the hotel bar until 6 a.m.

Mark Bosnich gave a great pre-kick off speech to our team, which really inspired the lads. I was gutted to be sitting on the bench, but I still wanted my team-mates to do well. Twenty minutes into the game, Bosnich went off injured, which meant that Terry Alderton had to come on to replace him. I was so pleased for him, since he was a great 'keeper and it was his time to shine. He made a great couple of saves and then suddenly the Legends scored, courtesy of a Gary Pallister strike.

The ex-pros played amazingly well that afternoon. While they were past their prime professionally, their brilliant football brains still remained and gave them the edge. It was noticeable that they gave Ralf a very tough time –no doubt having heard his disparaging comments about Viv Anderson – and every time he got the ball they went in extremely hard on him. Things got a bit nasty on other areas of the pitch, too, particularly between Harvey and Ian Wright (at one point their feud nearly descended into a mass brawl). Ex-Arsenal player Nigel Winterburn went in studs-first on Phil Oliver – it was right in front of our dugout - which was totally uncalled for.

It was 1-0 at half-time, and I was as eager as hell to get on the pitch. I sat there feeling increasingly pissed off as Graham changed things around, bringing on Gary Lucy and switching Rocky with Lee Latchford-Evans from Steps. Eventually, with about twenty-five minutes to go, he brought me on for Ben Shephard. Ben had played brilliantly, and as he came off he wished me all the best. I slotted into the right-back role and Rocky moved into midfield. I soon realised that I'd be marking Matt Le Tissier, who just happened to be one of the best English strikers of his generation. Eeek.

I remember Graham telling us that, when we were on the pitch, we'd hardly hear the noise of the crowd. He was so right; I was so focused that I managed to block out all the noise. I tried to keep things simple, getting in a few good challenges now and again and playing a few decent passes. Eventually, with about fifteen minutes to go, Jonny Wilkes bagged us an equaliser which – although he maintained it was a shot – looked suspiciously like a cross. A goal's a goal, however, and we celebrated like crazy while the ex-pros shook their heads.

Time was starting to ebb away, and we knew we'd have to do our utmost to cling onto the draw. The Legends brought off Gazza, which was a massive boost to us since he'd been brilliant from kick-off.

'How long's left?' I remember asking the referee.

'Five minutes plus injury time,' he replied.

Seconds later, Ian Wright had got the ball and was just about to shoot. I knew that if I mis-timed this challenge it would be a penalty, so I slid at the side of him just as he was about to aim and got my tackle in. The ball went out for a corner and, as I got up, Ian congratulated me on my good challenge.

Terry Alderton sustained a knock during the corner, and I remember telling him to stay down in order to waste a bit of time. Yet another corner came in; it was whipped in by Ally McCoist, the smallest man on the pitch, who headed it in to make it 2-1. The ref blew and it was game over. The Legends were brilliant in the aftermath, and all came over to congratulate us and shake our hands. Most of the lads swapped shirts and, knowing that Degs was a massive Matt Le Tissier fan, I exchanged mine with his (my mate still has it... I wonder what Matt did with his?).

The atmosphere in the dressing room was one of relief and disappointment. Sky TV were delighted, though, informing us that the show had attracted great ratings, with over 1.5 million viewers. The next day a few of my team-mates and I got the train back to London, and I remember Ralf, Harvey and Darren boasting that various clubs had been on the phone, asking them to play for them.

'I've had a club on to me, too,' I said. 'Stringfellows.'

While I was really sad that *The Match* had come to an end, I wasn't going to miss these egos one bit.

CHAPTER 25

Phone Hacked

In 2004 I'd been doing panto in Stevenage along with Lucy Benjamin from *Eastenders*. We were both single so I asked if she fancied going out one night. We exchanged a few text messages but kept things between ourselves as we didn't want people to know. One morning, however, she arrived at the theatre looking annoyed.

'Why are you telling people about us?' she said.

'I haven't told a soul,' I assured her. I'd not said a word – or shown our texts - to anyone, so it was all a bit confusing.

We did eventually go out for dinner, and then on to a club called Roadhouse in Covent Garden. We were having a great night until she got a call from her agent, asking her if she was out on the town with me. It seems he'd received a call from a journalist, and we assumed some punters in the club had recognised us both and tipped off the tabloids. We both decided to leave the club, and got a cab to her flat. I left Lucy's really early that morning, since I had a football match and she was flying out to Dubai. Our friendship soon fizzled out, however, and although I liked her a lot I decided not to pursue things.

It was only years later that I learned that our mobile phones had been hacked by the *News of the World*, hence the leaked sightings and the unwanted attention. The reporter in question had been arrested, and mine and Lucy's contact details had been found in a book, and our texts and voicemails had been logged. When I attended the police station to make a statement, I discovered that they'd intercepted a whole host of messages to other girls, too.

'D'you want to press charges?' asked the police officer.

'Damn right I do,' I said, and a few months later I was delighted to learn that the reporter had gone to jail.

It doesn't matter whether you're in the limelight or not, privacy is privacy and I was really angry at this blatant breach. It was bad enough I'd been set up previously, but this was going even further and I was really grateful that friends of mine hadn't had anything about their private lives revealed as a result of this intrusion.

I continued to work on *Richard & Judy*, and one week myself, Gaz and Uncle Rod were despatched to Japan to cover the world science expo in Nagoya. I was so excited – I'd never been to Japan before – but I knew it was going to be hard work, since we'd been asked to film five reports. Also, as there were just three of us (plus a fixer) we were a man down, meaning that Rod had to do both sound and camera.

We learned a lot about the Japanese culture and customs. Lateness was seen as hugely disrespectful, so if you were asked to be on location at nine o'clock you'd have to be there at 8.45 a.m. We were also told to put people's business cards in our top pockets – near our hearts - as it was an insult to stuff them into your back pocket, near your arse. Thinking about it, that's actually a really nice custom although there are several I've had in the past that definitely belong in the latter!

Japan seemed to be so far ahead with technology, and yet many of their amazing ideas ended up being refined by British scientists and engineers. We did a piece about a brand new, futuristic car that didn't need to be steered. We arrived at Nissan HQ fifteen minutes early and, for the next hour-and-a-half, had to sit through a full explanation of the car's workings (I was falling asleep, and Gaz had to keep nudging me). Eventually we went out in the car which, thanks to hi-tech sensors, tracked lights on a motorway and didn't need steering. The only problem was that it didn't work during rainy weather, and on the day we were filming it was pissing it down. This being the case, I had to get a (very embarrassed) technician to hold the bottom of the steering wheel so it looked like it was steering itself.

We spent a day filming at a place called Akihabara which, apparently, was one of Alan Sugar's favourite places in the world. It's an area of Tokyo famous for state-of-the-art electronic goods, and we visited a store that comprised seven floors of amazing gadgets including rocking horses, massage chairs, remote controlled vacuum cleaners, you name it, we filmed it. We featured the top five gadgets and got one of the workers to do the countdown in English while sat on a rocking chair. It was hilarious; proper TV gold. We also filmed mobile phones that you could watch TV on, which seemed revolutionary in those pre-iPhone days.

Japan was an amazing place, and we all loved it. Gaz developed a sushi addiction (he had it morning, noon and night) and Uncle Rod became a local hero (everyone wanted a photo with him since his blond hair was a rarity over there). The place was so safe, too; we'd ask our fixer to keep an eye on all our stuff, but she'd frequently tell us that no one would touch it, and she was right. I remember leaving my jumper on a bus one day, and mentioning it to the hotel when we got back, not ever thinking that I'd ever see it again. That night, after dinner, I went up to my room to find a box on the bed, inside which my neatly-folded jumper had been placed.

'You wouldn't get that in England,' I explained to the hotel staff. 'You'd probably get on the same bus the next day and see the driver wearing it.'

One day, Gaz and I had a massive fight. It was the first time in God knows how many years we'd had a humdinger and everyone on a packed Japanese commuter train was staring at us as we went for it.

'You fuck off!'

'No you fuck off…'

'You can stick this shoot up your arse…you're fired...'

I honestly can't remember what it was about, but Uncle Rod said it was the funniest thing he had seen in ages. I think it was as a result of tiredness, and by the next day we'd kissed and made up. We were like a married couple; the odd barney now and then, but deep down we both loved each other.

It was while we were in Japan that we met a very interesting guy called Doctor NakaMats. He was an inventor who'd created the floppy disk and the karaoke machine, so he was a bit of a national legend. We were invited to his house to film all his inventions and it was like a treasure trove; he had a chair that you sat in that apparently replaced your brain cells, as well as a ghost detector which we took away with us. It kept going off – *bleep, bleep, bleep* – yet, funnily enough, when we filmed in a cemetery it didn't make a bloody sound.

****

When I returned to England a guy called Danny Fenton, from a production company called Zig Zag, asked if he could meet me. The firm had been commissioned by Challenge TV to make a programme called *House of Games*, to be filmed at Maidstone Studios and to feature families competing in Olympic-type events at home (sofa jumping, plant pot throwing and so on). It wasa great concept for a game show, and they wanted me to host it, alongside the fantastic darts commentator Sid Waddell.

'Why not,' I said. 'Sounds like fun.'

My first task was to film some links with Sid, but the script they gave me wasn't funny at all.

'Just let Sid say something in his Geordie accent, and then I'll come in and ad lib,' I told the producer. It worked brilliantly, as I knew it would. Sid would say something like 'Why-aye, man, welcome to this next event... it'll be a corker...' and I'd walk in and say 'Now if you have any idea what Sid has just said, write it on a postcard and send it to me, Mike McClean, at *House of Games*.' Other times I'd just walk in, look at the camera and shrug my shoulders. I remember Michael Caine once saying that you don't always have to speak - just a look to camera can say it all - and he was so right.

House of Games was a good laugh, and was pretty easy to present. I was in my element because I was doing what I do best, just being myself and having fun with the punters. They wouldn't let me have a writer – many other shows had a team of them - so I had to do all the gags myself.

I was so busy filming *House of Games* and *Richard & Judy* that I didn't have a single day off for two months. I had to sort a panto out – as well as all my admin and invoices – and

I became shattered and ratty. Now my friends might say that they wouldn't have noticed a difference but I knew in myself that I just wasn't "me". Even when you're doing what you love, you still need time off and away. I did like *House of Games*, though, and felt fortunate to work with a great team. We'd play football outside the hotel in Maidstone, and enjoyed lots of dinners and drinks together. Our director, John F Norcott, was renowned for ranting and raving; I'd seen him in action during a celebrity singing show (I'd been a guest) and had heard him through my earpiece, yelling at the crew and presenters. There was no need, as far as I was concerned; we were making TV programmes, not saving lives, so nobody needed to get all stressed out. When I discovered he was the *House of Games* director, I thought it best to have a quiet word.

'Right, John,' I said. 'There's going to be no shouting at me or any of the crew, not even the cleaner,' I said. He looked at me, stunned.

'Well, that's me told,' he said.

'Yes, it is,' I replied.

And guess what? He never shouted once. Just goes to show what you can achieve if you set the right expectations. I'm sure it was probably a relief for him not to have to either, as it must be exhausting.

At the end of the filming, Challenge TV had forgotten to record any trailers, which meant that they needed me in for an extra day, from 9 a.m. to 6 p.m.

'So what about my fee, then?' I asked, knowing full well that they were going to try and pull a fast one and not pay me.

We had a bit of a wangle back and forth and I actually got what I wanted, although to be fair I'd probably have settled for their first offer, but a man has to live!

I was getting tired of negotiating my own deals, however, so went to speak with Noel Edmonds' company, Unique Management. Years ago they'd not been very keen to represent me, but they'd since changed their tune.

'I'm not giving you anything from *Richard & Judy* but you'll get fifteen per cent of any jobs you find me,' I told them.

My new agents got me a few castings but nothing substantial. They did get a meeting with Quiz TV, though, and I'd assumed it was about hosting some television show. It turned out to be a job for Gala Bingo, calling out numbers on TV. I was fuming afterwards.

'Do I look like I want to be a fucking bingo caller?' I yelled, telling them in no uncertain terms that I wanted to be on ITV, BBC or even Channel 5. My relationship with Unique didn't last long after that. Then my friend David Hahn rang, asking to meet up for a coffee.

That's not like David to offer to buy me coffee, I thought, only for him to tell me that he'd meet me in McDonalds (and that's why I loved him). It transpired that he'd been approached by Mersey TV, who made *Hollyoaks* and *Brookside*. They wanted me to present a new Manchester-based music and comedy show and Dave reckoned it was right up my street. It would go out live every Thursday on Granada, and would feature new bands and comedians from the north west.

'I don't know the fee yet, but I'll arrange a meeting,' he said.

We travelled up to Mersey TV on the train, and spent the whole two-and-a-half hours chatting and telling gags (Dave had great comedy timing and delivery and always had a good joke up his sleeve). We were met in Liverpool by a casting director, a woman who'd gained a bit of a bad reputation for herself, to be honest. Some actor friends of mine had told me how she'd taken a cut out of their personal appearance fees despite not being their agent, so she wasn't the most popular person in entertainment circles.

I was introduced to the show's producer, who was a big fan of mine and had loved my work on the *Big Breakfast*. He asked me to do a screen test in the studio with Jackie, who was going to be our music guru, as well as a guy called Terry Titter who was going to handle the comedy element of the show.

'What screen test?' asked David, who was unhappy that they'd sprung this upon us with no prior warning.

My task was simple enough; I had to introduce the show, run down the menu and hand over to Jackie and then the comedian. Then I had to welcome the first act, give out the phone number and then link into a break.

We returned to the Mersey TV office and the casting director asked David to wait outside while she chatted to me. This blatant snub made him so cross I could virtually hear his blood boiling.

'It's a six-week contract, and the fee is two hundred pounds per show,' she said. I nearly spat my tea out.

'Erm, I think I may need to discuss this with David,' I explained.

David went fucking spare. He marched back in and tore a strip off this woman, telling her that this derisory fee had insulted us both.

'I can tell you now that Mike will not be presenting your show. I wish you all the best,' he said, before gesturing for us to leave.

I felt like a naughty schoolboy whose father was dragging him out of school. We waited outside for cab, and I don't think I'd ever seen David so angry.

'How fucking dare she,' he kept saying.

By the time we caught the train David had calmed down, and we had a good chat.

'I really want to do this show, though,' I said forlornly.

'I know,' he said. 'Just trust me. She'll ring back.'

David's judgement was rarely wrong, and a few days later this woman called back to apologise, upping the original offer to £500 per show.

'Thanks but no thanks,' was his response, and she countered with an offer of £800 a show, plus our travel expenses, which I gladly accepted.

CHAPTER 26

Carter & Cooper McClean

In 2003 David had spent some time in Marbella with actor-comedian Mike Reid, filming a movie called *Oh Marbella*! It was a comedy, financed and directed by a guy called Darren Welch. Darren came from a wealthy family, apparently, and spent all his money making films on the cheaper end of the scale. Over lunch, David and Darren had chatted about his next film and, when David asked if I could have a part in it, the director agreed.

'Let's get ourselves to Marbella for a weekend so you can meet him,' said David when we next hooked up in London. A few weeks later we flew over, spending the first evening with Darren and his partner, Dave Mahoney. Without even auditioning me – no screen test, no read-through - Darren offered me the part of a drugs dealer in a film called *Slave*. David said he'd negotiate a fee but, to be honest, I wasn't too bothered as I was just happy to have got a part in a movie.

It took ages for the filming dates to be confirmed, and it turned out I'd only need to be in Spain for a week. Not only that, I wasn't going to be playing a drug dealer after all, and had been given the less glamorous-sounding role of 'ship captain'. I was a bit pissed off, but didn't say anything. I told Gaz all about the film, and explained that I'd need a week off *Richard & Judy*.

'Brilliant,' he said, adding that he'd sanction a behind-the-scenes feature about the film's progress. This pleased Darren no end, and he gave Gaz full access to the set and told us we could interview anyone we wanted. Once we arrived in Marbella it soon became clear that this was a real low-budget affair, featuring crappy film actors who were doing it just for the experience (only the lead actors were getting paid, it seemed). One was called Natassia Malthe, who liked to party (as they say) and her co-star was Sam Page, an actor who had been hotly-tipped to play Superman. Playing the villain, Mohamed Aziz, was a lovely guy called David Gant.

When we arrived on set, however, hardly anyone was prepared to be interviewed, which pissed off Gaz, particularly since Darren had promised him access. Then filming started, and I knew damned well that this film was going straight to DVD and, after that, straight to a supermarket bargain bin. The fact Gaz couldn't stop laughing when I filmed my first scene didn't bode well, either.

The storyline had described how Natassia was going to be spirited away on a speed boat and I, the captain, was going to let her go. However, since Darren hadn't located a speedboat, they tried to hire a jet-ski. That proved fruitless, so they ended up 'borrowing' one from a nearby boat yard (it was without the owner's consent, so it was technically thieving). When it came to me letting her get away, the fact that this speedboat had no power meant that the camera had to zoom off it to make it look like it was leaving.

To be honest I never had any expectations, the world of movie making sounds very glamorous but unless you're picked up by a big studio it's more *Hollyoaks* than *Dallas*! I've had opportunities come up like this quite often and initially you think 'Wow! Hollywood here I come.' Only to have it fizzle out within a few months.

The film did end up in a bargain bin, by the way. Yours for 99p.

****

Not all of my gigs were business related and in 2005 I had the pleasure of being best man at Les's wedding.

Throughout the day people kept coming up to me saying *I cannot wait to hear your speech*. I have honestly never felt so nervous, I must have been on the toilet about 5 times! There's far more emotion involved when it's personal and truth be told I did feel under pressure to be "funny". I did his speech and it was brilliant if I do say so myself! Obviously I ripped him to bits, but at the same time said what a good mate he was. Everyone was rolling about laughing, I remember looking out and seeing people crying. I looked at Les's Mum and she was crying, I ad-libbed a bit with her and it went down brilliantly. After I finished, I dashed off to the toilet again, a women stopped me and said *you should do stand up, you're really funny…*

****

By October 2005, I'd noticed that I wasn't being booked for many reports on *Richard & Judy,* and had gone from doing four per week down to two per week. According to Gaz, Channel 4 had a new commissioning editor who wasn't a fan of mine and wanted a wider selection of reporters. When I dug deeper, however, I was horrified to learn that this man didn't like me because he reckoned I was homophobic. He didn't know me, and he'd hardly worked with me, yet he'd made a totally false and baseless assumption. It really upset me. When I told my gay friends they were went crazy, and couldn't believe how wide-of-the-mark he was. I don't give a rats who you're in love with as long as you're happy.

I could only watch on, frustrated, as other comedians filmed reports for *Richard & Judy* which, in my opinion, weren't a patch on mine (although I admit I could be biased..). John Maloney may have been a great stand-up comic, but he just couldn't get to grips with stopping people in the street and chatting to the public. He just didn't have that warmth, that common touch.

Soon, Judy Finnigan got wind that this Channel 4 bigwig was curtailing my appearances, and apparently decided that she'd confront him in the green room. From what I gather, she fought my corner and gave him a good telling off. It was so nice to know that I had the support of Judy (and Richard, apparently) because their opinions mattered to me so much.

****

In 2006 it was time for Degs to get married and once again I was honoured to be best man. This time it was even harder to get the speech right as I didn't want him to think I'd cheated by using the same gags I'd used for Les! It was a fantastic day and I'm pleased that the speeches went so well.

****

However it wasn't all rainbows and love for *Richard & Judy* as on the show, things didn't seem right, and something seemed afoot. All became clear when Paul O'Grady revealed that he was leaving his ITV chat show – *Richard & Judy's* main rival - and would be defecting to Channel 4 to present a new programme. As you can imagine, Richard and Judy weren't at all happy (neither were Simon and Amanda at Cactus) since their offerings were so similar. It was eventually decided that, for the next eighteen months, *Richard & Judy* would air for three months, followed by three months of Paul O'Grady's show.

This was catastrophic for Cactus employees. They were now effectively out of work for three months, and many producers and researchers had no option but to look for new shows to work on. I had a feeling that the *Richard & Judy* show's days were numbered.

At that point in time though I had more pressing things to live for as my first son, Carter Michael McClean was born in Basildon hospital on 30th November at 11.47am, weighing seven pounds and seven ounces. I watched the doctors deliver Carter and I couldn't believe that I was going to be a Dad. I remember looking over as they cleaned him up and seeing the biggest bollocks on a baby I had ever seen (sorry Carter, that comment may come back to embarrass you at some point!)! The nurse passed him to me and I remember just looking at him and saying "*Hello Son.*" I just fell in love with him instantly. He was so cute, I thought *wow I am a Dad this is my Son. SHIT!* I always knew I wanted children and I always had it in my mind that whilst I would be a fun Dad, I'd also be strict but fair. I knew I was going to make sure that for any children I had, their lives would be filled with laughter. I remember him running out to phone my Mum and Dad to tell them that they had a grandson, then I sat in the toilet and cried and prayed and thanked God for a healthy baby.

****

My mate Gaz was discovering that more and more comedians were landing good television gigs because they were talented stand-ups. Producers felt they'd hit the jackpot when they found a comedian who could also present. Alan Carr, for example, had cracked it, although I suppose you could say I had a hand in that. I'd been due to present a live outside broadcast from the Trafford Centre but couldn't make it, so Alan was apparently drafted in as my replacement (I think he even mentions it in his book). He did a great job by all accounts, and the rest, as they say, is history.

'You need to start doing your stand-up again, Mike,' said Gaz, but I wasn't having any of it, for a variety of reasons. First and foremost, my on-stage confidence had definitely taken a battering and the idea of getting back on stage filled me with dread. Stand-up had changed a lot too, in that everyone now tended to write their own observational routines, whereas I was a gag man who liked a punchline, pure and simple.

Gaz wouldn't let it lie, though. One day he rang me up to tell me that he'd sorted me a ten-minute gig at The Hob in London.

'Don't even think about backing out,' he warned.

In the meantime, Richard and Judy's final show was broadcast. I found it all so sad; they aired a montage of some of my best bits, which made me realise what a brilliant time I'd had - despite all the hard work – and just how lucky I'd been to meet some fantastic (and bizarre) people as I'd travelled around this great country of ours. Ricky Gervais was the show's main guest - it was a running joke that he'd always be on the final edition – and it was lovely to see him again.

Ricky was in the middle of a national tour, and he put Gaz and I on the guest list for his show at the Hammersmith Apollo. He was just brilliant, and it made me realise that I really ought to give stand-up another try. I told Gaz that I would definitely do The Hob, but only on the proviso that he came with me.

On the night itself, not only did Gaz come along, but so did Charlotte (the celebrity booker from *Richard & Judy*) and a couple of others. I was third on the bill and I was absolutely shitting myself. I felt sick, actually, haunted by visions of my last stand-up disaster.

I went on, did ten minutes, and I was as pleased as punch when I came off. I couldn't believe I'd done it, to be fair, and Gaz and Charlotte were so complimentary. If I'm honest, I had a strong six minutes, and an average four minutes that were nothing to write home about. I'd riffed with the punters and thrown in some old standard lines, but they'd worked and had got me some laughs. I was proud of myself, as was Gaz.

News soon filtered through that *Richard & Judy* were decamping to the new Watch channel, and that I wouldn't be joining them. More than ever, I was in need of a decent agent, so I spent a day meeting various companies to see who'd be the best fit. Among them was Karushi Management - run by Lisa Thomas – who represented big names like John Bishop, Jason Manford and Mackenzie Crook. I liked Lisa's attitude – she was really keen for me to pursue my stand-up – and we agreed to work together.

Within two days Lisa had secured me a gig. It transpired that Jason Manford was leaving the Xfm Manchester breakfast show, and the radio station bosses wanted to know if I'd consider becoming his replacement. I wasn't totally new to radio – I'd done a Saturday show on Crawley FM to get some experience, and get my foot in the door – and it all sounded good to me. I was ready for a brand new chapter in my life, and radio was something I'd always wanted to get into.

I drove up to Manchester to meet with the programme director – a City fan called Matt Whyatt – and we got on really well. I had a good feeling about Xfm, too; it was a pretty forward-thinking station that focused on good music and comedy, although it would take me a while to get used to listening to indie music (much to my surprise, I'd end up loving it).

Following the meeting, Lisa rang to say that the job was mine if I wanted it. It was a good earner which made it even better and I was to start in a couple of months' time. I decided that it was a good offer, although it would mean living in Manchester from Monday to Friday, and coming home for the weekend. I was pleased that I had a whole year's-worth of work scheduled, though.

Then, as luck would have it, I received a call from the Travel Channel who were seeking a team of presenters for a new series called *Essential,* reporting from various worldwide locations. I had a meeting with them and, since it wasn't a regular gig (one show per two months) it wouldn't interfere too much with my Xfm job. My first location was Las Vegas – I filmed for a fortnight, with a great director called Adrian – and as soon as I returned to the UK it was straight up to Manchester to begin work on Xfm.

Around the same time, however, I was devastated to hear the sad news that my former *Big Breakfast* producer Ed

Forsdick had died of testicular cancer. He'd gone on to become executive producer on Ant and Dec's *Saturday Night Takeaway*, and was really making waves in the television industry. I always remember on the *Big Breakfast* if an item was rubbish he would say, *get the dwarves in*, and he would, for some reason it made the item funnier. He just knew when somthing was funny and something wasn't. It was a tragic loss and my heart went out to his family.

Xfm was a cool place to work. Everyone walked around in cool clothes, with cool haircuts, saying cool things. I was introduced to the breakfast show team, which included my producer, Jim, and the newsreader-cum-sidekick, Julia. When I first saw the radio mixing desk, though, a chill ran down my spine. *There's no way I'm going to get the hang of this*, I remember thinking. It looked like the cockpit of a plane – there were so many knobs, buttons and controls – and I reckoned it was way beyond my brain capacity. That said, I was determined to get to grips with it so I could be in full control of my timing and output. If someone else worked the desk for me I'd have to cue them in, and it would create unnecessary confusion. Luckily, within a fortnight I'd mastered it.

It was great being back in Manchester, apart from the bloody weather (I'd forgotten how much it rained). I loved being on the Xfm breakfast show - it was a brilliant new platform for me, and I learned so much – and for the first six months I was blissfully happy. Being away from the family was a struggle, though; Carter was growing by the day, and we had a new arrival due with a due date of April 2009 for his sibling.

My next shoot with the Travel Channel had me flying out to Africa, this time for twelve days, accompanied with a very chilled-out director called Ged. I got the chance to scuba dive in the Indian Ocean, but remember the instructor making the signal for 'shark' as we put on our dive gear.

'Hold on, mate, did I just see the shark signal?' I asked.

'Yes,' he replied, as I pumped some air into my dive suit. 'If you see one, just keep calm and relax.' Luckily the sharks swam elsewhere that day.

I also fulfilled a life-long ambition to go on safari, and seeing lions, elephants and hippos in their natural habitat was awesome. I stayed in an amazing tent in the middle of the safari, and one night was disturbed by two noisy lions, only a matter of feet away. We'd been told not to leave our tents in any circumstances, and there's no way I was going out to ask Mr Lion if he could possibly keep the din down since I had a busy schedule of filming the following day (we always had to be up at 5 a.m. for filming, as it just got unbearably hot after midday). The next morning, our safari guide informed us that the lions had been mating, hence all the screeching and grunting. To be fair I'd heard worse on a night out in Essex…

By the time I returned to Manchester, Xfm had been taken over by a media company called Global. A lot of people were made redundant, including my co-presenter Julia. I'd be lying if I said we'd developed a great chemistry together, but I felt sorry for her because she'd moved lock, stock and barrel to Manchester from Southampton, only to be fired after four months. Suddenly, our once-bustling studio seemed quiet and dead.

Not unlike Old Trafford on a match day dah bum tis!

Sadly, my working relationship with my producer, Jim, started to deteriorate. I had a feeling that he'd gone behind my back on a few occasions, and for that reason I'd lost trust in him. He also kept kyboshing my content ideas, many of which had worked fantastically well on the *Big Breakfast,* whether they'd have translated to radio, I'm not sure but it would have been great to have given them a chance. I began to dread doing the show, and my enjoyment started to wane.

'What's up, Mike?' Jim had asked me one morning, probably sensing that I wasn't very happy. I told him straight.

'I think you're a frustrated presenter, Jim,' I said. 'Why don't you take over the breakfast show, eh? It seems to be more about you than me...'

It was while doing another *Essential* show – this time in Nova Scotia –that I came to the conclusion that Xfm was no longer for me. I'd had a lot of thinking time over there, and I realised that I'd lost interest in the breakfast show, and that I needed to seek pastures new.

Back in the UK, and after playing in a charity football match for Kevin Horlock, I reluctantly headed back to Manchester. As I did so, however, I received a phone call, telling me that I had to get my arse back to Essex as quick as I could, as I was going to be a dad again . I drove from Manchester to Basildon in three hours flat – I'd never driven so fast – because I was desperate not to miss the birth. I watched Cooper being born and he cried straight away, I thought *ok he's going to be the moody one* and I wasn't wrong! (Sorry Cooper but you know it's true!) They cleaned him up and handed him straight to me so I put him under my gown so it was skin to skin. On 27th April at 2.27 p.m., Cooper Michael McClean was born, weighing eight pounds and four ounces. Funnily enough, I just "knew" it would be another boy. He looked Chinese I thought they'd handed me the wrong baby. He had these gorgeous lips, as I held him and just like with Carter, I fell in love. HOLY SHIT! I've got two little mouths to feed. He was gorgeous too just like Carter. I was so pleased and blessed with having two healthy boys. I immediately phoned my mum and dad and told them they had another grandson. They were both delighted and couldn't wait to meet him. I drove back to my house to pick up Carter, then took him to meet his brother. He gave him a lovely kiss when he saw him and said *hello baba*. I am pleased to say they are so solid, they are best mates.

CHAPTER 27

Back Doing Stand Up

I travelled back to Manchester following Cooper's birth, knowing that I only had a few months left on my Xfm contract, which I doubted would be renewed. It was Matt Whyatt who confirmed the inevitable, and to be honest I didn't really care. I'd had enough of working with Jim and wouldn't have accepted a contract extension even if one had been on the table. One morning, I remember looking across into the next studio with envy as I saw Galaxy FM's breakfast show team - Nigel, Rachel and Rob – having a great laugh. Gone were the days when I'd had such fun. I finished Xfm that summer; I didn't even have a leaving do, and just went for a night out with the Galaxy lot.

The work offers reduced to a trickle. Lisa had got me a part in the gritty Manchester-based drama, *Shameless*, playing a priest called Father Tony, but as the year went on my phone just stopped ringing. I had no work and I hated it. So after some thought, I became a stay-at-home dad which in some way was a blessing to me as it meant I had more time with the boys, I felt like I just wanted to hold Cooper forever, I missed out on a lot of the baby cuddles with Carter having worked away. I hold my hat off to mums as I realise being a full-time parent was probably the hardest "job" I have ever done. It took me a few weeks to get the routine right. I would get up feed them both then take Carter to nursery, he would cry every time I left him, (which broke my heart and made me feel like the meanest Dad alive), then go home to play with Cooper, go out do my shopping and take him either swimming or for long walks. Then I'd be back collecting Carter, head back home feed them both, then back out to the park to play either football or push them on the swings. Then it was back home to get dinner ready. I honestly have never been so knackered. A bloody far cry from my working days and a total shift of mindset.

While working on *Richard & Judy*, I'd remembered my good friend Dino looking really haggard one day, and him explaining that it was all down to the stresses of parenting. Not until I had my own kids did I fully understand what he meant.

I can't begin to tell you how different my life was. Would I change it? Ooh that's a difficult one. I wouldn't for one minute give away the time I got to spend with the boys, but was I incredibly sad and frustrated that I was steadily losing what I loved dearly and had worked so hard to achieve.

A short while later Kevin Wood – the boss of First Family Entertainment - offered me a panto season, asking me to play *Aladdin*'s Wishee Washee at Manchester's Opera House. I wasn't massively bowled over with the £1,500 per week fee, but I needed the work and signed on the dotted line. To be fair, I'd always wanted to perform at the Opera House, so here was my chance.

I filmed a few more *Essentials* travel shows, including one in Ecuador. It was an amazing place, and they gave us such a lovely welcome (the local press followed us for a few days and featured us in the paper). The head of tourism told us how programmes like ours helped to raise awareness of their country, especially as they were keen to disassociate themselves from Colombia and its drug-related problems.

We stayed at a place called Sasha's Lodge in the middle of the Amazon jungle. It was a fantastic place, but sleeping became problematic with all the wildlife activity outside, from noisy crickets to screeching monkeys.

I was filmed fishing for piranhas – the river was full of them – at one point our guide fished one out and when he pulled its mouth open I could see how ferociously sharp its teeth were.

When we finished the shoot, Ged the director reckoned it would be a good idea to film me diving into the water, which could be used as a link into a break.

'Hang on a minute,' I said, convinced that he was taking the piss. 'You want me to dive into that piranha-infested water?'

He was deadly serious. Our guide convinced me that it was safe – 'they won't bother you,' he said - and performed a demonstration dive in order to prove his point.

'Okay, sod it,' I said, and dived in as requested, but not before pretending that I was being attacked by the flesh-eating piranhas. It was a masterclass of acting. Ged and the crew nearly shit themselves.

****

One day, I was reading an article in *Magic* magazine, written by a guy called Graham Haye, that contained a few gags that made me laugh out loud. I asked my agent to get in touch with him to ask if he'd consider helping me write my stand-up act. I knew in my head that I wanted to do something linked to mind-reading, having seen the popularity and success of Derren Brown's shows.

I met with Graham in a hotel near Bradford, and we clicked instantly. He agreed to write and produce an act for me, and within a week had come up with some great ideas (including a brilliant opening gag that I'll be eternally grateful for}. His jokes were exactly what I wanted – quick, clever and – more to the point – very, very funny. We concluded that, if I was to do this properly, I needed to spend a full week practising and rehearsing until I got it right, and preferably away from any distractions. Graham was based in York, and asked the manager of the nearby Pocklington Arts Centre if we could rehearse there.

We spent five days going over the routine, drinking lots of tea, and laughing like drains. Graham was a very talented performer himself, and proved to be a brilliant producer, too. We worked so well together, and I learned so much more about the writing process. Many a time I'd throw in an ad-lib and he'd laugh and say 'That's funny, Mike... write it down and use it.' I learned the importance of logging those throwaway asides and weaving them into my act. Graham and I became firm friends, and it's been like that ever since.

I left York feeling confident and headed back to London. I stopped off in Lincoln to meet my old friends Craig and Pam; Craig as you might remember, had helped me get my first panto, but had since become a motivational speaker who specialised in Neuro-Linguistic Programming (he has now written a great book, *Improve Your Life,* which is well worth a read and is on Amazon. *Can I have that tenner now Craig?*). He assured me that he'd help me overcome my fear of dying on my arse, and showed me a few brilliant techniques and strategies, some that I still use to this day.

I phoned Emma at The Hob and explained that I wanted to showcase my new act at the club, because the place meant a great deal to me. She agreed. John Mann – who'd once worked with me at the *Big Breakfast* - was top of the bill, and I was first on stage after the interval. I knew that my act was good enough – and that it contained enough laughs – but that didn't stop me feeling as nervous as hell. I was, however, determined to put all my hard work into practice.

The Hob was packed - Gaz and his lovely wife Jo were in the audience - and before I knew it the compere, Chris Neill was welcoming me onto the stage. I did my opening gag and it got a laugh – not a massive laugh – but I was up and running. A twenty-minute gig turned into a twenty five-minute gig, and I was flying. All the lines that Graham and I had rehearsed were going down a treat, and the mind reading element of the act was really well received. While I wouldn't say I stormed it, I came off the stage feeling happy that I'd got through it all, and had not died on my arse.

A very excited Gaz came up to congratulate me afterwards – as did the owners, Emma and Ron – and I stayed to watch John Mann. He was fantastic that night; a joy to watch.

Later that week, Emma phoned to ask if I'd like to compere the next two Saturdays, and I bit her hand off. The first of those nights saw Micky Flanagan trying out his new stuff – as well as his famous 'out-out' routine - and he unsurprisingly brought the house down. Emma continued to give me gigs at The Hob and I got better with each performance, my confidence soaring as time went on. I'd also record myself on my phone, spending the next day listening back and noting down which bits worked and which bits didn't. It was only by doing this that I realised I needed to slow my delivery down, and to stop having a go at the audience.

I needed more gigs, though, so I did my best to put my name about and stopped asking for silly money. I had to come to terms with the fact that, even though I'd been on the television, I had to accept the dosh that was being offered, even if it was a hundred quid. It couldn't be about the fee; it had to be about getting back on the horse. Because my act was little different, the bookings started to flood in.

By this time, however, I'd been dropped by Lisa (I'd begun to despise agents all over again) but I realised that – with all these gig offers - I needed representation. Most of the agents I met with wanted to put me up for various celebrity-led pro-grammes, which I'd frankly had enough of. I wanted either presenting work, acting jobs, or stand-up gigs. I decided to join forces with a top London agent – Can Management – but after three months of feeling like the small fish in a very large pond I decided to part company with them, too. Ideally, I needed a smaller-scale outfit that specialised in sourcing work for comedians and, during a trawl on the internet, I stumbled across Charlotte Hamilton Productions. As soon as we met, I knew Charlotte was the agent for me.

'I only wish you'd been with me all those years ago,' I re-member telling her following our long chat. They say you should never regret things in life, but I regret not having Char-lotte as my agent during the *Big Breakfast* years. I think she'd have secured me loads more work and would have got me straight back into stand up.

She was keen to see me do my new show, so I invited her to The Hob where I was doing another spot. Despite my nerves – I was desperate to impress - my new agent loved my act. She set to task to get me some more gigs, and told me to contact a guy called Ian Franklin, who ran The Comedy Club in Colchester, Essex. Ian had some great comics on his books and he had worked with all the biggest names. Charlotte explained that, even though I'd made a good name for myself, I still had to audition for him.

I went to see him on a very warm Sunday evening, and he seemed really impressed with my set – he liked the fact it wasn't your typical stand-up – and told me that he'd be able to put some dates in my diary. His colleague Craig – who dealt with the corporate side of things - explained that, as much as companies love a good comedian, they were always asking for something a bit different, and that my comedy-cum-mind-reading act fit the bill. Ian was true to his word and before I knew it I had about seven gigs in my diary.

The spring in my step had returned. I'd fallen back in love with stand-up, and had realised why I'd loved doing it all those years ago. I was now gigging with comedians who'd been on circuit for a good few years, some of whom had only seen me presenting on telly and were surprised that I was among their ranks.

'I never knew you did stand up,' one would say, probably remembering me from Nickelodeon and the *Big Breakfast* but not realising that my career was rooted in comedy.

'I can't believe you're doing gigs for two hundred quid, Mike...' another would say.

'I've got a family and bills to pay,' I'd reply. 'I'm more than happy to work my way up again.'

A lot of them were really nice about it, and said they admired my honesty.

In July 2010 I didn't have that much in my diary, other than a few stand up gigs and one or two corporate events, including Pizza of the Year awards at the Grosvenor Hotel in London. I thought it was a joke – it wasn't - but there was a big smile on my face when they paid me two grand to host it.

I'd also sorted out my panto for the year; I was off to Lowestoft to star in *Snow White and the Seven Dwarfs* with *Eastenders'* Stephen Booth and *Hi-De-Hi's* Nikki Kelly. Our producer was Paul Holman, one of the nicest panto supremos in the business, and our director was the legendary Ken Old-field, a dancer and choreographer who'd worked with big names like and Ronnie Corbett. I was really excited to be working with Ken and we got on brilliantly from day one (he loved my northern wit, apparently).

Charlotte continued to do a sterling job and began to get me castings for various advertisements and dramas, having forged great contacts with various producers and casting agents. I'd always craved to worked with someone like Charlotte; she was always ahead of the game, regularly kept me informed and constantly looked for ways to get me noticed.

She got me a casting for E4's smash hit drama, *My Big Fat Diary*. It was only a small role, as Finn's dad.

Bloody hell, I remember thinking. *I'm so old I'm now being asked to play a father...*

On the day of the audition, however, my son Cooper was off school. I was going to send my apologies, but a little voice told me to go for it. I took Cooper along too (clutching his iPad) and gave him strict instructions to stay put. I must have done a good audition, because a few hours later Charlotte rang to tell me that I'd got the part. I think Cooper was my lucky charm that day.

CHAPTER 28

The End… Sorry

I was now gigging most weekends and, during the week, continuing with my stay-at-home dad duties. I was growing with confidence on the stand-up circuit; my act was working and evolving and I no longer felt intimidated by other comedians. Graham was writing for me, my old *Big Breakfast* mucker Paul Connolly was sending me ideas and some brilliant gags, and I was coming up with a few lines of my own, too. I began to make friends with my comedian colleagues, like Sam Avery (a very funny Scouser), Kevin McCarthy, John Ryan, Jeff Stevenson, John Newton, Ryan McDonnell and Gerry Kaye.

Craig & Martin from The Comedy Club rang to offer me an afternoon gig at Butlin's in Skegness, as part of their regular '90's Weekender' event. The venue was packed out – there must have been about 1,500 people in this room - and I was shitting myself as I'd never performed in front of such a big crowd. And I was the closing act, too.

Is a mind-reading act with jokes going to work here? I recall thinking at the time.

As soon as I walked on I got heckled, but managed to fend off the fella nicely. This guy wouldn't shut up, though, and I knew I only had two more heckler put-downs in my locker. If those didn't work, I was fucked. Luckily my next comment did the trick.

I completed my set, finishing off with a number prediction. When I revealed the correct number, one bloke shouted out 'FUCK OFF, HOW THE HELL DID HE KNOW THAT?' I left the stage to a massive round of applause, and felt really good about myself. I knew that if I could make a room full of people laugh, while at the same time leaving them baffled, then I was on to a winner.

After the Butlin's gig, Ken Oldfield offered me a panto, *Dick Whittington* at the Assembly Rooms in Derby. The deal was done, but then the bombshell was dropped that I'd be starring with Linda Robson again... and Paul Nicholas. At first I thought it was a wind-up, but it was indeed the case. I was happy to be working with Linda though; she was lovely and we had a laugh together, despite the presence of our stroppy co-star.

As it happened, my relationship with the Assembly Rooms continued for four years. One year I was even asked if I'd do a Saturday night post-panto show for adults; Charlotte suggested we call it *Not So Clean McClean* and not only did it sell out, we had to put on an extra show on the Sunday, which also sold out.

In 2012 I was offered *Peter Pan* in Derby with one of the nicest men I have ever worked with: step forward Mr Larry Lamb. Larry had starred in some great TV shows, including *Eastenders* and *Gavin and Stacey,* and had even had roles in my favourite films, *Superman* and *Superman 3*. He was to play Captain Hook and I was to be his Smee. Larry was just brilliant; so funny and – as we say in luvvie-land - just a *darling* to work with.

Peter Pan that year broke all box office records; over 50,000 people came to see the show and it earned countless rave reviews. The chemistry between Larry and I was great, and our final show will live long in my memory. Everything went wrong that night but it made for one of the funniest shows to date. Larry is without doubt one of the nicest people I have ever worked with (and his sister makes the best Christmas cake I've ever tasted).

Charlotte was now getting me seen by West End directors, and I went up for a part in *Billy Elliot* playing the boxing coach, the final hitch being that it was a twelve-month contract, which was just too long for me. The rest of the year flew by, though, with more auditions, more castings and more gigs. Charlotte secured me a guest spot on the BBC kids' show, *Dick and Dom*, which I leapt at because my boys were huge fans. It was the first time they'd seen me on television, and I couldn't wait for them to tell their friends at school.

My stand-up act was getting tighter, and as a performer I was becoming stronger. I was working regularly with Gerry Kaye, who reached the final of Jimmy Carr's *Find Me A Comedian* competition which (in my opinion) he should have won. Gerry and I have become really good mates and, along with Ryan McDonnell, we do a podcast called *Slack Men* (find us on Twitter!).

In February 2013 I was contacted by a Florida-based agent called Roy Yates. Roy ran a company called Open Wide Entertainments and was booking acts for the Princess, Celebrity and Royal Caribbean cruise liners.

'I was just wondering whether you'd be interested, Mike?' he said.

I spoke with my fellow comic Jeff Stevenson who regularly worked on the cruise ships.

'Ships are the new clubs,' he said, explaining that, for him, the choice of blue oceans, fine dining, and decent wages - as opposed to grubby clubs, gobby hecklers and crap fees - was a no-brainer.

So I did a couple of cruise gigs, but I hated them. I told Roy that it wasn't for me, but – Roy being Roy – he persuaded me to give it another go. He booked me in for six more Princess Cruises, and I had a blast. Roy bombarded me with more bookings on various ships, and I've not looked back. To date, I've visited forty-six different countries, have performed on some of the biggest cruise liners in the world, have met some amazing people and have earned good money. Life on the ocean wave is great, trust me.

****

If I'm totally honest, I think my television journey has probably come to a natural end. I haven't totally given up hope of working on another TV show, though, and still cross my fingers that I'll get another opportunity. In 2016 I was asked to apply for *Britain's Got Talent*; I thought about it for a few seconds, before saying a polite thanks, but no thanks. The time wasn't right for me then but never say never in this industry, mind you it would be just my luck to lose to a collie dog or a puppet! I do think that it's a great platform for people who are starting out and are looking for their first break.

I don't watch television much these days. Not because I don't want to, but because I'd rather be outside with my boys. When I do watch TV, I find I'm seeing the same old faces appearing on panel shows, or the same presenters appearing on entertainment programmes. I watch *Live From The Apollo* and it's the same comedians, week-in, week-out, yet I've worked with some amazing funnymen who'll never get the chance because they're not championed by the 'big boys'. Companies like Open Mike, Avalon and Off The Kerb are the mafia of these TV shows, and their producers haven't got the balls to go to clubs, watch other comics and cast their net further. In my opinion, today's producers are lazy and are not giving enough chances to fresh new talent. If a show doesn't get over a million-and-a-half viewers, it's seen as a disaster, and everyone's become far too risk-averse.

There's far too much shit on television today, I reckon, a case in point being *The Only Way Is Essex* or Life on Marbs (what's the appeal of someone like Joey Essex, for God's sake?). Shows are given to personalities like Rylan Clark, who is probably a really nice fella, but for me has zero talent. People have become famous for being famous, and talent shows like *The X Factor* and *Britain's Got Talent* have been milked to death. I see fame-hungry people on shows like *Big Brother* or *The Apprentice*, the same people who publish their autobiographies at the age of 22, when they've basically done fuck all apart from getting themselves a new, white, gleaming set of teeth.

Some time ago I was asked to teach a presenter's course and the ten attendees clearly just wanted to be famous. They weren't interested in craft or graft, they just wanted to be in *Heat* magazine and go to showbiz parties. Sad, really.

It's funny, I was on a train once, eavesdropping on two blokes chatting about how modern TV had become boring, and about the lack of genuine 'stars' on television. Years ago, millions would tune in to watch talented all-rounders like Michael Barrymore or Bob Monkhouse larking about, or the general public making fun of themselves on *The Generation*

Game, *Beadle's About*, or even *Noel's House Party*. I dearly wish that Channel 4 would resurrect the *Big Breakfast*, as I honestly believe that it would still command a huge audience and would trounce every other breakfast show.

****

I have ticked so many boxes doing the job I love. I've appeared on iconic TV shows. I've played alongside and against some football legends. I've done the London Marathon and the Great North Run (twice). I've travelled the world. I've performed in some brilliant venues. I've covered the Oscars. I've met some of the world's biggest stars (and Dale Winton). I've worked with some amazingly talented people, on-screen, on-stage and behind the scenes. I've also worked with some of the biggest arseholes in showbiz (they know who they are).

I've also seen my beloved Manchester City win the League three times (as well as the Carling Cup and the FA Cup) and now have a lovely little gig hosting City Square on match days, which allows me to watch the Blues while getting paid.

But, as I've got older, I've realised that life is not easy, and doesn't come with a trouble-shooting manual. It's a game that throws many obstacles your way, and you have to deal with them as you see fit. I always knew what I wanted to do, though, and I always knew I was going to do it. You can achieve anything in life if you want to; don't dwell on what you CAN'T do, concentrate on what you CAN. I wanted to make people laugh and see them laugh, which I hope I've done. I wanted to be on television and on stage, and it happened. I wanted to pay off my mortgage (and my parents') and I've done that, too. I also wanted to get my golf handicap down (okay, I've not managed that yet).

I count myself incredibly lucky to have two brilliant sons. They are my life, and I thank God every day for them, they're very funny, cheeky and healthy boys. Like their dad they love their football, and if they end up playing for Manchester City then I'd be the happiest man alive (if they play for United they'd better not come back home). I cried when they both became City mascots; it was definitely one of the proudest days of my life.

Whatever Carter and Cooper choose to do in the future I will back them one hundred per cent. It may be showbiz-related, who knows; they have both been in few adverts and, even at the age of six, Carter was telling the ad director what would be funny. I'm trying to bring them up well; if they want something they have to earn it by washing my car or doing little jobs around the house. Every day I tell my sons I love them – something that my dad didn't always do - and I'll carry on doing so, even when they're older.

I have now met someone who is just amazing. Kate is very funny, super-intelligent, a great cook and a football-lover (I'll just about forgive her for supporting Chelsea).

As for the rest of my family, both my parents are fit and well and still living in Manchester; one's deaf, one's forgetful, and both drive me mad, but I wouldn't have it any other way. I have a lovely, funny sister, Aurora, who has supported me during some tough times, and for that I will always be grateful. I am also very proud of my niece Nicole. She's like a daughter to me and has now become a mother herself, to Olivia and Sophia. She sent me a lovely Facebook message on Father's Day which made me cry like a baby; I love her so much.

I really do count myself a very lucky man to have such good mates that have stuck by me no matter what I've done, namely Degs, Les, Darwood, Stevie, Phill, Andy and Sizz, Tommy C ..Worthy. My friends are very funny and it's always great when we get together, we literally just rip the piss out of each other. We have a WhatsApp group and if I could print that or make it into a book it would be hilarious reading. I listen to them and get some good material. Don't get me wrong, I occasionally will chip in with a funny gag but not as much as they do. If I do chip in nine times out of ten they will just say *is that in your act? It's shit.* We have been mates for years and its always a joy when we get together and I love it.

I've really enjoyed writing this book, because it's brought back some happy memories and has made me realise what I've achieved in my life so far. But now it's time for the only son of Peter and Pari from Levenshulme to sign off. I need to go upstairs and get ready because I'm on stage tonight, doing what I do best.

Making people laugh.

See ya x

Lightning Source UK Ltd.
Milton Keynes UK
UKHW02f0619100818

327043UK00008B/272/P